Techniques of Dressmaking and Soft Tailoring

Also by E. Lucy Towers

STANDARD PROCESSES IN DRESSMAKING

E. Lucy Towers is a First Class Diplomée of the
Training College of Domestic Subjects, London, in
Dressmaking, Needlework, Tailoring and Millinery;
she was formerly Lecturer in Dressmaking and
Needlework at The Polytechnic, Regent Street, and
at Chelsea Polytechnic, London.

Techniques of Dressmaking and Soft Tailoring

E. LUCY TOWERS

 University of London Press Ltd

to my friend, Helen Lewis,
who inspired and encouraged me to write this book

The author and publishers would like to thank the
International Wool Secretariat for help with the pro-
vision of woven fabrics and related diagrams for pho-
tography (plain weave manufactured by James Hare,
twill weave by Digoloom, and herringbone weave by
Hunt and Winterbotham), and Mr Eric Keates and the
Leicester College of Technology for help with the text,
diagrams and samples of material relating to knitted
fabrics.

ISBN 0 340 08021 3

First published 1968
2nd impression 1972
Text and diagrams copyright © 1968 E. Lucy Towers
University of London Press Ltd
St Paul's House, Warwick Lane, London EC4

Printed in England by
Hazell Watson and Viney Ltd, Aylesbury, Bucks

This book is intended to be a sequel to *Standard Processes in Dressmaking* but it can be used quite independently of the previous book. It deals with some of the more advanced parts of the craft.

Included are chapters on 'Fibres and Fabrics' and their influence on choice of style, cutting out, stitching and pressing. The development in this field alone during the last two decades has been enormous, and makes an interesting study. Competition between weavers and knitters, and between natural and man-made fibres is a stimulus to the textile industry. New developments continue.

The improved performance of modern sewing machines has given fresh encouragement and interest to women and girls who want to make clothes, yet need time-saving methods. Devices for neatening raw edges or working buttonholes by machine overlocking, using the zigzagger, and the one-sided presser foot for stitching close to zip teeth are instances, as well as reverse stitching which enables seams and darts to be finished securely.

Soft tailoring has been included at the request of students and teachers of the craft. With shorter working hours many women and older girls have more leisure. The subject of dress is universally popular, and for those who are already quite proficient in dressmaking, the successful achievement of making a suit or slacks brings great satisfaction.

'Do it yourself' is a popular slogan today. The diagrams of the various processes have been drawn with self-help in mind. Where hand stitches are introduced, working diagrams have been drawn in stages so they can be followed easily. In the case of tailored lapels and collar, drawings show the position of the hands holding the work, while in pressing the iron is shown in the correct position for particular parts such as collar or sleevehead.

Couture finishes are emphasised in layering turnings, strengthening or giving firmness where necessary by interlining or lining garments. Invisible joining of lace is illustrated and advice given in dealing with more difficult fabrics.

E. LUCY TOWERS

CONTENTS

Changing values of distance and time, due to the recent tremendous increase in the speed of travel and communications, have influenced developments in fashion and fabric in the mid-twentieth century. Air travel, radio and television have linked the world. The pace of modern living is increasing and with it our habits are changing ever more rapidly.

The demand for lightweight, easy-care, crease-resistant fabrics has been answered to a large degree by the scientific development and production of man-made fibres, and the finishes devised to improve the properties of fabrics after they have left the loom or knitting machine. These in turn influence fashion, since the properties of fabrics must be taken into account when designing and making styles.

But although the passing of the years brings fresh developments which influence the creation of garments, the four main factors remain the same: the wearer, the occasion, the style and the fabric. Each must influence the final product.

The Wearer

The personality of the wearer is reflected in her clothes. Wise choice can enhance good points, and this must be the aim of the dressmaker who should be ready to modify fashionable styles to achieve a pleasing, uncluttered line and good proportion when clothes are worn. Wise judgment and common sense are necessary when dealing with varying builds and ages, e.g. the hem level for youth is not always desirable for older women (though both are influenced to some degree by fashion). Height also influences hem levels. Very long legs are emphasised by very short skirts, but so are extremely short legs, so it follows that extreme

contrasts emphasise some points that would be better disguised by a happy medium that is still in keeping with fashion.

The Occasion

A well chosen outfit for work or sport must be easy to wear as well as smart, so that the wearer does not feel restricted and yet has the assurance of looking right for her job. Suitable and pleasing clothes give poise and confidence. Over-dressing can cause self-consciousness or give a vulgar impression. Unsuitable dressing can cause acute embarrassment and spoil an otherwise pleasurable occasion.

Well chosen accessories form part of planned wardrobes as well as matching or contrasting separates which team together successfully. One well cut suit or dress of good fabric with couture finish can be worn with different hats, costume jewellery, shoes, handbag, gloves, etc., to suit various occasions.

The Style

Choice of style is influenced by the fashion of the day. Usually designers suggest styles to suit a variety of figures and age-groups. Hence the choice of silhouettes in a collection. Divisions within the silhouette break up the figure into sections by means of seams, yokes, pleats, contrasts of colour or texture, etc. The dressmaker must use her knowledge of the effect the direction of lines has upon figures, e.g. vertical lines lengthen and horizontal lines widen. Used alone either can become monotonous, but in proportion some of each can give interest and variety to a design. Diagonal lines need to be studied in relation to the general visual effect; V chevrons are wider at the top, whereas Λ widen at the base.

The original lines of a dress designed for a figure of average height and build may need to be modified to suit a taller, more heavily built woman, or a shorter person who might be stout or slim. Here are some simple examples:

(a) A boat-shaped neckline may be drawn in the original fashion sketch, but is not a wise choice for a person with a short, thick neck. Hence it might be possible to change the neckline to a V shape, giving a more flattering line to the wearer without spoiling the style.

(b) Higher necklines may be in vogue, and a close-fitting turndown collar might be shown in the original design. A suitable modification for someone with a long neck would be a built-up collar like the mandarin, or military type.

The Fabric

Fabric and style are so closely linked that each must be suitable for the other, whichever is chosen first. Together they should look right on the wearer, e.g. the design and texture of a fabric suitable for a tall, well-built woman might be quite the wrong choice for a smaller, more fragile-looking person, although the same style of dress may suit both people. The former may be able to wear boldly patterned fabrics, wide stripes or large plaids successfully, whereas the latter's choice might be a plain material of interesting texture in a becoming colour or a smaller, more closely spaced print, stripe or check.

Muted colours are less conspicuous than sharp, bright contrasts. Clever blending of fibres and dyes give soft, pleasing effects as in some interesting striped and checked fabrics such as woollens or wool blends. On the other hand some stripes and other designs can be startling because of their width or size and colour contrast and need careful discrimination in buying and making up successfully.

Remember the ability and skill of the garment maker, particularly her finger skill and pressing ability, when choosing both style and fabric. It is a great disappointment when a dress fails to come up to the expectations of the maker or wearer because of insufficiently skilled workmanship. The art of dressmaking needs much patience and perseverance. Success with simple creations means encouragement to try more difficult ones. There are really no short cuts to good dressmaking with a professional finish, and elementary stages must be mastered before progressing to advanced work. Dislike of dressmaking is often caused by beginners attempting too advanced work and failing.

Allow sufficient time and thought for buying the fabric. Hurried choice often leads to disappointment. Choose materials in a good light (daylight, or, less satisfactory, a daylight lamp for day wear; and the appropriate kind of artificial light for evening wear). Colours often change considerably under some forms of modern artificial light, and can prove very misleading if this is not taken into account. When matching material for linings, sewing threads, buttons, bindings or zips, etc., act on the same advice.

Always buy enough material for the style and size allowing for matching designs in patterned fabrics. Although wastage must be avoided, garments can be spoiled through insufficient length of fabric. There should be enough for adequate turnings and hem allowance so that both fit and finish will be satisfactory.

Look at the weft threads of the fabric. If they are badly 'off grain', i.e. not at right angles to the selvedges, avoid purchasing, if possible. (See diagrams and notes on 'straight grain', pages 29–30.)

Feel the fabric and decide if it will make up successfully in the chosen style. Draping needs a supple fabric that will hang well in the required folds, e.g. ring velvet, jersey, chiffon, etc. These need skilful handling in making up, the last being particularly difficult owing to its fine texture and slippage. More tailored styles require fabric with a firm handle, yet pliable and not too harsh to the touch.

Tailoring terms
and their equivalents in dressmaking

Tailoring	Dressmaking
Basting	Tacking
Drawstitch	Slipstitch
Flash basting	Diagonal tacking
Forepart	Front
Forearm	Front of arm
Hindarm	Back of arm
Scye (this originally meant 'arm's eye')	Armhole
Tailor tacking	Tailor tacking
Vent	Slit with an underlap to cover the back of it

(Tailor's buttonhole has a different knot to dressmaker's or needlework buttonhole.)

Abbreviations

RS — Right side
WS — Wrong side
RHS — Right-hand side
LHS — Left-hand side
CF — Centre front
CB — Centre back
SG — Straight grain

FIBRES

Cutting and treatment when making up clothes have been influenced by developments in the construction of modern fabrics. The familiar ones, made from fibres which have stood the test of time (cotton, linen, wool and silk) are still proved favourites; but where each of them had certain weaknesses as regards clothing, scientific research has found answers to these problems by various treatments or by mixing with man-made fibres.

Clothing fabrics are usually either woven or knitted from lengths of yarn. Yarns are produced from fibres. These may be of one variety which are twisted or spun together, such as cotton, which is a vegetable fibre, or nylon, a synthetic fibre, or a blend of various fibres, e.g. wool and Terylene (animal and synthetic), or nylon, viscose rayon and cotton (synthetic, regenerated and natural fibres).

To understand something of the treatment required for modern materials, it is useful to have some knowledge of the origin and properties of various fibres. The sources of those in common use today are divided into two groups: those from natural sources and those made and developed by man. Natural fibres are again divided into two main groups: those obtained from animals—wool, hair and silk; and those derived from vegetable or plant sources, cotton and flax being the main ones concerned with clothing fabrics. The history of these natural fibres being used for cloth dates back to something like 8000 B.C., when it is recorded that spinning and weaving were practised in Egypt, and to 5000 B.C. when silkworms were reared in China.

The development of fibres made by man has been mainly in the present century, though research was carried out in the nineteenth century. Man-made fibres are also sub-divided into two groups: regenerated fibres, i.e. those whose basic components have been derived from natural sources, like wood or cotton (viscose rayon, both di-acetate and tri-acetate, are in this group) and synthetic, e.g. man-made from a mineral origin (like nylon and Terylene and acrylic fibres).

Staple fibres and continuous filaments

With the exception of silk, both animal and vegetable fibres are short, coming in various lengths. These are called *staple fibres*. The longest are the best in quality and are used to make the more expensive fabrics.

Silk is wound off the cocoons of the silk moth in single, long threads called *continuous filaments*. It was through the study of the habits of silkworms that man first developed the idea of producing artificial fibres which could be made into fabric. All man-made fibres imitate the silkworm in producing continuous filament fibres by squirting a solution through microscopic holes called *spinerettes*. If needed these filaments can be cut into short lengths at a later stage to form staple fibres. (See page 20.)

It is useful to remember that fabrics made from man-made filament yarns are those which resemble silk, e.g. taffeta, satin, etc., and have a smooth, lustrous appearance. Fabrics made from man-made staple yarns look similar to those produced from natural staple fibres, e.g. wool, cotton or linen.

Fabrics containing different fibres may be:

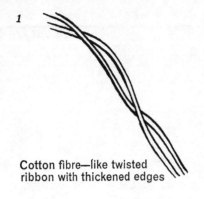

Cotton fibre—like twisted ribbon with thickened edges

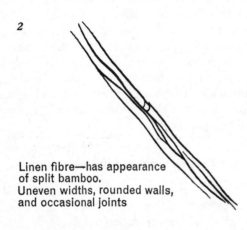

Linen fibre—has appearance of split bamboo.
Uneven widths, rounded walls, and occasional joints

Natural fibres
as seen through a microscope

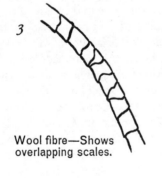

Wool fibre—Shows overlapping scales.

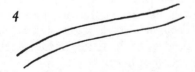

Silk fibre—like rounded glass rod

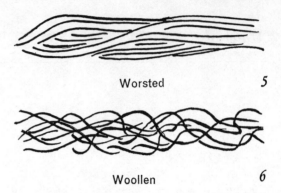

Worsted   5

Woollen   6

1. Woven with one kind in the warp and another in the weft.
(These are *mixtures*, e.g. acetate rayon warp and viscose rayon weft produce a 'shot' effect.)
2. Woven from yarns which contain mixed fibres spun together, e.g. rayon staple and wool, or rayon staple, nylon staple and wool.
(These are *blended yarns*.)

Blending or mixing fibres or yarns may produce fabrics with better weàring or washing qualities. This helps to keep the selling price low.

Wool and cotton mixtures

Both fibres are of natural origin (animal and plant). They combine the warmth of wool and the strength and smoothness of cotton, as well as their hygienic qualities. Their price is lower than 'all-wool' fabrics of similar quality, the cost being in proportion to the amount of wool in the mixture. The higher the percentage of wool content, the higher the price per yard.

When making up the fabric into garments, pressing is needed, and the temperature of the iron must be regulated. Wool scorches at a lower temperature than cotton, therefore heat the iron gently for wool.

Wool and Terylene

These combine natural and synthetic fibres. The warmth and hygienic qualities of wool are teamed with the strength and hardwearing properties of Terylene, together with their thermoplastic and heat-setting features. During the pressing of garments this fabric can have

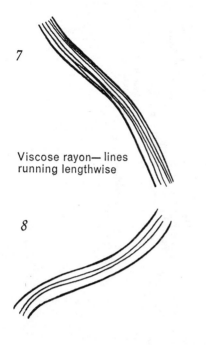

7

Viscose rayon— lines
running lengthwise

8

Acetate—fewer lines running
lengthwise than viscose,
otherwise similar

Regenerated fibres

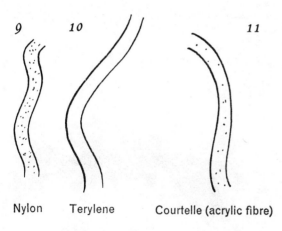

9   10   11

Nylon   Terylene   Courtelle (acrylic fibre)

Synthetic fibres

wool, so 'all-wool' cloth can be shaped by tailor pressing more easily than the Terylene-wool fabric which will appear more stubborn. Shaping of the latter will depend more on suppression of fabric by means of darts and seams.

The charts (pages 16–25) are intended to give useful information on individual fibres and the fabrics made from them. This knowledge helps in the cutting and making of clothing, especially when choosing, buying and using fabrics made from a variety of yarns and fibres.

Only simple tests are mentioned, which can be carried out at home òr in the classroom.

1. *Handle* or *feel* of cloth or fibre: soft or stiff, cool or warm, springy or limp; harsh, smooth or uneven; cold or warm when wet, or damp, whether absorbent or not.

2. The *look* or *appearance* of cloth or fibre: dull or lustrous; straight or crimpy; dead white or creamy in its natural undyed state.

The drawings of the appearance of various fibres when seen under the microscope show interesting distinctions in the look of natural fibres, but synthetic fibres are not so easily distinguished from one another (Diagrams 1–11).

3. *Reaction to heat*: burning test (carried out over suitable protective covering of table or surface). Apply a flame to the end of the fibre. Note if it flares quickly (e.g. cotton) or smoulders (wool), or melts (nylon). Note the smell, e.g. of burnt paper (cotton or linen, vegetable fibre), or of burnt feathers (wool or silk, animal or protein fibre), and the residue or ash left, if any.

4. *Reaction to simple chemical tests.* It will be found that, as a general rule, strong alkalis (e.g. caustic soda) dissolve animal but not vegetable fibres. Acids will cause damage to vegetable fibres but, if weak, will not affect animal fibres. Acetate will dissolve in acetone. Terylene is unaffected by most chemicals.

creases set permanently at given temperatures. These will not be disturbed unless higher temperatures are used to remove them. In this case care is needed not to melt the fibre of Terylene or scorch the woollen one. Terylene fibre will not respond to moulding as much as

For burning or chemical tests it is advisable to separate fibres to find their individual reaction. Take a piece of yarn first from the weft threads of the fabric, and then from the warp. Untwist each yarn and separate the fibres using a needle or pin with a sharp point.

Cotton

SOURCE AND COUNTRY WHERE FOUND	WHERE MANUFACTURED IN BRITAIN	TESTING	ADVANTAGES FOR USE AS CLOTHING	DISADVANTAGES FOR USE AS CLOTHING	FABRICS FOR CLOTHING MADE FROM COTTON FIBRES
COTTON fibre is of vegetable origin. Ribbon-like fibre in seed pod of cotton plant. Grown in tropical climates. West Indies grow sea-island cotton of finest quality. Egyptian cotton is also of finest quality. United States of America is one of the largest producers of cotton. India and Pakistan also grow large crops of cotton.	LANCASHIRE Raw cotton is shipped in bales to Lancashire for manufacture, because of its damp climate. Here it is cleaned, spun into yarns, and woven into cloth. NOTTINGHAMSHIRE is noted for its manufacture of lace and net.	*Handle* of fabric Cool and smooth (except brushed cotton). *Look* Under a microscope untreated cotton fibres look like twisted ribbon with thickened edges (Diagram 1). *Burning* of fibre Cotton burns rapidly unless rendered flame-proof. Leaves grey ash. Smells of burnt paper. *Chemical test* Cotton will decompose in concentrated hydro-chloric acid (spirits of salt), but it is not affected if boiled in 5% caustic soda (alkali).	Comparatively cheap and plentiful. Strong when wet and when dry, therefore hardwearing. Resistant to alkalis, therefore washes well. Can be boiled if white or fast dye. Hygienic. Can be starched to stiffen. Good conductor of heat and absorbent, so cool in summer. Easy to handle and make up into clothes. Can be given finishes to render it: crease-resistant, shrink-resistant, stain-resistant, flame-proof, moisture-repellent. Stretch and elastic recovery properties are also being developed.	Creases badly unless given modern treatment to counteract this tendency. NOTE: *Poor* grade cottons are weakened when treated with resins for crease-resistance. They appear much better than they are, but tear or split very easily in wear. Cotton may shrink unless given anti-shrink treatment. Cold to the touch in winter, or if wet with perspiration, with the exception of cellular-type cotton fabric. This is comfortable to wear next to the skin, and hygienic because it can be boiled. Inflammable, unless treated with anti-flame finish, especially brushed cotton, *e.g.* winceyette and flannelette. Subject to mildew if left damp.	*Fine or lightweight* Cambric, lawn, organdie, muslin, voile—for lingerie, baby wear, linings, blouses, children's dresses. Stiffened lawn for inter-linings. *Medium weight* Gingham, zephyr (plain or woven into stripes or checks), printed and plain dress cottons with satin or glazed finish. Poplins, piqué, sateens for linings. Lace flouncing or piece lace. *Heavy weight* Corduroy, denim, drill, sailcloth, velveteen—for hard-wearing clothes, *e.g.* skirts, shorts, jeans, etc. *Brushed* Flannelette, winceyette—for nightwear, shirts, etc.

Linen

SOURCE AND COUNTRY WHERE FOUND	WHERE MANUFACTURED IN BRITAIN	TESTING	ADVANTAGES FOR USE AS CLOTHING	DISADVANTAGES FOR USE AS CLOTHING	FABRICS FOR CLOTHING MADE FROM LINEN FIBRES
LINEN fibre is of vegetable origin. Inner parts of stalk of flax plant. Smooth, strong fibres of varying sizes. Ireland and Belgium produce the best quality flax. Other countries where flax is grown for commercial purposes: France, Holland, USSR, USA.	IRELAND	*Handle* of fabric Cool, firm and strong. *Look* Rather more lustre than cotton. Single threads are uneven in thickness. Under a microscope linen fibres have the appearance of split bamboo (Diagram 2). *Burning* of fibre Similar to cotton but burns more slowly. Leaves grey ash. Smells of burnt paper. *Chemical test* Not affected if boiled in 5% caustic soda (alkali). Will dissolve in concentrated acid, *e.g.* spirits of salt (hydrochloric acid.)	Stronger when wet than when dry. Very hard wearing. Resistant to alkalis. Will wash and boil well (if dyes are fast). Good conductor of heat, therefore cool and comfortable to wear in summer, also absorbent. Easy to handle. Makes up well in tailored styles. Threads are strong enough to be withdrawn for drawn-thread work. When mixed with Terylene, linen fabrics have greater crease-resistance and recovery, and are lighter in weight.	More expensive than cotton because much of the preparation and manufacture has to be done by hand. Creases badly unless specially treated. Cold to the touch in winter. Not a good draping fabric for swathed styles.	*Fine linen* Linen lawn— for embroidered blouses and baby wear. *Medium weight* Dress linens. *Heavy weight* Tailoring linens.

Wool

SOURCE AND COUNTRY WHERE FOUND	WHERE MANUFACTURED IN BRITAIN	TESTING	ADVANTAGES FOR USE AS CLOTHING	DISADVANTAGES FOR USE AS CLOTHING	FABRICS FOR CLOTHING MADE FROM WOOL FIBRES
WOOL is an animal fibre, coming from the fleece of sheep or lambs. Chief countries where sheep are reared are: Australia, New Zealand, South Africa, South America, British Isles, Spain.	YORKSHIRE is the chief county in Britain where wool is cleaned, spun and woven into cloth of varying weights. Two main varieties: woollens and worsteds. *Worsteds* Long wool staple fibres go through a combing process which causes them to lie parallel to each other, and discards the shorter fibres. Worsted yarns when magnified show this parallel structure (Diagram 5). They are tightly twisted and make smooth, even, compact cloths. *Woollens* Shorter wool fibres are used in woollens. Instead of lying parallel, they mingle in all directions, and are more loosely twisted, giving a shaggy appearance under the microscope (Diagram 6). Different finishes give 'soft' woollens as in dress fabrics, or rougher ones, such as tweeds.	*Handle* of fabric Warm and hairy, soft or springy according to fabric. *Look* Dull and hairy surface, crimpy. Scaly surface of wool fibres can be seen through a microscope (Diagram 3). *Burning* of fibre Wool fibres smoulder but do not flare. Leaves slightly brittle beads at end. Smells of burnt feathers. *Chemical test* Wool fibre will dissolve in 5% hot solution of caustic soda. Acids will turn wool yellow but not dissolve it.	*Warm* Wool is a bad conductor of heat. Scaly surface of wool fibres entraps air causing air pockets which help to keep the body warm and give ventilation. *Hygroscopic* Wool will absorb 30% of its own weight of moisture without feeling damp to the touch. *Flame-resistant* Wool will scorch and smoulder but not flare. These qualities make it suitable for underwear, especially for babies, children and old people, and for winter outerwear. Very good fabric for tailoring, especially worsteds and tweeds, as it is *thermoplastic*. Woollen and worsted fabrics can be shaped or moulded by careful and expert treatment of heat (iron) and moisture (damp rag)—(tailor manipulation). Hard wearing, particularly tweeds and worsteds. Soft and lightweight dress woollens will drape to a certain extent. Australian process is being developed giving woollens washable, drip-dry, non-iron qualities similar to cotton and synthetic fabrics. Wool is resilient and has great powers of recovery	*Cost* Wool is inclined to be expensive. Shrinks and felts easily unless treated to counteract this. Needs careful washing, since too strong alkalis affect wool adversely. Great heat will scorch, so irons must be moderately hot. The hairy surface sometimes affects sensitive skins. Smooth linings can counteract this. Wool can be damaged by moths, unless specially treated for resistance.	WOOLLENS (from woollen yarn). *Lightweight* Wool crêpe, wool lace, angora, wool delaine. *Medium weight* Crêpes, facecloth, flannels, jersey, tartans, tweeds. *Heavy weight* Wool coatings, *e.g.* velours, tweeds, etc. WORSTEDS (from worsted yarn). *Lightweight* Wool georgette, cashmere, nuns veiling. *Medium weight* Barathea, gaberdine, serges, suitings. *Heavy weight* Barathea, coatings, suitings.

Silk

SOURCE AND COUNTRY WHERE FOUND	WHERE MANUFACTURED	TESTING	ADVANTAGES FOR USE AS CLOTHING	DISADVANTAGES FOR USE AS CLOTHING	FABRICS FOR CLOTHING MADE FROM SILK FIBRES
SILK fibre is of animal origin. Produced by the silkworm when spinning its cocoon. Inside the cocoon the change from silkworm to chrysalis takes place. The cocoons must be baked or steamed to kill the insects inside before the silk filament can be reeled off. There are two kinds of silkworm in general use for the production of silk: the *cultivated* and the *wild* silkworm.	'Sericulture' and silk weaving were first known in China about 3000 B.C. Afterwards it was practised in Japan and India, then introduced to Europe, in Italy, France, England.	*Handle* of fabric Soft, warm to the touch. Pure silk is usually light in weight and firm and flexible in texture. Luxurious feel. *Look* Soft lustre. Under a microscope silk fibres have the appearance of smooth glass rods (Diagram 4). *Burning* of fibre Burns quickly and melts. Very little flame. Leaves a bead of brittle ash. Smells of burnt feathers. *Chemical test* Silk will dissolve in a hot solution of 10% caustic soda. Acids affect silk also. Concentrated hydrochloric acid (spirits of salt) will dissolve silk.	Good draping fabric. Does not crush badly and recovers quickly when hung. The beauty of silk fabrics makes them ideal for evening wear and dresses for special occasions in both natural and artificial light. Soft and warm. Light and firm. Washing silks make excellent fabrics for blouses or overblouses, underslips and other lingerie. Smooth silks do not soil readily. They have good wearing qualities. Silk is a bad conductor of heat, and absorbent, so if damp with perspiration it does not feel clammy when worn next to the skin. Silk is *hygroscopic*: it will absorb 33% of its own weight of moisture without feeling damp to the touch.	*Cost* Silk is expensive because of the cost of rearing the silkworms and producing the yarns and fabrics. Silk is affected by iron-mould and mildew. Silk cannot be boiled or bleached. Too great heat in pressing or ironing will scorch. Some silks show watermarks if damped. (NOTE: Shantung and tussore must be pressed or ironed quite dry. *No* damp rag used.) White silk tends to become yellow, either with careless laundering or with age. Heavily weighted silks are likely to crack or split (*e.g.* weighted taffetas).	*Lightweight* Ninon, chiffon, georgette, tulle, net—for diaphanous evening wear and lingerie. *Medium weight* Crêpe de Chine, foulard, Jap silk, silk satin, silk taffeta, silk faille, silk velvet —for lingerie, blouses, evening wear and special occasion dresses. *Heavier weight* Street velvet, brocades, silk moiré—for suits and evening coats and dresses. *Wild silk* is made into spun tussore and shantung silks—for blouses and dresses. (NOTE: Use pure silk for stitching silk fabrics.)

Rayon and Viscose Rayon

SOURCE	TESTING	ADVANTAGES FOR USE AS CLOTHING	DISADVANTAGES FOR USE AS CLOTHING	FABRICS FOR CLOTHING MADE FROM RAYON FIBRES
RAYON is made from cellulose, of vegetable origin. Cellulose is found in cotton linters (the fibres which are too short to be spun into yarn) from cotton-growing countries, or in wood pulp from spruce or pine trees grown in Scandinavian countries and Canada. This is termed *regenerated cellulose*. It is used in the production of both kinds of rayon which are widely used for clothing in Britain. These are classified as *viscose* rayon, or *acetate*, the latter being divided again into Di-Acetate and Tri-Acetate. VISCOSE RAYON was the first man-made fibre and a British discovery. Courtaulds are the main producers in Britain, having started developing it in 1904. After passing through various chemical processes a treacly substance is formed called *viscose*, hence the name viscose rayon. The liquid is squirted through microscopic tubes to form a thread which solidifies under further chemical treatment. This is called *continuous filament fibre*. Viscose rayon filament can be cut into short staples of equal length and spun similarly to cotton and wool. These are called rayon *staple fibres*. They can be used separately or mixed or blended with other staple fibres both natural and synthetic. The producers are continually experimenting and improving viscose rayon. A crimp has been introduced, resulting in further wool-like characteristics and warmth without weight.	*Viscose* rayon made from continuous filament fibre. *Handle* of fabric Cold to the touch. Not so soft as acetate. *Look* More lustrous than silk, but if de-lustred looks more dull than silk. Appearance of fibre striated under microscope (Diagram 7). *Burning* of fibre Burns quickly like cotton with a bright flame, leaves very little ash.	*Cost* Because of large production viscose rayon is comparatively cheap to buy. Appearance is sometimes better than cheap cotton of similar price, though wearing qualities may not be so good. Wide variety of choice in colour and design; mothproof; resistant to mildew; absorbent. Viscose rayon staple fibres are mixed with natural staple fibres of wool or cotton to produce many of our modern fabrics more cheaply. Continuous filament fibres can be mixed with those of silk or nylon. *Draping qualities* Viscose rayon hangs well but crease-resistant finish should be obtained. Viscose rayons can be treated to render them: crease-resistant, shrink-resistant, stain-repellent. NOTE: The synthetic resins used in these finishes render viscose rayon stronger when wet than when dry, and garments keep their shape well.	*Laundering* Viscose rayon is a weaker fabric for washing and ironing. It will not wear as long as cotton or nylon. (Research is remedying this former weakness.) *Time factor* Takes much longer to iron than nylon or drip-dry cottons. Crinkles or withers under too hot an iron. Frays badly, and in filament form is slippery to handle. Slippage causes seams to split and wear out more quickly. Filament fabrics are cold to the touch. Viscose rayon creases badly unless treated to counteract this tendency.	Most fabrics that were originally made from silk are produced in rayon at a much lower price. Examples are: *Lightweight* Rayon georgette, chiffon. *Medium weight* Rayon crêpe de Chine, foulard, poult, satin, spun, taffeta, ring velvet. De-lustred rayon has the appearance of wool fabric. Brushed rayon has a fluffy surface. *Heavier weight* Rayon street velvet (water-repellent), rayon marocain. Further developments incorporating a crimp in viscose rayon fibre is enabling new fabrics to be produced with 'warmth without weight' and 'easy-care' properties at reasonable prices.

SOURCE	TESTING	ADVANTAGES FOR USE AS CLOTHING	DISADVANTAGES FOR USE AS CLOTHING	FABRICS FOR CLOTHING MADE FROM ACETATE FIBRES
DI-ACETATE is a British discovery. British Celanese Ltd are the main producers in Great Britain, Celanese being acetate. It was developed as a clothing fabric after the First World War. It is made from cellulose + acetic acid and consequently called cellulose acetate or di-acetate. This is the liquid forced through spinerettes to form continuous filament fibre. Special synthetic dyes are used for acetate. This makes production costs high, and prevents it being used to mix with natural fibres taking different dyes. Acetate filament fibre can be converted into staple fibre in a similar way to that of viscose rayon.	*Look and handle* of continuous filament acetate. Lustre and handle nearer to silk and softer than viscose rayon. Under microscope appearance similar to viscose but fewer lines (Diagram 8). *Burning* of fibre Will melt under too hot an iron. Leaves *hard*, dark bead of ash (not brittle like silk). Tricel rolls back from flame leaving hard bead. *Chemical test* Acetate will dissolve in acetone: di-acetate in 70% acetone, tri-acetate in 100% acetone.	Acetate drapes well and has more natural crease recovery than viscose rayon. Acetate has a richer appearance than viscose rayon, hence its use for such fabrics as brocades. Acetate is absorbent but not so much as viscose rayon and therefore dries more quickly when wet. Mothproof; resistant to mildew.	Although stronger in water than viscose rayon, acetate can be damaged by too great heat such as too hot water for washing. It melts if too hot an iron is used. De-lustred acetate may show watermarks if damped down before ironing. Acetate tends to accumulate static electricity. This makes the fabric cling to the body or clothing. Frays badly and is slippery to handle in silk or satin form. Creases badly unless treated to counteract this tendency.	Acetate is used largely in the making of brocades, moirés, satins, taffetas.
TRI-ACETATE is a development of acetate. It is cellulose treated with acetic acid and acetic anhydride obtained from petroleum. The three combine together to produce tri-acetate. It combines the properties of di-acetate + heat-setting crease-resistant, non-stretch and non-shrink properties. It can be permanently pleated and is quick drying. It is stronger than di-acetate. The tri-acetate fibre developed by British Celanese Ltd is Tricel (registered trade name). The filament fibre can be converted into staple fibre and used by itself or with other staple fibres.		TRICEL made from tri-acetate resists hot, wet conditions to a much greater degree than di-acetate. It resists soiling, and is easy to wash and quick drying. Cheaper than some of the synthetic fibres and fabrics. Blends and mixes with other natural, regenerated or synthetic fibres. Tricel can be permanently pleated because of its heat-setting property.	Frays badly, especially silk or satin types which are slippery to handle and sew.	Tricel, the fibre made from tri-acetate, is manufactured as fabric in a great variety of forms, either by itself or in blends or mixtures with natural, regenerated or synthetic fibres, giving many 'easy-care' fabrics at reasonable prices.
FIBROLANE is made from casein, which is a by-product of milk. It is therefore of animal origin and is a *regenerated protein* fibre. Fibrolane is the registered trade name. It is produced in staple form only, and used to blend with other natural and man-made staple fibres such as wool, cotton or nylon. Fibrolane resembles wool in its warmth and resilience and the way in which it can absorb water without feeling wet. It loses strength when wet, and so is used mainly in blends with other fibres. It is non-irritant and adds softness and resilience to fabrics.				

Nylon

SOURCE	TESTING	ADVANTAGES FOR USE AS CLOTHING	DISADVANTAGES FOR USE AS CLOTHING	FABRICS FOR CLOTHING MADE FROM NYLON FIBRE
NYLON is a synthetic fibre derived from air, water and coal, and called a polyamide fibre. It was discovered and produced first in the USA between 1928 and 1938. Nylon polymer chips are made in Britain by Imperial Chemical Industries Ltd. Nylon yarn is spun from the nylon polymer.	*Handle and look* Although appearance is deceptive, many nylon fabrics look very like silk or rayon, but they are much firmer and stronger. Pull fabric both warp way and then weft. Under microscope nylon fibre has the appearance of a glass rod—sometimes speckled (Diagram 9).	Durable: strong yet light. Easy washing; retains strength when wet. Quick drying; little pressing or ironing is required. Non-creasing. Unaffected by moth and mildew.	*Cost* Nylon fabric is more expensive than many rayons and cottons. Some of the smooth, close weaves are non-absorbent, and therefore unsuitable for wearing next to the skin. Many nylon fabrics fray badly.	*Lightweight and diaphanous* Nylon chiffon, organza, voile, lace, net. *Medium weight* Nylon seersucker, taffeta, satin, paper nylon, spun nylon.
Nylon polymer chips have the appearance of white marble. They are melted and forced through spinerettes. Air then cools and solidifies.	*Burning* of fibre On contact with a flame nylon fibre melts, becomes treacly, and hardens into a bead. Smells of celery.	Will not *spread* fire. Nylon yarn will melt at 480°F. but will not flare. Nylon net is not called 'flare-free'. It is specially treated to withstand flames. Sewing thread and trimmings should be of nylon or Terylene also. See note on 'Thread for Stitching', page 37.	Slippage causes weak-nesses at seams unless sufficient turnings are allowed. Attracts dust and there-fore tends to soil quickly. White nylon discolours.	*Heavier weight* Brushed nylon, nylon velvet. Banlon (like ribbed jersey).
Through a process of stretching called 'cold drawing' it is converted into a textile fibre which is further processed to become continuous filament fibre.	*Chemical test* Nylon fibre dissolves in 90% formic acid or in 100% hydrochloric acid (spirits of salt.)	Perspiration does not rot nylon.	Some plain weave, firm nylon fabrics need careful adjustment of the sewing machine to prevent puckering.	
Nylon staple is continuous filament fibre cut into short lengths for hand knitting yarns, or for mixing with natural fibres, *e.g.* wool, cotton, flax, or with regenerated staple fibres. It can also be used alone.		Bulked nylon yarn makes suitable knitted or woven fabrics for under and outer wear, *e.g.* Banlon.		
Permanent crimp can be put into nylon staple fibre making it feel like wool. Crimped nylon is used for 'stretch' fabrics.		Nylon can be permanently pleated, because of its heat-setting property.		
The strength of fabrics made from natural or regenerated fibres can be increased by the addition of a small percentage of nylon staple, or nylon filament fibre.		Good draping qualities; nylon hangs in folds well and does not crease.		
Nylon fabrics can be 'heat-set' by steam-heating. Thus shape and size can be retained, making them crease-resistant and non-iron. This property also enables permanent pleating to be given to nylon fabrics and garments.		If white nylon discolours, it can be dyed another colour.		
Nylon has a low moisture absorption, and fabrics dry quickly when wet.		Nylon can be stiffened to use for interlinings or linings.		
Nylon can be bulked (see note on page 27).				

If too hot an iron is used in pressing, nylon fabric will melt.

Terylene

SOURCE	TESTING	ADVANTAGES FOR USE AS CLOTHING	DISADVANTAGES FOR USE AS CLOTHING	FABRICS FOR CLOTHING MADE FROM TERYLENE FIBRES
TERYLENE is a synthetic fibre derived from ethylene glycol (better known as anti-freeze) and terephthalic acid, which are derived from petroleum. It was a British discovery during the Second World War. Imperial Chemical Industries Ltd manufacture the fibre in Britain. Terylene is the registered trade name. The fibre is classed as polyester. Terylene polymer chips appear as tiny cubes of white marble. They are melted and forced through spinerettes in a similar way to nylon. Eventually they are converted into continuous filament yarn used for smooth surfaced fabrics. Terylene staple fibre is derived from continuous filament fibre and is suitable for mixing with natural or regenerated staple fibres, or for use as 'all Terylene' fabrics. Terylene has been difficult to dye, but continued research is being made in this field, and new dyeing techniques are being developed. Terylene can be heat-set, enabling the fabric to be permanently pleated or creased, by heat- and steam-setting. As with nylon, shape and size can be retained, making the fabric crease-resistant and non-iron. Terylene has low moisture absorption and dries quickly when washed or wet. Unaffected by many chemicals it is useful for protective fabrics for clothing. Terylene can be bulked (see note on page 27) and crimped. *Dacron* and *Fortrel* are polyester fibres similar to Terylene, and made in the USA.	*Handle* of fabric Terylene is very strong and tough. *Look* It is difficult to distinguish between Terylene and nylon fibres. Under a microscope, Terylene fibre appears like a glass rod (Diagram 10). *Burning* of fibres Both fibres melt forming a hard bead. Faint smell of mushrooms. *Chemical test* Terylene will *not* dissolve in formic acid, or hydrochloric acid, whereas nylon will do so.	Hardwearing; light yet strong. Strong when wet or dry—washable yet quick drying—time-saver as little or no ironing is required; practically unshrinkable. Crease-resistant because fabrics are heat-set in finishing. Can be permanently pleated. Fire-resistant; the fibre will melt if it contacts a flame, but it will not flare easily. Unaffected by moths or mildew; unaffected by seawater, so used a good deal for swim wear. Low water uptake and so is quick to dry. Resistant to sunlight. Good draping qualities; Terylene hangs well, yet is resilient, so creases little, and recovers quickly. Fibres can be mixed with other man-made or natural fibres to improve the strength and wearing qualities of clothing fabrics. Bulked Terylene yarn makes suitable knitted or woven fabrics for underwear or outerwear. Crimped Terylene is used for 'stretch fabrics'.	*Cost* Production costs are still high, so that Terylene fabrics are comparatively expensive. Non-absorbent; closely woven fabrics of Terylene are unsuitable to wear next to the skin. Attracts dirt. The difficulty encountered in dyeing Terylene limits the variety of colours at present, but research is continually developing this side of production. In tailoring, Terylene resists shrinking and stretching (tailor manipulation). It requires special styling to cause the desired shape and fit. All Terylene fabric has a harder feel than wool or worsted cloths. Terylene will melt if too hot an iron is used for pressing or ironing.	From Terylene continuous filament yarn, sheer fabrics are made for lingerie, baby wear, blouses and dresses. From Terylene staple fibre opaque and heavier fabrics are made for skirts, dresses, suits, etc. Terylene mixed with wool, worsted, cotton or linen gives strength and resilience to the fabrics. Terylene petersham for waistbands will not shrink or stretch. As it resists stretch, Terylene sewing thread is good for stitching both Terylene and nylon. Terylene yarn is used extensively in making net and lace; also Terylene jersey (called Crimplene).

Courtelle, Acrilan and Orlon

SOURCE	TESTING	ADVANTAGES FOR USE AS CLOTHING	DISADVANTAGES FOR USE AS CLOTHING	FABRICS FOR CLOTHING
COURTELLE, ACRILAN and ORLON are acrylic fibres produced from acrylonitrile, derived from by-products of either coal or petroleum. Courtelle is a British fibre made by Courtaulds. Acrilan originated in the USA and is now produced in the United Kingdom. Orlon is another acrylic fibre produced in the USA and used for making fabrics and knitting yarns. The filaments are drawn together and after further processing are cut into staple fibres for use in fabric production, either woven or knitted. Fabric may be 100% Courtelle or Acrilan, or blended with wool or cotton or other man-made staple fibres.	*Look* Microscopic view of Courtelle fibre like glass rod slightly speckled (Diagram 11). *Burning of fibres* Acrylic fibres melt like tar leaving hard, cinder-like beads. They are slow to ignite, melting point being reached before ignition. *Chemical test* Acrylic fibres have considerable powers of resistance to alkalis. They are not soluble in 1–5%, and their strength is only slightly impaired. Their resistance is lowered in hot, concentrated alkalis. Orlon can be differentiated from other acrylic fibres as well as nylon and Terylene by testing in 5% caustic potash when it will turn orange brown, whereas the others will not.	Light in weight yet warm. Strong and hard wearing. Non-irritant. Crease-resistant. Unaffected by moths or mildew. Resist damage by acids. Can be permanently pleated because of their heat-setting properties. Easy to wash and dry. Do not shrink.	Tailored garments of Courtelle cannot be shaped by steam-heat process, so need careful styling and fit. Attracts dirt. Perspiration and body oils may penetrate fibres and be difficult to remove. Knitted fabrics must not be stretched in making up or the finished result will be unsatisfactory. Easily puckered when machining. Test tension (medium) and stitch (medium) first and use medium speed. Use Terylene sewing thread. Test for heat when pressing. Use a cool iron and *no* moisture. Press dry.	Courtelle 100%, *e.g.* double-knit Courtelle. Acrilan 100%. Blends and mixtures of these acrylic fibres with natural and/or man-made fibres are continually being tried, developed and improved. Both woven and knitted fabrics are produced under the name of Courtelle, and for other acrylic fibres such as Acrilan and Orlon. Choose simple, uncluttered styles when making 100% Courtelle into garments.

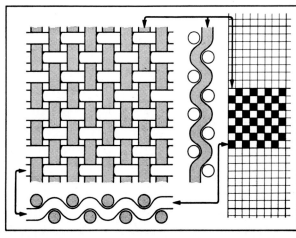

1. **Plain weave**

2.   **Twill weave**

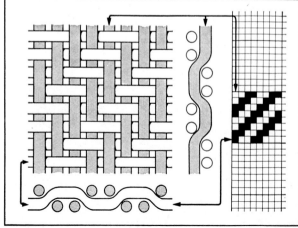

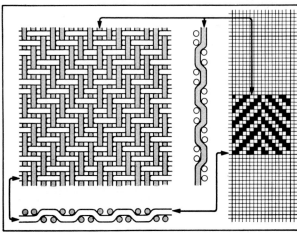

3. **Herringbone weave**

4. Satin weave

RIGHT SIDE Coarser threads are unravelled to show the density of the fine, closely set warp threads which run parallel to the selvedge.

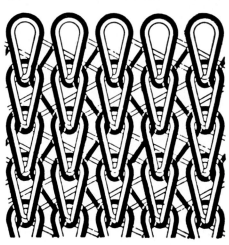

5. **Warp locknit**

6. Weft knitted jersey

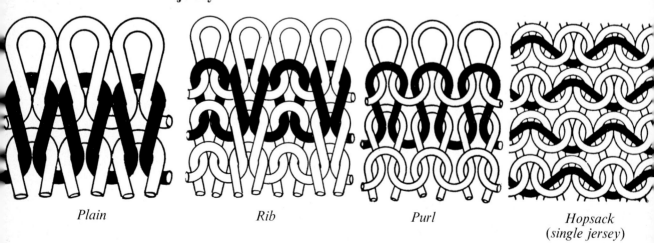

Plain *Rib* *Purl* *Hopsack (single jersey)*

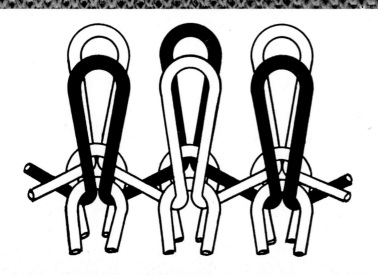

7. **Plain double jersey**

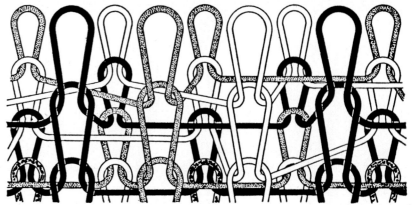

8. Rib jacquard
   (three colours)

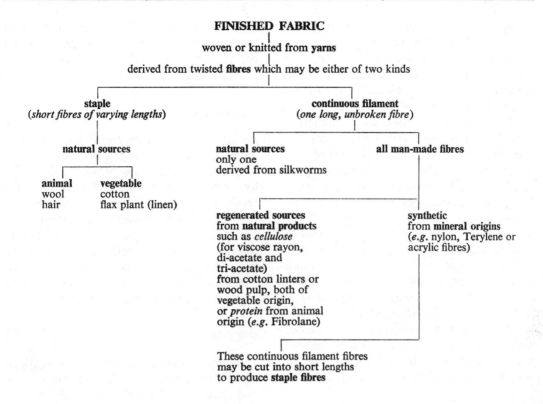

FINISHED FABRIC

woven or knitted from **yarns**

derived from twisted **fibres** which may be either of two kinds

staple
(*short fibres of varying lengths*)

continuous filament
(*one long, unbroken fibre*)

natural sources

natural sources
only one
derived from silkworms

all man-made fibres

animal
wool
hair

vegetable
cotton
flax plant (linen)

regenerated sources
from **natural products**
such as *cellulose*
(for viscose rayon,
di-acetate and
tri-acetate)
from cotton linters or
wood pulp, both of
vegetable origin,
or *protein* from animal
origin (*e.g.* Fibrolane)

synthetic
from **mineral origins**
(*e.g.* nylon, Terylene or
acrylic fibres)

These continuous filament fibres
may be cut into short lengths
to produce **staple fibres**

FINISHES

Besides having some knowledge of the fibres contained in modern fabrics, the needlewoman should know how cloths are finished to give more practical and economical wear. Fabrics that are well made and well chosen can still prove unsatisfactory if, when making up or laundering, they are badly handled and carelessly treated. Some of the fabric finishes affect methods of applying heat and moisture, and can be damaged or even destroyed by ignorance or careless usage.

Crease-resistant finish

This is the finish given to cotton, linen and rayon which, as untreated fabrics, crease badly. When treated by impregnating the fabric with synthetic resin it is less likely to crease, and any creases disappear after the garment is hung up for a time (as with wool). This is called 'recovery' from creasing. Great heat can affect the resin, so that when pressing, washing or ironing, it is wise to use lower temperatures than for untreated cotton or linen. Nylon and Terylene are made permanently crease-resistant by means of pressure and heat, as long as the temperature does not exceed that given to the finish.

'Minimum-iron'

These fabrics must be able to resist, and recover from, creases when wet as well as dry, to retain smoothness in drying and so justify the claim of 'little or no ironing'. Synthetic resin is used for this. It has been developed from the crease-resistant process first invented by a British firm in the 1930 era. Some *embossed* fabrics, where raised designs are impressed on cloth by means of heat and pressure, are crease-resistant and 'non-iron' because of their thermoplastic properties and heat-setting method of finishing.

Labels carrying instructions for washing, such as 'wash as wool', attached to many ready-made garments should be carefully noted. These fabrics often contain modern finishes such as crease-resistant, minimum-iron, flame-resistant and stain-resistant. Too little rinsing of garments to rid them of soap or synthetic detergent, and too high temperatures of water and iron, can impair the special finish. Any points regarding heat and moisture should also be carefully noted.

Most fabrics bearing labels or marks of quality tests related to brand names have been subjected to rigorous tests according to fabric and use. It is wise when buying clothing fabrics to realise this, for although the price may be higher than similar cloth which carries no label, there is more guarantee of satisfaction with the labelled fabric in appearance, wearing qualities and durability of finish. Time is usually well spent in making up such fabrics.

Water and stain-repellent finishes

These can be given to various fabrics by means of silicones or resins. Instead of the fabric absorbing liquid, the silicone or resin finish repels it, so that globules are formed which can be shaken off and the fabric sponged clean straight away. The liquid finish, chemically produced, forms a sheath on individual fibres which can then be spun and woven into cloth. This finish improves the appearance and draping qualities of the fabric. It will withstand washing provided the fabric is well rinsed, but soap, synthetic detergents, fat or grease left in the cloth will cause the stain-repellent finish to deteriorate.

Moth-proofing

Several trade finishes make wool permanently resistant to moths and are suitable for all woollen goods, clothing and furnishing fabrics of wool, yarn, etc. They are a great boon to the woollen goods trade as well as to the dress-maker and housewife. Other moth-proof finishes are resins which discourage moths, but garments treated with most of these need re-proofing after dry-cleaning.

Permanent pleating

Fabrics made from synthetic fibres such as nylon, Terylene or regenerated fibres such as tri-acetate or Tricel are permanently pleated by steam- and heat-setting. Pleat creases are retained so long as the fabric is not subjected to a higher temperature than that used in the finish. Rayon staple, wool and worsted cloth can be treated by a chemical solution to give a permanent finish to the pleated fabric. By using resin and applying heat-setting treatment, cotton can also be permanently pleated.

Stiff finishes

These finishes are generally given to synthetic fabrics which are used for collar interlinings and crinoline underskirts. The fabrics are impregnated with synthetic resin and subjected to special heat treatment so that the fabric finish, as in paper nylon, will stand up to pressing and laundering. Cotton can also be processed with this stiff finish, but the cheaper kinds are inclined to go limp after being worn for a time. Stiffened cotton lawn is similar to organdie and if it is of good quality, it will keep its crispness when laundered.

Bonded fabrics

These fabrics are non-woven and may be used for interlinings. They are made of short cotton fibres mixed with man-made fibres which are held together by a bonding agent. They have no warp and weft, which makes these fabrics economical to cut as there is no 'grain' to study.

Anti-shrink finishes

These finishes can be applied, under various trade names, to wool, cotton, linen and rayon fabrics. If such fabrics are not pre-shrunk, they may shrink when washed, or if too much water is used in damp pressing when garments are being made up.

Fire-proofing (non-flam)

It has not been possible so far to make inflammable fabrics like cotton net, flannelette and winceyette proof against fire, but finishes have been devised which will make them smoulder instead of flaring up quickly when they are brought into contact with a flame. Some of these finishes will deteriorate as a result of frequent washing, but research continues to improve them. There is also a chemical solution on the market which can be used to spray or respray garments or fabrics to make them flame-resistant. NOTE: It has been proved that clothes of the pyjama or jeans type are less likely to catch fire than loose-skirted garments like long nightdresses, a thing worth noting when clothing children. 'Flare-free' is a trade name given to nylon and Terylene fabrics like lace, net, taffeta, etc., which have been given flame-resistant treatment. These fibres melt but will not flare up. Hence nylon net is much safer than cotton net for bouffant dresses and underskirts. It is important, however, that sewing thread and trimmings such as lace and ribbon should be of similar synthetic fibre like nylon or Terylene. See notes on *Thread for stitching*, page 37.

Bulked fabrics

These fabrics, such as bulked nylon or Terylene, are crimped to give stretch, and the surface of the yarn is fluffed up to give extra 'loft' and absorbency, which removes transparency and gives warmth and softness instead of a cool, smooth surface.

Stretch fabrics

Yarns are crimped to give stretch: warp stretch pulls lengthwise, parallel to the selvedge; filler stretch pulls widthwise; and two-way stretch pulls both ways.

Laminated fabrics

These, called foam laminates, are backed with a chemical foam to give insulation and warmth without weight.

Polyurethane is one of the plastics used for foam backing fabrics. Polyester resin, or polyether, combine with isocyanates to produce polyurethane foam. The foam has a cellular structure making it porous and hygienic to wear. Grades and thicknesses vary according to quality and purpose. The high grades have closer cellular construction than the lower, more open grades, and qualities which enable the backing to stretch where required for movement, e.g. sleeves, where arms bend at elbow joints.

The foam is attached to WS or back of clothing fabrics by a process called 'laminating'. The foam backing gives resilience and shape retention as well as warmth without weight.

The wise buyer will look for labels of quality and fitness in foam back fabrics. This is one of the most recent developments in fabric production and finishing, and it is still being improved.

The work of the dyer and finisher of fabrics is both a science and a craft. Research and development continue daily to improve quality and wearing properties, as well as appearance. More synthetic fibres are being discovered and introduced. In mixing and blending these with fibres already known, much scientific knowledge and skill is required. Just as there are degrees of quality in natural fibres, so too in finishing there are low and high grades. For instance, the application of some resins tends to make a fabric weaker, and cheaper, poorer grades of cotton with this finish may tear easily in wear, although their appearance and glossy finish may be attractive. It is wise to look for well known and proved brands of finishing.

CUTTING OUT

In considering lays and cutting out in more advanced materials, attention should be paid to the following points:

1. *Construction* of fabrics affecting lays—woven, knitted or twisted (e.g. cloth, jersey, lace);
2. *Texture* and surface interest and effect on made-up garment (velvet, mohair, facecloth, satin);
3. *Pattern design* of fabric—affecting balance of design, balance of colour and correct matching of pattern.

Construction

WOVEN FABRIC

Yarns cross each other at right angles, those running the length of the piece of cloth being called warp or selvedge threads, while yarns crossing the fabric from side to side are called weft threads. Different ways of intersecting the yarns are called 'weaves' of fabric. These may be plain, or give surface interest by the method of weaving or the patterns formed by variations of interlacing the threads. (See Plates 1–4, showing fabric construction.)

Plain or tabby weave is the basic one and the simplest, both warp and weft threads interlacing alternately over and under each other. This weave will produce strong *tightly woven* fabrics like gingham, calico and canvas as well as plain surface fabrics such as taffeta or organdie. There may be variety in the thickness of warp and weft, or in the type and quality of the yarns; these may be smooth, uneven in thickness, loosely or tightly twisted or woven. *Ribbed weave*, sometimes called 'rep' weave, illustrates this. The fabric may have fine warp yarns set closely together, and much thicker weft yarns. When woven, a ribbed effect is produced as in grosgrain, marocain, poplin, etc. The thick yarns are entirely covered by the fine warp yarns. This is the reason why some fabrics of this nature become threadbare if subjected to continual friction or strain. The fine yarns fray away, uncovering the thick ones underneath, e.g. wool reps. Slippage of fabric at seams occurs in such materials, where there is extra strain through tight fit and movement of figure, e.g. across hips and seat of skirts. (NOTE: *Slippage* is a term used when threads of fabric move or 'slip' from their

Fabrics with twill weave

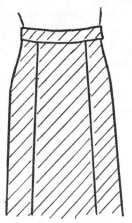

Right—twill weave must run in same direction on each panel.

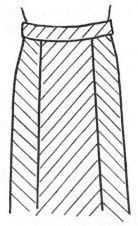

Wrong—twill weave runs in opposite directions on side and centre panels.   *12*

correct position, leaving a threadbare space.) The rib weave of this type of fabric shows clearly in garments emphasising grain faults in cut or making up. In some fabrics the heavy weft yarns give a somewhat stiff feel, as in poult or grosgrain. This would influence choice of style, as such fabrics have not the draping quality of softer materials.

Twill weave is another standard weave. The intersection of yarns in this case forms steps, giving the effect of lines running diagonally across the fabric. Care should be taken to find the *right* and *wrong* side of the fabric before cutting out. Usually, when worn the twill should run downwards from left to right on the right side of the fabric, but there may be exceptions to this rule. The twill must follow the same direction in all parts of the garment in either case (Diagram 12). Examples of fabrics with twill weave are: gaberdine, serge, Viyella, foulard, and many suitings. *Herringbone weaves* incorporate *twills* and *reverse twills* causing V shapes where they join.

Satin weave is the third basic weave. Satin, noted for its lustre, has a different construction to give this effect. One set of yarns (usually the warp) forms the surface, being bright, fine, and closely set, producing a slippery, mirror-like effect. The second set of yarns forms the back, and are usually thicker and duller than those of the warp or first set. This gives a definite right and wrong side to the fabric. Because of the nature of the weave, the surface threads of satin are easily caught up and damaged by friction, blunt or too thick needles or pins. The fabric drapes well, but is slippery and needs skilful handling in cutting out and making up to preserve good shape and line. In garment lining, slipperiness is a desirable quality and satin is often used for this.

These are the three basic weaves. There are many variations used in modern fabrics.

STRAIGHT GRAIN

In cutting out garments the straight grain of the pattern and fabric is all-important. The correct hang of the made-up garment depends upon the accurate judgment of the cutter in preparing the material before planning the lay of the paper pattern.

When laid correctly upon the cutting-out table, the weft grain should lie at right angles to the warp. A good test is to see whether warp and weft threads are parallel to the squared table ends (Diagram 13). If the weft threads are crooked, i.e. not at right angles to the warp, they are called 'off grain'. They should be pulled, or stretched carefully, from corner to corner in the opposite direction to correct the angle before planning the pattern on the fabric (Diagram 14).

If the fabric is very obstinate, and it is possible to anchor the corners and weft edges at the correct angle to a squared table or hardboard surface by such means as drawing pins, this will hold it in position. Lightly press the surface (WS uppermost if possible) with a partly damp cloth (but *not* wringing wet)

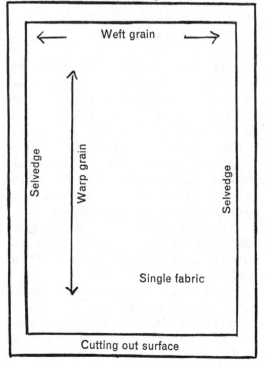

Correct placing   *13*

Weft grain at correct angle

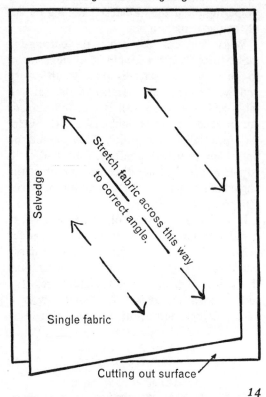

Weft grain at wrong angle

Selvedge

Stretch fabric across this way to correct angle.

Single fabric

Cutting out surface

14

between the iron and the fabric. NOTE: The preservation of the fabric is essential, so test on a small piece first for reaction to heat and moisture. Allow the fabric to dry before releasing the edges, so the threads are stabilised.

Note also that some crease-resistant fabrics, or those with special finishings such as glazing or polishing, cannot be straightened without losing the special qualities given to them. Do not buy fabric which is badly 'off grain'.

The importance of straight grain is emphasised in Chapter Fifteen, Jackets (cutting out), page 172, Skirts (cutting out), page 195 and Slacks (cutting out), page 200.

The following idea for an improvised cutting-out and working surface may be helpful to those people who live in flats or bed-sitters and have no room for large tables, or whose table surfaces need protection from scratching.

Obtain a piece of hardboard or beaverboard, 36 or 54 inches square. It can be in two pieces, hinged together with plastic or adhesive tape on the under side for convenient storage. The board can then be opened out and placed on a table top or other flat surface. If the sharp corners tend to catch in clothing when the work table is being passed, they can be rounded off to avoid this nuisance.

Texture

Texture in fabric is produced by the method of construction, e.g. openness or closeness of the weave or type of knitted fabric, as well as by the type of fibre or finish. The feel or handle of the fabric may be smooth or rough, firm, supple or fluid (e.g., chiffon). Each of these characteristics affects both choice of style and construction of garment.

Surface interest involves nap or pile. *Nap* means that the surface of the cloth has fibre ends raised, cut evenly, and brushed smoothly one way, e.g. mohair, facecloth, wool or nylon furcloth. *Pile* is the name given to the surface. of velvet, velveteen or corduroy, where fibre ends are upstanding and closely cut.

These fabrics are termed 'one way' when planning lays of garment patterns, since each part must be cut with the nap or pile running in one direction to gain the desired effect when made up.

When nap or pile runs upwards the fabric appears darker; when smoothed downwards, the effect is lighter. The usual practice is for the nap to smooth downwards in garments of napped surface cloth such as mohair or facecloth, and to smooth upwards in velvets, velveteen, or corduroy.

Pattern design

In fabrics patterns are divided into two groups:
1. *Woven* into the material, as in stripes, checks and plaids or jacquard loom designs;
2. *Printed* on the surface.

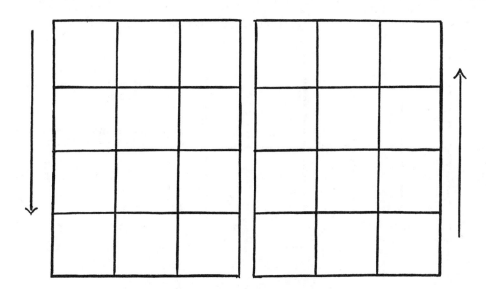

Paper patterns can be laid either way, when
fabric is reversed top to bottom the lines will
match to give correct appearance on garment.   *15*

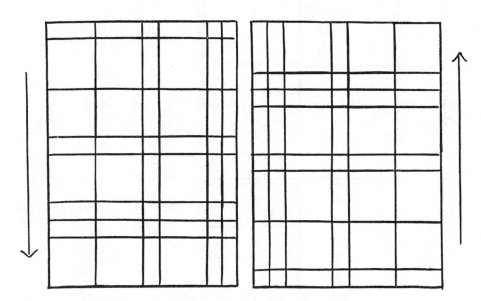

Paper patterns must be laid one way only if
reversed top to bottom lines cannot be matched
for correct appearance of design on garment.   *16*

WOVEN DESIGNS

Even stripes, checks and plaids have no up or
down (Diagram 15). In this case paper patterns
can be dovetailed. *Uneven* stripes, checks or
plaids must be treated as 'one way' fabrics
(Diagram 16), and paper patterns placed
accordingly.

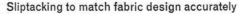

Sliptacking to match fabric design accurately

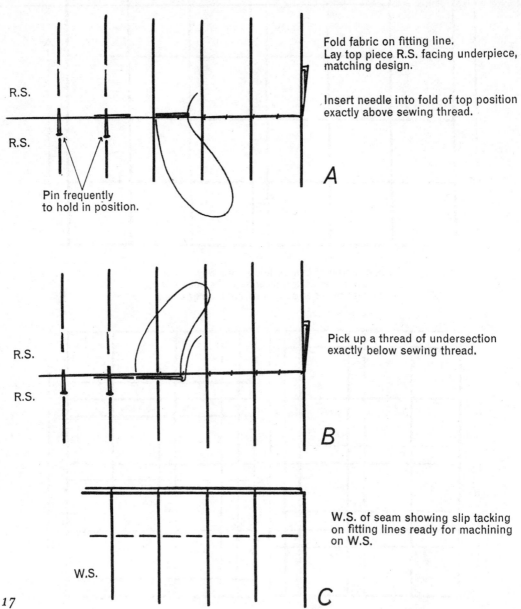

Fold fabric on fitting line.
Lay top piece R.S. facing underpiece, matching design.

Insert needle into fold of top position exactly above sewing thread.

A

R.S.

R.S.

Pin frequently
to hold in position.

Pick up a thread of undersection exactly below sewing thread.

B

R.S.

R.S.

W.S. of seam showing slip tacking on fitting lines ready for machining on W.S.

C

W.S.

17

Choose suitable styles for checks or stripes. They cannot be matched easily on bias seams. Some paper patterns state 'not suitable for checked or striped fabric'. When buying the pattern, be sure to look for such notes and avoid those styles.

In both cases careful planning is required to balance the fabric design on the figure, and match it on seams, so that horizontal lines appear to continue round the figure and are at the same level on bodice and sleeve, especially in front and at fastening edges. Centres of collars and bodices should match or complement each other. Prominent vertical lines should balance and complement each other on both sides of the figure.

In matching stripes or plaids, seams must be constructed where stripes or checks meet in chevrons. The exact matching of the woven lines of the pattern at the correct angle is essential. For this purpose, and also in matching horizontal or vertical lines of fabric together, sliptacking is illustrated in Diagrams 17a and b. Work on RS so that the visual appearance is correct when assembling the seam. Use small stitches to hold the design firmly and prevent slippage. The seam can be machined on WS afterwards, as shown in Diagram 17c. This method of sliptacking is most useful whenever it is advisable to watch the right side for correct effect when assembling parts of garments.

PRINTED DESIGNS

It is advisable to purchase a little extra fabric (¼ or ½ yard) when choosing:
1. A large design, where planning the lay of the paper pattern involves careful arrangement so that motifs and colour are balanced well in the finished garment;
2. A repeat design, where matching the pattern is necessary in joining seams, as shown in Diagram 18;
3. A 'one way' design, when all pieces of paper pattern must be laid in one direction on the fabric and cannot be dovetailed for economy.

When using fabric with 'one way' designs or nap surfaces, note that it cannot be folded as illustrated in Diagram 19 or one half will be upside down.

The paper pattern must be planned on single

18

Repeating patterns

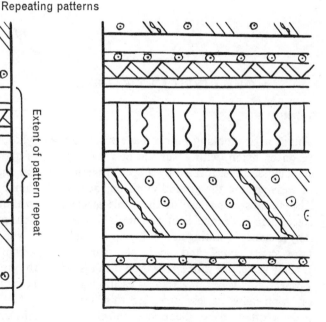

Where pattern repeats must match, allow **extra** fabric when buying.

An exact length as shown here may be insufficient to match the pattern design on fabric.

33

material. Where pieces need to be duplicated, cut out the first portion, leaving the paper pattern pinned on top. Lay it with WS facing a corresponding section of correctly patterned or napped fabric in order to cut the second portion.

Alternatively, duplicate the pieces of paper pattern by cutting them out again in paper. Mark 'right' and 'left' sides on each piece. Then plan the whole paper pattern of the garment on single material.

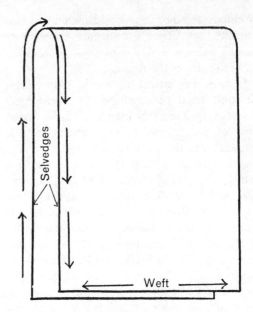

When fabric is folded double like this any pattern design or pile surface (nap) is reversed, as shown by the direction of the arrows.

Fabric with one-way design or nap must not be folded in this way, or the result will be upside down on one half of the garment.

19

MORE DIFFICULT FABRICS

Velvet

This is a rich-looking fabric made from silk, rayon or nylon, with a surface of close, up-standing cut pile, formed by a special method of weaving into the ground cloth or backing. The pile must lie *one* way on the whole garment since there is definite light and dark shading. Any mistakes in cutting or making up would be most conspicuous, and spoil the garment. Usually velvet pile runs *upwards* on the finished garment. Silk velvet fingermarks easily. Rayon or nylon velvet is less prone to this. Dressmakers often make themselves finger stalls of the fabric to prevent marking when handling costly velvet. Fine needles mark less than pins and silk thread marks less than cotton or sylko, when fixing patterns or assembling parts of garments. Avoid if possible machine stitching on the right side of the fabric. Seams should be few and as inconspicuous as possible to allow the material to show its full beauty and richness. It lends itself to folds and draping.

Velvet is often lined with fine silk-type lightweight material, e.g. chiffon or similar fabric, to prevent double parts of the pile surface being used.

Use pure silk thread for hand and machine stitching, fine, sharp machine needles, medium size machine stitch and rather loose tension to avoid puckering seams.

Pressing velvet is described on pages 42–3.

Transparent fabrics

Some of these fabrics are fairly firm and easy to handle, e.g. organdie or voile. *Chiffon, georgette, ninon,* and similar *fine* diaphanous fabrics with a fluid characteristic need special care and handling when cutting out and making up. Lack of firmness and a tendency to slip causes difficulty. The following suggestions may be found useful:

1. Cover the cutting-out surface with large sheets of smooth tissue paper as wide as the material.
2. Pin the fabric to the paper to hold the grain in position, before planning the lay of the paper pattern. Use very fine pins or needles. Fix the selvedge of the fabric to the straight edge of paper with the weft threads at right angles. If necessary to hold the fabric flat in position, pin down the centre as well as all round.
3. Plan the lay of the paper pattern on the fabric. Pin in position.
4. Cut out both material and tissue paper together and treat as one fabric.

Threadmark the fitting lines of pattern to fabric through the tissue paper as well. Assemble the pieces with tissue paper attached. The thin paper backing gives the firmness required to retain shape and grain correctly and to prevent incorrect stretching. If and when fitting is required, carefully detach the paper by cutting or tearing away, leaving a border of at least one inch either side of seam lines. When stitching permanently, machine through the paper as well as the fabric. This gives firmness and avoids puckers. The paper can be torn away afterwards.

Lace

Threads are twisted together in lace making. Dress lace usually has a net or mesh background through which designs are worked giving a light, delicate appearance. Because of the transparency of lace it is often lined with a firm fabric such as taffeta or a bright surfaced material such as satin. Contrasting colours or textures can give pleasing effects, e.g. black, dull-finished lace over vivid-hued satin. The two fabrics can be made up together, or as two separate garments, i.e., foundation and lace overdress. Lace may be made from various fibres—cotton, rayon, nylon or silk, or mixtures such as silk net background and viscose rayon design. Wool lace is also made, often containing a percentage of cotton or nylon fibre as well to give added strength.

Wide lace is often made and sold as 'flouncing'. This kind has one straight edge and the other scalloped. The width is usually 34 to 36 inches. It is made in lengths of approximately five yards. This length may be sufficient for short length dresses but more would be required for those of ground length depending on the style. (NOTE: Manufacturers are beginning to produce longer lengths.)

On the right side of lace the pattern is usually more raised than the wrong side, which feels smoother. In some cases, however, it is quite difficult to detect. The scalloped edge of flouncing may be used as a decorative edging to a full skirt, or it can be cut away if not required by the style. Attractive neck or sleeve finishes can be made by using the scalloped edge shaped and appliquéd to the bodice or sleeve. Other wide lace is termed 'allover lace'. *Bobbin net* is used to strengthen lace where a transparent effect is required. Dance dresses of lace often have layers of net under the skirt to add to the effect. The lower edges of lace dresses can be finished with a band of net. Nylon net is more durable than cotton or rayon and is much less inflammable (often sold as flare-free) and therefore safer for party or theatrical wear.

If the lace is to be mounted on either matching or contrasting fabric, e.g. taffeta, poult or net, the two fabrics can be cut out and made up as one. This makes handling and construction easier since the two fabrics together are much firmer than lace alone. It will be found, too, that seam turnings do not show through· and hems can be attached to the lining fabric only, avoiding any stitched appearance on the right side of the lace.

Lay the lining fabric on the cutting out surface with selvedge and weft grains correctly running at right angles to each other. Press out any creases. On top lay the lace in position. Join the two fabrics by pinning and tacking across both width and length. After this, treat the two as one fabric. When each piece has been cut out threadmark the fitting or stitching lines by tacking them carefully together through double fabric. Proceed to make up the garment as for single material.

When lace is cut out by itself, choose simple styles that will show the beauty of the fabric without too many seams to break the lace design. If the lace is not wide enough and requires joining across the fabric, as, for instance, in full length evening or bridal dress skirts, use the method for invisible joining of lace by the design, as illustrated in Diagrams 233 to 238 on pages 156–8.

The twisted or looped threads which form the design are worked over a warp base. So, in cutting out, treat the lengthwise direction of the fabric like selvedge grain in other woven fabrics. For pressing lace, see page 42.

Jersey fabrics

These fabrics are knitted both on the warp and the weft principle. A warp knitted fabric is made up of a number of vertical threads, where each thread, as in hand crochet work, makes only one loop in a horizontal row of knitting; in a weft knitted fabric, the complete horizontal row is worked from a single thread, as in hand knitted stocking-stitch. (See Plates 5–8, showing fabric construction.)

1. Locknit, used mainly for women's lingerie, is made on the warp knitted principle.

2. Weft knitted jersey fabric may be divided into three types: plain, rib and purl. For *plain fabric*, the loops on one set of machine needles are drawn in one direction only. *Rib fabric* is knitted on two sets of needles so that the loops may be drawn to the front of the fabric (plain loop) or the back (rib loop). A *purl fabric* is knitted on a special machine with double-headed latch needles so that one row

may be worked with the loops drawn to the front and the next with loops drawn to the back. This fabric has the same appearance as hand knitted garter-stitch.

Modern jersey fabric by the yard is produced mainly on circular knitting machines with a finished open width of 58–60 inches depending on the machine and the kind of stitch. If the machine has only one set of needles, it produces *single jersey* and if there are two sets, the fabric is *double jersey*. A single jersey fabric may incorporate a laid-in yarn which reduces the lateral stretch of the fabric and gives it a woven appearance so that it is very suitable for women's lightweight dresses. A typical fabric of this kind is weft knitted hopsack. (See Plate 6, showing fabric construction.)

3. Apart from the simple rib shown in Plate 6 one of the most common types of double jersey is *interlock* (Plate 7) which is two simple rib fabrics locked together. Before 1950 nearly all interlock was in cotton and used for all types of underwear. Since then, however, interlock has become very popular in the dress trade and is knitted from worsted yarn and many man-made fibres spun on the staple principle. There are many variations on standard interlock. *Milano rib* and *ponte di Roma* are now extremely popular. These two fabrics have a slight ripple effect on the right side.

4. *Rib jacquard* is a popular fabric of varying texture where up to four colours are worked into the design by using several sets of needles, each set knitting or missing according to the pattern. It has no floating threads on the wrong side as the rib needles knit them in at the back to give a striped or twill effect in the colours of the face pattern. Plate 8 shows the structure of three-colour jacquard with a twill backing. Ripple and blister (cloqué) effects may be produced in jacquard fabrics and certain machines can knit reversible jacquard in two colours.

Jersey fabric of all kinds is very popular. Both wool and man-made fibre jersey packs easily into a small space, and much of it is crease-resistant or, at any rate, recovers quickly after being unpacked and hung up.

CUTTING OUT JERSEY FABRICS

Find out if the fabric is circular or flat. The advantage of circular jersey is that long seams can be avoided. Suppression of fullness in shaping can take the form of darts, gathers or soft unpressed pleats.

The rib in jersey corresponds to selvedge grain in woven fabric. It is also the right side of the fabric. The straight grain symbols on paper patterns must be placed parallel to the ribs to ensure the correct hang of the garment. The cut ends corresponding to weft grain should be squared across, i.e. cut at right angles to the ribbed edges.

Research goes on to improve jersey fabric as it is inclined to stretch. Double knit jersey is firmer and less likely to stretch than single.

Allow generous turnings. Sometimes jersey fabric drops after hanging. This could prove disastrous if garments are close-fitting, unless forethought in cutting out has provided for such an emergency. This applies particularly to garments cut in one with no waistline. Cut edges tend to curl. See Chapter Five, Seams, page 58. After cutting out portions of garments, preserve the shape and measurements of important curved lines by staystitching near the fitting lines on the turning side. This is preferably done by hand for less experienced workers. More skilled workers might prefer to use machine staystitching—but unless this is carefully done, further stretching could occur.

Linings or part linings are advisable to preserve shape, especially in the case of single jersey fabric. See Chapter Fourteen, Linings, page 159.

Stretch fabrics

These must *not* be stretched when patterns are being pinned on. Select styles designed specially for stretch materials. Pin frequently to hold the pattern firmly in position. Hold the fabric down flat on the cutting surface so that it cannot stretch. Use scissors with good sharp blades that cut evenly. After cutting out the material, staystitch it immediately round the neck, armholes and shoulders to prevent loss of shape through further stretching.

Laminated fabrics

These are insulated with a backing of chemical foam to give warmth without weight. They are therefore thick to cut out and make up. Choose styles specially designed for these fabrics, with few seams which are as straight as possible. Adjust paper patterns carefully before cutting out the fabric, to avoid alterations after fitting.

Lay the paper pattern on the right side of the fabric, as this is the only side on which to see and plan the grain in conjunction with the grain symbols on the paper pattern. Pin securely. Cut out with sharp scissors or shears. If the foam fabric tends to stick under the presser foot of the sewing machine, lay tissue paper on each side of the fabric to help it pass through more smoothly. Use a medium stitch (about ten stitches to the inch) and a fine needle.

Thread for stitching

Buy the same type of thread as the fabric to be sewn, e.g. cotton or sylko (mercerised or satinised cotton) on cotton, vegetable fibres sylko on rayons (regenerated cellulose), synthetic (e.g. nylon or Terylene) on synthetics, and silk on wool (animal fibres). The reason is that in sewing and pressing, wear and washing or cleaning, the thread reacts in the same way as the fabric.

Another important reason for 'safety first' has resulted from research by a well-known firm of sewing thread manufacturers. As the result of a burning accident they discovered that if synthetic material such as nylon was sewn with cotton thread it could (and did) cause a serious burning accident through the sewing thread igniting. The flame travelled up the seam stitching, raising the temperature of the synthetic fabric to ignition point, which is higher than melting point in nylon and Terylene.

The golden rule is to stitch synthetics with synthetic thread and reduce the risk of burning accidents through clothes catching fire.

A well pressed garment has a smart finish, but the professional appearance of a well made garment is spoiled if it is poorly pressed.

A good dressmaker presses each part of the garment as she works. Skill in pressing is acquired by the correct use of pressing apparatus on a wide variety of fabrics and garments.

APPARATUS

Irons should be thermostatically controlled if possible, recording the heat required for various fabrics. Otherwise great care is needed not to overheat irons. Besides possible scorching, some man-made fibres melt under too great heat with disastrous results.

Use lightweight irons for thin or light fabrics, organdie, thin silks, rayons or nylons. Heavier irons are used for fabrics needing heavier pressure, e.g. wool and Terylene mixtures, worsteds, heavier cottons, silks or mixture fabrics.

The surface of the iron must be kept clean and smooth. If it is spoilt by pressing fabric containing size or dressing which may leave a film on the iron, clean it with fine steel wool and soap while it is still warm.

Steam irons are useful when pressing fabrics needing a little moisture in their treatment. Woollens, wool or wool mixture fabrics, which need shrinking in the piece before cutting out, may be methodically pressed all over with the steam iron to ensure this. The same treatment is also used to avoid watermarking fabrics which need damp pressing in the making-up. See *Choice and preparation of fabric* on page 171.

20

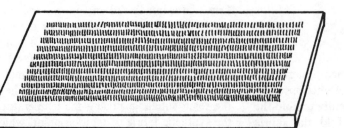

A   Wire needleboard mounted on wooden base

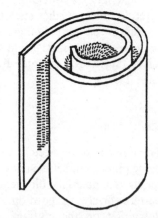

B   Wire needleboard on flexible base rolled up for easy storage

Plastic foam pressing pad

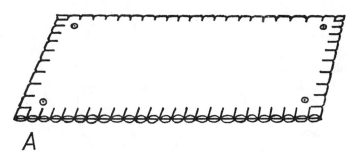
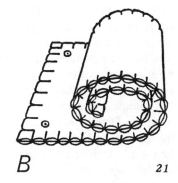

A   *B*   21

Skirt or sleeve boards should be covered with blanket or felt pads and washable cotton covers with smooth surfaces. *A pressing table,* similarly covered, is useful when a larger surface is necessary, e.g. for shrinking lengths of fabric.

Pressing cloths of clean, white or unbleached cotton or linen both thick and thin are used dry or damp on various fabrics.

Wire needleboard, often called *velvet pressing board* is used for pressing pile surfaced fabrics such as velvet or corduroy (Diagrams 20a and b). These may be purchased in various sizes suitable for either sleeves or skirts, and can be laid on top of the ordinary skirt or sleeve board when in use. They are expensive to buy, but a boon for pressing pile surfaced fabrics, for the 'needle' side of the board preserves the character of the material. (See pressing velvet.)

Store needleboards in a dry place when not in use to prevent rusting. As bits of sewing thread are liable to become embedded in between the wires, it is possible to purchase wire cleaning brushes to extract them.

A plastic foam pressing pad (Diagrams 21a and b) specially prepared for pressing is most useful when a well padded under layer is required for fabrics such as lace or embossed materials, which are pressed on the wrong side. The raised surface sinks into the cushioned side of the plastic foam pad leaving the wrong side smooth.

When pressing fabrics such as poult or faille which mark easily and show the impression

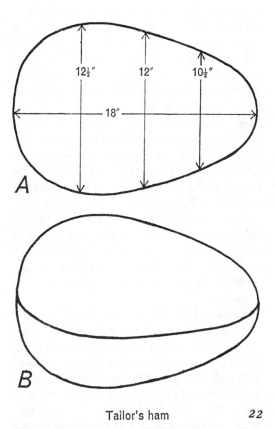

Tailor's ham   22

of seams and hems on the right side, try pressing on the right side, with a dry cloth between the iron and the fabric to avoid shine marks. The wrong side will be next to the foam pad and the impression of the thickness of seam or hem turning will sink into the pad leaving a flat surface on the right side.

A tailor's ham (Diagram 22b) is useful when tailor pressing curved surfaces in bodices such as bust darts or seams. It can be made quite easily as follows: cut a paper pattern to the shape and measurements shown in Diagram 22a. From this pattern cut two pieces of strong, firm, washed cotton or linen, such as calico, sheeting or holland. Allow turnings extra. Machine together round the edges leaving an opening. Turn to RS and stuff very firmly till quite hard with dry sawdust, cork shavings, kapok or small bits of cloth cuttings. Sew up the opening.

A sleevehead pad can be made similarly by using the top part of a good sleeve pattern. Alternatively an oval of thick white felt (or several layers) covered with firm clean cotton has been found most useful as a pressing pad for sleeve tops and other curved edges. Diagrams 23a and b give measurements and shape. Cut the top cotton to the size of the felt with good turnings and draw the edges in on the underside so it fits tightly and smoothly over the felt. Cut the cotton under cover for the second side to the exact size of the felt. Turn the raw edges to WS and fell it to the underside as shown in Diagram 23b.

A tailor's clapper (Diagram 24) is an excellent help when steam pressing tailored garments of wool cloth and similar fabrics. It consists of a single block of wood shaped at the top and sides for the fingers to grip it when being used. (See page 43.)

A roller can be used for pressing open seams on its curved surface without the turnings making an impression on the garment. Diagram 25 shows an ordinary wooden rolling pin covered with a piece of wool blanket or flannel stitched tightly round it. Diagram 26 shows a piece of thick white furnishing felt (of similar length to the rolling pin, e.g. 12 to 14 inches) rolled tightly into a pad and held in place with herringbone-stitch.

Pattern for oval pad of felt

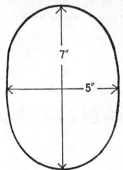

A   Top or right side showing smooth surface and no stitching

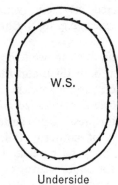

Underside

B   The cotton is drawn smooth over felt and held taut with a smaller oval on W.S.   *23*

24

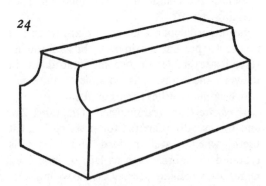

Tailor's wooden clapper, shaped for easier holding when in use

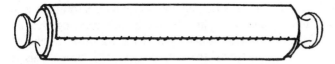

Wooden rolling pin covered with blanket   *25*

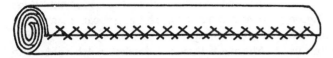

Thick white furnishing felt rolled into a pad
and held in place with herringboning   *26*

USEFUL GUIDING POINTS ON PRESSING

Time factor

Good pressing needs care, thought and plenty of patience. Try to arrange pressing so that sufficient time is available to carry out the process satisfactorily. Experience helps considerably but some fabrics with delicate surfaces or springy natures need extra time spent on them in pressing.

When moisture is required, allow sufficient time for the fabric to dry so that shape and finish will not be marred. Some materials stretch when in a damp condition and may look rough-dry, with consequent loss of good finish.

Retaining good shape

The position of the garment, or part to be pressed, on the ironing board is most important. Shape, or run of seam lines, can be ruined by ignorant or careless placing before pressing. Make sure that the parts to be pressed are in the correct position first. Support surplus fabric that may add weight and cause movement or stretching. In pressing avoid stretching the fabric out of shape. This is all too easily done. Work in the direction of the grain as much as possible. *Remember that pressing is not ironing*, as in laundry. The iron should be lifted and pressed upon the required part, not smoothed to and fro.

Heat and moisture

According to the fibres contained in the fabric, regulate the heat of the iron, and use discretion in judging the amount of moisture, if any, which is required. Always test for these reactions on a spare piece of the garment fabric. When a fabric contains blended yarns or mixtures, regulate the heat of the iron to suit the fibre requiring the lowest temperature, e.g. for cotton, wool and viscose rayon, heat required is for viscose rayon. Higher temperatures would damage the rayon fibres. Some of the easy-care, or crease-resistant finishes to fabrics are affected by the temperature of the iron in pressing, and can be destroyed if this is too high. NOTE: 'Damp' rather than 'wet' pressing cloths should be used. Never use a soaking wet pressing cloth. It is often the cause of spoiling the appearance of fabric, leaving a rough-dry look.

Wring the pressing cloth out tightly after immersing it in water. Then press it with a hot iron to get rid of surplus moisture, leaving the cloth damp, but not wet.

Light

Press in a good light. Remove tacking from seams or darts before pressing. Remove pins which might mark the fabric. Press on the wrong side of the garment as a general rule. If it is necessary to press on the right side, use a pressing cloth between the iron and the fabric.

Special parts of garments

HEMS

Press the crease line edge of hems *before* stitching permanently. This helps to avoid the stitching line showing on the right side. In this case it will be necessary to retain the tacking holding the hem in position. If any tack marks show on the finished hem, remove them by steaming. To do this, lightly cover the portion of hem with a damp cloth. Allow the hot iron to touch the cloth to produce steam, but do not press at all. Quickly remove iron and damp cloth and lightly brush over the surface.

SEAMS

Use the point of the iron to press open the actual stitching line. Look on RS to make sure the seam line is flat before pressing heavily on WS. It is easy to leave a groove instead of obtaining the correct flat finish unless this is watched. To avoid seam turnings showing through on RS of garment place fairly wide strips of brown paper, or similar thickness, between the turnings and the garment. Press in the usual way. The paper can then be removed ensuring a satisfactory finish on RS. Alternatively, use a wooden or felt roller with curved surface under the seam (Diagrams 25 and 26).

DARTS

After a light press on WS make sure the stitched line of the dart is quite flat on RS before pressing more firmly on WS. As in seams it is easy to leave a groove, giving a faulty unprofessional finish, unless care is taken. See Chapter Fifteen, pages 176–7 for pressing darts over a tailor's ham.

PRESSING MORE DIFFICULT MATERIALS

Lace

Many laces have a raised surface on the right side. Use a plastic foam pressing pad (Diagrams 21a and b) or several layers of blanket or turkish towelling placed on top of the ironing board. Lay the lace WS uppermost so RS sinks into the thickness of the padding. Press dry on WS. Some lace is liable to shrink if moisture is used. Regulate the temperature of the iron to the fibre in the fabric and test on a spare piece. Lace may be of rayon, cotton, nylon, wool, silk or blends of these fibres. Press lightly. Avoid stretching. When pressing lining and lace together, keep both layers flat. Use a dry pressing cloth between the iron and the lining fabric.

Embossed or embroidered fabrics

These should be pressed face downwards on a thick pad similarly to lace.

Chiffon, georgette, ninon

These may be of silk, rayon, nylon, or other synthetic man-made fibres. Use a well padded board with smooth surface (see pressing lace) and a lightweight iron regulated to the correct heat. Press dry, except in very special circumstances, and then use moisture very sparingly. These are very light fabrics, so use light even pressure and press the way of the straight grain whenever possible. When pressing hems lay the part to be pressed on a flat surface and support the rest of the garment so that no stretching occurs. Take care to place seams in their correct positions before pressing, e.g. straight lines or smooth curves, because these fabrics are fluid, and slip out of place so easily.

Velvet

The pile surface must be protected and preserved. Use a wire needleboard if possible (see page 38, Diagrams 20a and b). Lay the velvet with pile surface RS downwards, facing the wire or 'needles' which will protect it. Press lightly using a damp cloth between the iron and WS velvet. Do not use too much moisture, and be very careful in placing the part to be pressed in the correct position to ensure good lines in the finished garment. If no wire board is available stand the heated iron on its heel, or get a second person to hold it inverted. Over the iron place a well damped cloth to cause steam. Hold WS of velvet by the seam or part to be pressed, and pass it to and fro over the cloth. The action of the steam passing through the fabric flattens the seam without pressure being used. A stiff brush, either wire or stiff bristle, inverted, makes a useful substitute for a needleboard for small parts of garments. Steaming is also useful for removing marks which may be left by tacking or pins. Velveteen or corduroy can be pressed or steamed in the same way as velvet. In each case light handling is essential to prevent marking the fabric.

Wool

Lightweight dress woollens are sometimes difficult to press. Use a dry pressing cloth over the wrong side of the wool fabric first, then place a damp cloth on top. The moderately heated iron touches the damp cloth first and steam penetrates the dry cloth to give slight moisture to the stitched part being pressed. Too much moisture may shrink the part being pressed, causing seams to cockle. To avoid this, remove surplus water from the wrung-out damp rag by ironing over it separately until it is damp but not soaking. Then place it on top of the dry cloth. Always test a spare piece of self fabric for reaction to heat and moisture. Use as little moisture as possible. Retain the correct shape of the garment by careful placing on the pressing board. Wool is a pliable fabric that will stretch, especially soft, loosely woven cloths.

If it is necessary to press on the right side of a wool garment, use a piece of self fabric next to the wool material (i.e. wool facing wool) then the two pressing cloths as before. The protecting piece of wool will avoid shine or press marks.

When tailor pressing heavier wool cloth, e.g. tweeds, suitings, flannels, press as directed above, for wool, using a heavier iron, if possible, and tailor's clapper (see page 40). As the iron is lifted after pressing each part, quickly remove the damp pressing cloth, and smartly bang down the tailor's clapper, holding it firmly for some seconds over the pressed section. This action helps to 'set' the seam or edge more professionally, for the steam is trapped a while longer, and the flat surface of the clapper and the pressure behind it ensures a crisper fold, or a flatter surface, whichever is required. Press the folds of pleats and the hem edges of jackets, coats and skirts like this, as well as seams, pockets and plackets as construction of garment proceeds.

Jersey

Avoid stretching. Press in the direction of the rib. Pressing across the rib may cause stretching out of shape. Careful positioning of the part to be pressed is essential if the garment is to retain its correct shape. Moisture should be used with discretion. Too much may spoil the nature of the fabric and give it an overpressed appearance. As for pressing wool, it may be found helpful to use two pressing cloths, one dry next to the jersey fabric, and the other damp (not wet) between the iron and the dry cloth.

NOTE: To avoid watermarking jersey fabric of wool in stage pressing of garments, lightly steampress the fabric in the piece before cutting out. A steam iron used over a dry cloth covering WS of fabric is a good method.

Jersey fabrics made of *acrylic fibres* such as Courtelle should be pressed dry on the wrong side with a cool iron. Do not use a damp cloth or steam iron. These are drip-dry fabrics which only need very light dry pressing on the wrong side after washing.

Nylon and Terylene

Trouble often occurs when seams have been machined with too tight a tension or too small a stitch causing the thread to spring back and pucker. No amount of pressing will rectify this. The remedy lies in adjusting the machine for correct stitching which will enable the seam or stitched part of garment to lie flat before pressing. The nature of the fabric is crease-resistant, and practically non-iron, but, as in other materials, light pressing is beneficial throughout the construction of garments and improves the finished appearance. Irons should be regulated to low heat and used carefully. Avoid pressing in a crease by mistake as only by raising the temperature of the iron can it be removed. Both these fibres melt in too great heat. If dampness is required in pressing, use it with caution. Test on a spare piece of the fabric first, for its reaction. Faults due to the use of too much moisture are very difficult to remedy.

NOTE: When nylon or Terylene is used in conjunction with natural or man-made fibres, the utmost caution is necessary in regulating the amount of dampness and heat used in pressing. So much depends on the percentage of each fibre in one given fabric. Too much moisture could cause a rough-dry appearance.

Faille, poult or taffeta

See notes on using a plastic foam pressing pad to avoid seams and hems leaving an impression on the right side (page 39).

Foam-backed (laminated) fabrics

Use a cool iron and a damp pressing cloth, or a steam iron. Test for heat and moisture before pressing the actual garment.

STRENGTHENINGS USED IN DIFFERENT PROCESSES

Bias and curved edges easily stretch out of shape when making up a garment. These faults may spoil the finished effect and are difficult to rectify. Strengthen curves, corners, and bias lines of garments *after* cutting out and *before* assembling for fitting.

Staystitching by machine

Use matching thread and a fairly large stitch. Work on single fabric close to the fitting line on the turning side. Follow the exact shape of *curves*, e.g. neck and armhole lines (Diagrams 27a and b) or *bias edges*. Hand running stitch is an alternative to machining.

Before cutting *inside corners* into which the turning allowance must be cut, thus causing weakness (Diagrams 28a and b), staystitch each side of the corner just inside the fitting line on the turning side. The corner of a garment shoulder where the collar is cut in one with the front is also illustrated in Diagrams 28c, 195.

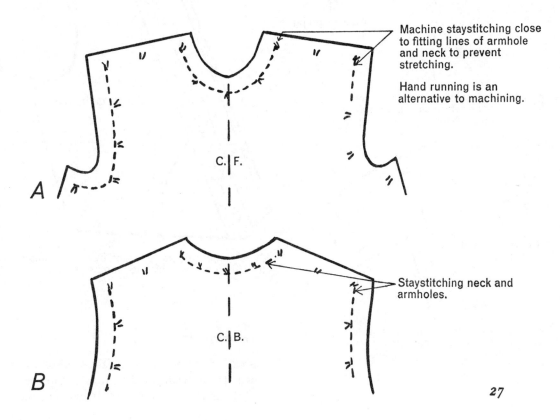

Machine staystitching close to fitting lines of armhole and neck to prevent stretching.

Hand running is an alternative to machining.

C. F.

A

Staystitching neck and armholes.

C. B.

B

27

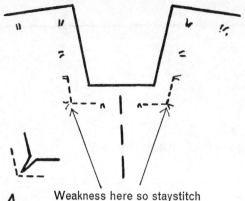

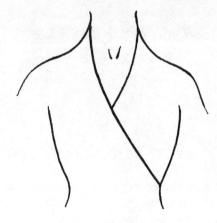

A Weakness here so staystitch inside corners *before* snipping

Finished crossover bodice   **29**

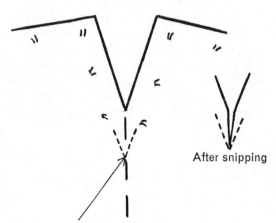

After snipping

B Staystitch front point of vee neck before snipping turnings near to centre point for fitting.

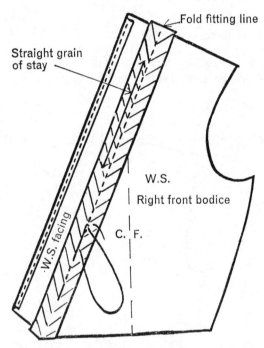

Centre crease of stay attached by hand running to fold fitting line which is on bias grain

30

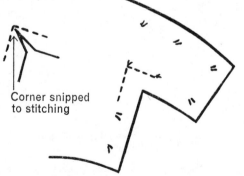

Corner snipped to stitching

C Where collar is cut in one with front staystitch the inside corner where collar joins shoulder.

28

Strengthening stays

These are made of firm, thin fabric cut on the straight grain. Seam binding tape is suitable, and colours may be chosen to match garment

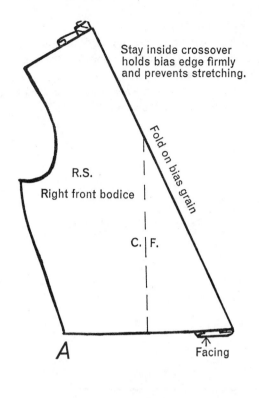

Stay inside crossover holds bias edge firmly and prevents stretching.

R.S.

Right front bodice

Fold on bias grain

C. | F.

A   Facing

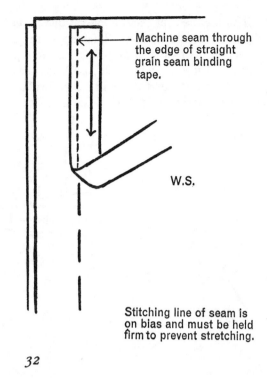

Machine seam through the edge of straight grain seam binding tape.

W.S.

Stitching line of seam is on bias and must be held firm to prevent stretching.

32

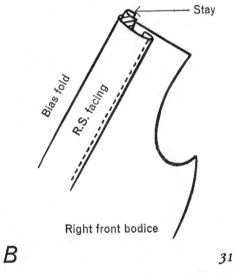

Stay

Bias fold

R.S. facing

Right front bodice

B   *31*

fabrics; or cut strips of firm cotton fabric such as lawn $\frac{1}{2}$ or $\frac{3}{4}$ inch wide. Shrink stays before using by thoroughly damping and ironing dry.

For a *bias fold*, e.g. crossover bodice, where the facing is cut in one with the front (Diagram 29), cut the stay to the required length. Fold it in half lengthwise and press in a crease down the centre. Matching the crease lines pin the stay to WS of the bias fold line. Using self-coloured thread attach the two crease lines together with firm but not tight hand running, picking up only a thread of the bodice fabric so the stitching is invisible on RS (Diagram 30). When the facing is finally neatened, folded, and pressed in position on WS, the inserted stay will prevent the bias fold from stretching (Diagrams 31a and b).

Seams of skirts in jersey fabrics have a tendency to stretch and also *bias seams* of skirts in other fabrics. Attach a stay of seam binding tape (on the straight grain) to the seam fitting line on WS of one side of the garment so that it is sewn in when the seam is machined (Diagram 32). See also the method of using seam binding tape to face the raw edges of seams with wide turnings, page 65.

Stays are used for reinforcing various parts of garments in soft tailoring. Reference to them is made in the following diagrams: curved zip openings, Diagrams 95 and 96; pockets, Diagrams 152a and b and 174; suit jacket 'bridle', Diagrams 266 and 267; pleats Diagram 132.

Strengthening tacks

Worked bar tacks are advised in numerous positions throughout this book for strengthening ends of seams, openings, or pleats. *Decorative tacks* such as *arrowheads* are also used for strengthening. See Diagrams 87 and 175.

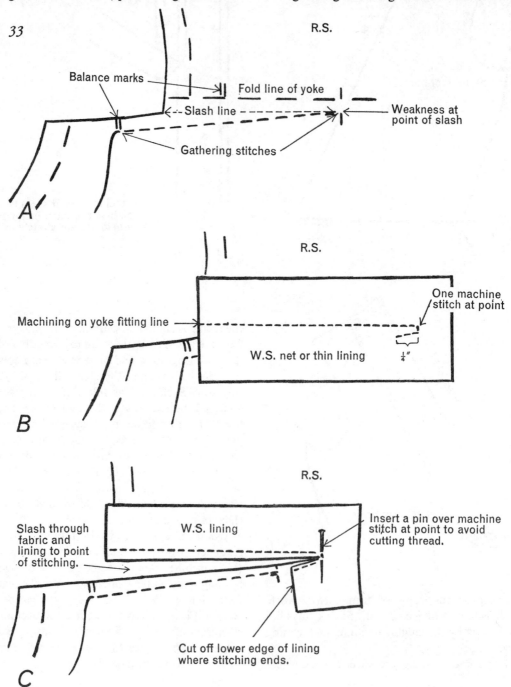

33

Balance marks

Fold line of yoke

R.S.

Slash line

Weakness at point of slash

Gathering stitches

A

R.S.

One machine stitch at point

Machining on yoke fitting line

W.S. net or thin lining

$\frac{1}{4}''$

B

R.S.

Slash through fabric and lining to point of stitching.

W.S. lining

Insert a pin over machine stitch at point to avoid cutting thread.

Cut off lower edge of lining where stitching ends.

C

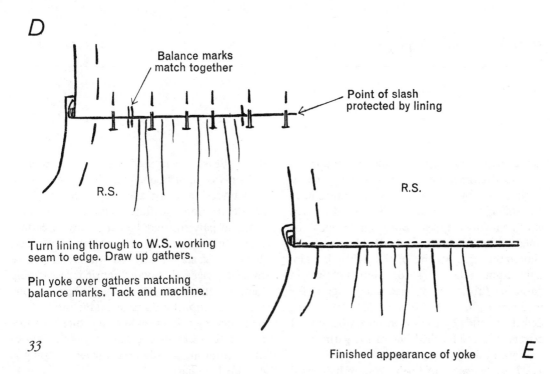

D

Balance marks
match together

Point of slash
protected by lining

R.S.

R.S.

Turn lining through to W.S. working
seam to edge. Draw up gathers.

Pin yoke over gathers matching
balance marks. Tack and machine.

33

Finished appearance of yoke   E

Lining

Inner corners may be reinforced by lining before
cutting the turnings. See lining the edges of a
gusset slash, page 155, Diagrams 230 to 232.
The same method may be used when gathers
are set into a *bodice yoke slash*. Line the top
edge and extreme point of the slash with thin
matching fabric or net. This will facilitate laying the yoke edge over the gathered portion
for stitching on RS later (Diagrams 33a, b, c,
d and e). Yoke and panel effects are seen from
time to time in garment styles. When making
up these fashions, inner corners have to be
dealt with (Diagram 34). Line these with thin
fabric or net before cutting the seam allowance.

Lining the edges of curved overlaid seams is
often more practical than trying to cope with
wide turnings. This is illustrated in the treatment of curved slot seams on page 61, Diagrams 58a and b.

Strengthening curved seams on WS such
as those of underarm seams (usually plain
open seams) in kimono or magyar styles, is
shown in Diagrams 54 and 55.

Lining inside corners

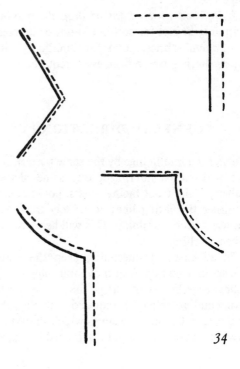

34

Good shape and crisp finish play an important part in dressmaking. Much can be done to achieve this by the skilful use of interlinings and stiffenings which can be divided into *woven* and *non-woven* types. Both kinds may be obtained in different weights. It is important to choose the right weight for the right job; thin, lightweight interlining for thin lightweight garment fabric, and medium weights for mediumweight materials. Too thick interlining defeats its ends by too much bulk with loss of crispness in the finished line of the garment.

Woven interlinings include:

1. *Tailor's canvas* of linen, wool or hair, used in soft tailoring where shaping by tailor manipulation is required. (Shrink woven canvas interlinings before using. See Chapter Fifteen, page 172.)
2. *Stiffened cotton lawn or organdie* making crisp interlinings for cotton blouses or dresses.
3. *Taffeta* fabrics, good for interlining silk type materials where firmness is required.

4. *Stiffened nylon*, used with nylon fabrics.

Non-woven or bonded interlining fabrics are sold under various trade names. See page 26 for description and fibre content. There is no grain so patterns may be cut in any direction, preventing waste, as cut edges do not fray. They are generally labelled washable or able to be dry cleaned. Bonded fabric is less pliable than woven canvas and shaping must be done in construction by darts or seams rather than by moulding using heat and moisture. For this reason they are used extensively with fabrics made from man-made fibres, where shaping is obtained similarly.

Both woven and bonded fabrics can be bought with adhesive backs, if required. These are pressed on to the wrong side of the garment portion with a moderately hot iron. In this case care is needed to use even pressure consistently over the required area, so that the interlining is fused to the garment fabric without wrinkles or creases.

GENERAL DIRECTIONS

Cut out the interlinings by the same patterns as the part to be interlined, e.g. same shape, collars, cuffs, front facings, belts, pockets, etc. Transfer the fitting lines accurately from the pattern to the interlining. This will help greatly when stitching.

In all cases of interlining keep the main object in mind, *preservation* and *support of shape* together with crisp finish. Accurate fixing and stitching are required with thought and care in trimming turnings which should be *layered* where necessary, i.e. trimmed in stages

to thin down the finished edge when turned. Too much thickness on edges and corners prevents slick shaping, whereas careless cutting of turnings too near stitching can be fatal. Diagrams 42, 199 and 269 illustrate layering turnings. Interlining edges are usually trimmed as near to the stitching lines as possible with safety. Turnings at corners must be cut across. Bad corners on garments may be the result of poor stitching lines, or too much thickness in the turnings, or seam lines not being carefully worked out on the right side.

Joins

In all cases the chief consideration is flatness of surface, with correct shape after any joins have been made.

METHOD 1

This is used for a flat finish, e.g. CB collar as shown for roll collar (Diagram 197). Lay the two fitting lines one on top of the other. Pin and tack together. Trim the turnings to ¼ inch on both upper and under sides. Catch-stitch each edge in position (Diagram 35) or fix by machining. The former gives a softer and more supple finish than machining. For working catchstitch, see Diagrams 36a, b and c.

Seam fitting lines overlaid and tacked together

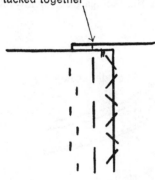

Overlaid join with turning edges catchstitched on each side

35

METHOD 2

For a plain open seam, machined on the fitting lines, turnings are pressed open and trimmed to ⅜ or ¼ inch. This is suitable for shoulder joins where a back interlining joins the front parts (Diagram 37).

Catchstitch

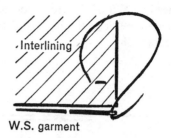

A   W.S. garment

Begin with a backstitch on double fabric. Take a very small stitch (two threads) on single fabric just below the edge of the interlining and a little to the left (Diagram a).

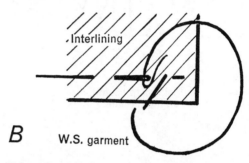

B   W.S. garment

Take a firm stitch on the interlining well above the raw edge and slightly to the left (Diagram b).

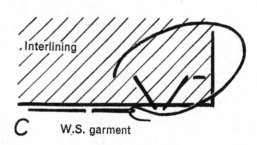

C   W.S. garment

Continue working (Diagram c).
                No stitches show on R.S.

36

Inserting interlining edges placed to folds

Where the interlining is not caught into a seam, e.g. where front facings for blouses or bodices are cut in one with the front pattern, the interlining provides one layer between the facing and the garment. Therefore one edge is fixed invisibly to the fold of the facing. It can be placed to WS of the front bodice itself, as in Diagram 39 or to the back of the facing, as in Diagram 38.

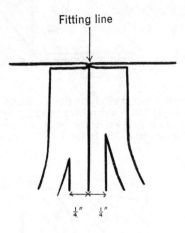

Fitting line

Plain open seam join
Turnings trimmed to ¼″

37

METHOD 1

When bound buttonholes are to be made, lay the interlining to WS of the front of the garment to give strength and support when the additional pieces for binding are stitched to the buttonhole positions. Diagram 39 shows the edge of the interlining catchstitched to the fold fitting line of the garment. Trim the opposite long turning edge to its fitting line. The stitching of the buttonholes holds both layers together. The free edge of the facing can be neatened separately as shown in Diagram 39. Note the position of the buttonhole slits indicated on the facings. Diagram 40 shows the front of garment with bound buttonholes made and facings folded back into position on WS garment. Note that the neck edge of the garment should be finished according to the style required before the backs of the buttonholes are cut on the facings and attached in position. This leaves the facings free for any manipulation required.

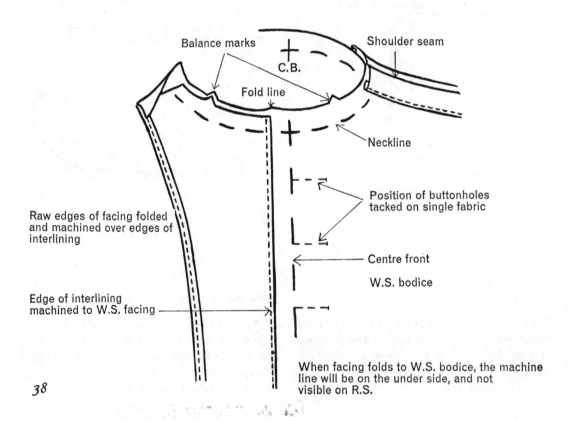

Balance marks

Shoulder seam

C.B.

Fold line

Neckline

Raw edges of facing folded and machined over edges of interlining

Position of buttonholes tacked on single fabric

Centre front

W.S. bodice

Edge of interlining machined to W.S. facing

When facing folds to W.S. bodice, the machine line will be on the under side, and not visible on R.S.

38

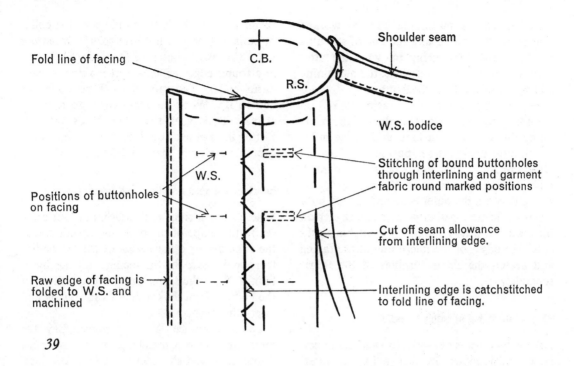

Fold line of facing

Shoulder seam

C.B.

R.S.

W.S. bodice

Positions of buttonholes on facing

W.S.

Stitching of bound buttonholes through interlining and garment fabric round marked positions

Cut off seam allowance from interlining edge.

Raw edge of facing is folded to W.S. and machined

Interlining edge is catchstitched to fold line of facing.

39

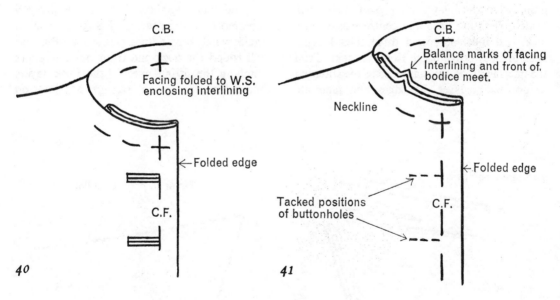

C.B.

Facing folded to W.S. enclosing interlining

← Folded edge

C.F.

40

C.B.

Balance marks of facing Interlining and front of bodice meet.

Neckline

← Folded edge

Tacked positions of buttonholes

C.F.

41

METHOD 2

Interlining is fixed to the back of the facing when buttonholes are to be worked from RS of the garment. Trim off the turnings on the two long edges of the interlining as far as

the fitting lines. Leave the turning on the neck edge as shown in Diagram 41. Lay the interlining to WS of the facing with the correct edge to the fitting line of the fold. Pin and tack this edge in position. For invisible fixing catchstitch the edge in position as for Method 1.

For quickness machining can be worked (Diagram 38). In this case the line of stitching will be on RS of the facing, but when the latter is turned to WS of the garment the machining will not show on RS of the front.

Fold the free edges of the facing to WS on the fitting lines enclosing the edges of the interlining. Pin, tack and machine on the edge, holding all three thicknesses in position as shown in Diagram 38. If this finish causes too much bulk, trim the turnings of the facing to the fitting lines on the outer edge and neaten both layers of fabric together with the zigzagger on the machine. If no zigzagger is available catch-stitch the edges of the interlining to the facing and neaten the single turnings of the fabric separately.

Simple interlining of collar or cuffs

Lay the two pieces of fabric, top and under collar or cuff together, RS facing. Lay the interlining as a third layer on top of these two. Match all fitting lines and centre marks. Pin, tack, and machine round three sides leaving neck or sleeve edge open. Remove tacks. Trim the interfacing turnings as close to the stitching as possible to layer the edges and facilitate

turning to RS. Trim the turnings of the collar or cuffs to $\frac{1}{8}$ or $\frac{1}{4}$ inch. Mitre corners to ensure good shapes as shown in Diagram 42. Notch any round edges as shown in making a mandarin collar (Diagram 188). Turn collar or cuff to RS. Work the seam edges to required shapes. Tack near the edge. Press on WS. Fitting lines of neck or sleeve 'setting on' edges should be clearly marked (Diagram 43).

Interlining shaped necklines and front openings

Where both facings and interlining fabric are cut to the shape of the neck and opening, join the shoulder or other seams of (a) the bodice front and back, (b) the facings, (c) the interlinings. Press the seams open. Neaten those of the bodice. Trim the turnings of the facing and interlining seams to $\frac{1}{4}$ inch.

Lay the bodice WS uppermost. Lay the interlining on top matching centre and neck fitting lines, and shoulder or other seam lines. Pin and tack together. Turn the bodice RS uppermost. Lay the facings RS facing bodice. Again match centre lines and seams. Pin and tack round the neck and front opening edges matching the fitting lines of the three layers (bodice, interlining and facing). Machine on

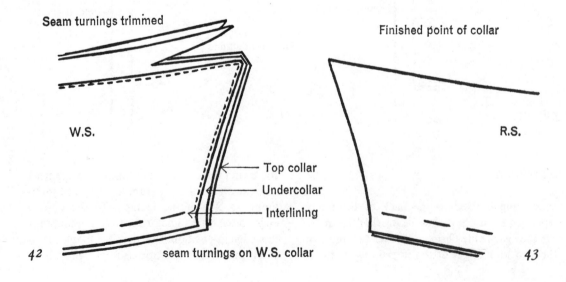

Seam turnings trimmed

Finished point of collar

W.S.

R.S.

- Top collar
- Undercollar
- Interlining

42   seam turnings on W.S. collar   43

the fitting lines. Remove tacks. Trim the turnings (diagram on opposite page), snipping or mitring corners and notching curves. Turn to RS and work the neckline and opening edges to good shapes. Tack in position and press on WS. (See Chapter Ten, *Neck Finishes*, Diagrams 182 to 186 for close-fitting round neck, where interlining can be added if desired, and Diagrams 194 to 204 for roll collar and front opening showing interlining inserted.) For interlining a jacket front with pre-shrunk linen or hair canvas, see Chapter Fifteen, page 176 (Diagram 266).

Interlining a full skirt with bonded fabric

Cut the interlining exactly the same shape as the skirt. Mark all fitting lines and balance marks. On a flat surface, e.g. a table, lay each interlining section. On top lay the corresponding fabric shape, RS uppermost. Match centre and fitting lines. Smooth the fabric so it is quite flat. Pin centres first then other edges and tack into position. Treat each portion similarly. Then continue to make up the skirt as for one fabric.

Interlining a skirt hem

The stiffening for this purpose, crinoline, horsehair braid or stiffinette, can be bought in various widths 1 to 4 inches. Choose one that is suitable for the style. Level the hemline with garment on wearer. Afterwards fold under the hem allowance to WS. Measure the width of turning for hem to include the strip of crinoline inserted into it. When joining the crinoline, overlap and catchstitch the ends for flat finish, as shown (Diagrams 44a, b and c).

Inserting steel tape into crinoline skirts

Steel tape can be obtained covered either with cotton or with plastic, approximately $\frac{1}{4}$ or $\frac{1}{2}$ inch wide. For this a casing of self fabric or matching material is fixed to WS of skirt in the required position. Through this the strip can be inserted. The casing can be arranged so

44   Hem interlined with crinoline

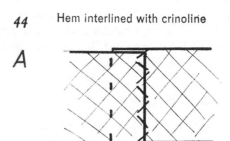

A

Join ends of crinoline by overlapping and catchstitching the raw edge on each side for flatness.

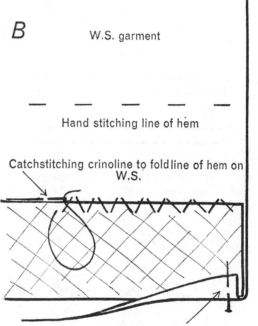

B   W.S. garment

Hand stitching line of hem

Catchstitching crinoline to foldline of hem on W.S.

Fold first turning of hem over lower edge of crinoline

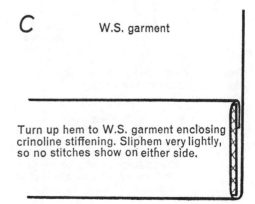

C   W.S. garment

Turn up hem to W.S. garment enclosing crinoline stiffening. Sliphem very lightly, so no stitches show on either side.

that it is stitched to the lining of the garment only. In this way no stitching will show on RS although the garment is held in the required shape (Diagrams 45 and 46).

Boning a bodice lining for a strapless top

The shape of the lining can be on princess lines to form seams on which to apply the boning (Diagrams 47 and 48).

Prepare the bodice by machining seams and darts. Neaten and press them open on WS.

Form casings for insertion of bones with either tape (single) or bias binding (doubled for strength). Cut the casing 1 inch longer at either end than the actual seam. With WS facing, pin and tack the centre of the casing to the centre of the seam. Care is needed in handling and tacking to regulate the fullness smoothly over the curves. Pin, tack and machine down each side of the casing. Remove tacks. Press carefully, using a rounded pad held in the

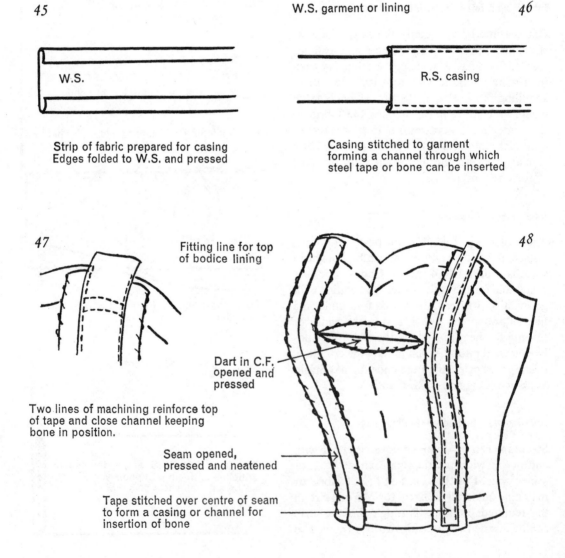

45

W.S.

Strip of fabric prepared for casing
Edges folded to W.S. and pressed

46

W.S. garment or lining

R.S. casing

Casing stitched to garment
forming a channel through which
steel tape or bone can be inserted

47

Fitting line for top
of bodice lining

Two lines of machining reinforce top
of tape and close channel keeping
bone in position.

Dart in C.F.
opened and
pressed

Seam opened,
pressed and neatened

Tape stitched over centre of seam
to form a casing or channel for
insertion of bone

48

hand under the bust shape and working the toe of the iron very lightly in a circular movement over the casing.

Tack across the top fitting line and ¼ inch below it. Machine on these lines forming a tiny oblong to reinforce the casing at the top and prevent the bone from poking through. Leave an opening at the lower end to insert the bone.

Prepare the bones by cutting each bone ¼ inch shorter than the required length. If bones just fit, they tend to poke out quickly. Cut and file the ends into smooth round shapes (Diagram 49). Any sharp edges hurt the wearer and cut the casing. Pad the tops of the bones with small pieces of cotton wool. Take care not to form lumps.

Insert bones from the lower open end of the casings. Secure at the base with an extra piece of tape or bias binding stitched twice for strength. If hooks and eyes are used for fastening a side placket which is boned, stitch a piece of plush or velvet ribbon over them as a guard to prevent them from hurting the wearer.

One classic bodice shape is shown in order to give the basic method for boning a bodice, but according to trends of fashion the method can be adapted to other shapes.

A second method is to prepare the bones as already described, and insert each one in a casing of its own as shown in Diagrams 50a and b. Each encased bone can then be attached to the turnings of whichever seam or part needs the stiffened support.

Several types of bone may be purchased:
White or black whalebone.
White or black feather bone. (This is softer bone which can be shaped by hand after heating slightly with a warm iron.)
Plastic bone. (This is rather stiff and not so pliable.)

ELASTIC SUPPORT

To hold strapless and other bodices with low necklines close to the bust fix the centre of an elastic band (¼ to ½ inch wide) to CF lining at bust level. Allow the elastic to be loose except for this so it can be passed round the body under the bust to fasten at the back.

Preparing bone

49

Insert bone here.

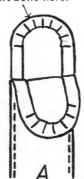

A

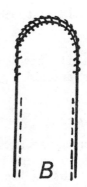

B

50

After inserting the featherbone, close the top edges and oversew them.

Subtlety of fit as well as good line and style can be achieved through seaming which may be simple or intricate. In each case good workmanship is essential to obtain a professional effect.

In this chapter the aim has been to help the craftsman to overcome the more difficult parts of construction, and to choose suitable methods of finish for the raw edges of seams in various fabrics. Treatment of curved edges, crossed seams, and seams running down into hems have been included. In addition piped and corded seams, and several tailored effects have been described, supplementing those given in *Standard Processes in Dressmaking*.

In neatening the raw edges of seam and other turnings, where hand stitching, such as overcasting or loopstitching (blanketstitch), is shown, a quick alternative method is to use the zigzag stitch on the machine. So many sewing machines have the zigzagger as a built-in device, and the size of the stitch can be adjusted according to purpose. For others a zigzag attachment can be obtained through sewing machine agencies.

Where raw edges are inclined to stretch or fray easily through being on the bias, or because of loosely woven or knitted fabric, stay the fitting line of the raw edge with straight machine stitching first as shown in Diagrams 64a and b or face the underside of the turnings (Diagrams 68a and b). For this use straight ribbon seam binding on straight edges and bias binding on curved raw edges.

DIFFICULT PARTS IN MAKING SEAMS

Crossed seams causing extra thickness

OPEN SEAMS

Diagrams 51a and b show diagonal trimming of single turnings at crossing points to eliminate thickness.

FRENCH SEAMS

Where the turnings are already double fabric in both sections, let the machine stitching continue in a straight line, but reverse the turnings at the crossing point (Diagram 52).

Curved seams

OPEN SEAMS

Turnings are pressed open and must fit flat to greater or smaller curves, e.g. short sleeved kimono or magyar underarm where there is no gusset. Diagrams 53a and b show how turnings must be cut almost to the stitching after machining, before they can be pressed open to lie flat against a greater curve. In this case the seam is weakened by the enforced snipping, so Diagram 54 shows how it can be reinforced with bias binding on the wrong side. This is best held in position by hand stitching so as not to show on RS and to be more flexible. The centre can be stabstitched through the seam itself for further firmness. Stitch invisibly on RS; allow longer stitch on WS. (See Diagrams 178 and 179 for stabstitch.) Diagram 55 shows alternative reinforcement, if desired, by machining close to seam line on RS holding turnings firmly to strengthening strip and so prevent splitting of seam.

A

Open seams

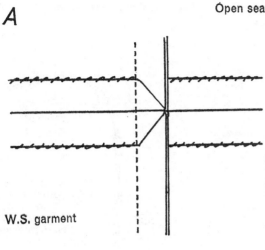

This reduces thickness at the crossings.

Crossed seam showing mitred turnings

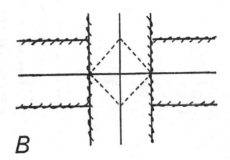

W.S. garment

51 **B**

French seams

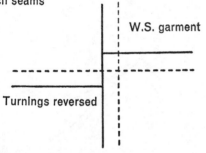

W.S. garment

Turnings reversed   *52*

Stitching of seams must meet exactly.
Turnings can be reversed as shown in
diagram to avoid bulk at the crossing point.

A

Underarm seam stitching

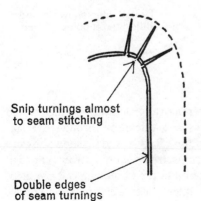

Snip turnings almost
to seam stitching

Double edges
of seam turnings   *53*

B

Turnings are pressed open and must fit flat
to greater or smaller curves. Snip as frequently
as necessary so they
can spread apart to
lie against a greater
curve, e.g. kimono or
magyar underarm
where there is no
gusset.

Seam pressed open

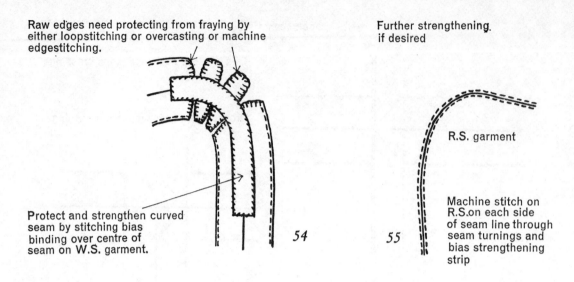

Raw edges need protecting from fraying by either loopstitching or overcasting or machine edgestitching.

Protect and strengthen curved seam by stitching bias binding over centre of seam on W.S. garment.

54

Further strengthening. if desired

R.S. garment

55

Machine stitch on R.S. on each side of seam line through seam turnings and bias strengthening strip

Seams on inner curves

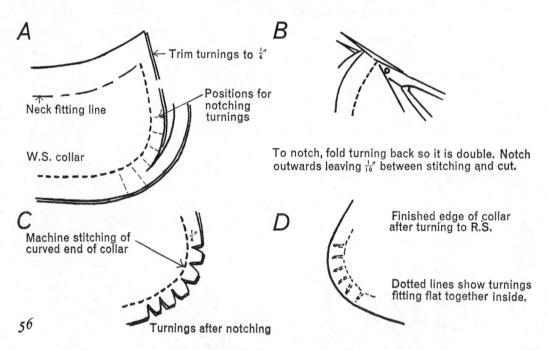

A

← Trim turnings to ⅙″

Neck fitting line

Positions for notching turnings

W.S. collar

B

To notch, fold turning back so it is double. Notch outwards leaving ⅒″ between stitching and cut.

C

Machine stitching of curved end of collar

56

Turnings after notching

D

Finished edge of collar after turning to R.S.

Dotted lines show turnings fitting flat together inside.

For long or three-quarter sleeved kimono or magyar bodice, see page 149 for setting in a gusset (Diagrams 217 to 232).

For seam turnings fitting to inner or concave curves, e.g. curved ends of collars, turnings must fit to a smaller curve, therefore it is necessary to remove surplus fabric which would cause bumps and thickness through overlapping. Diagrams 56a, b and c show how to trim the turnings reasonably narrow, approximately ⅛ inch and then notching out pieces of fabric at frequent intervals round the curves.

Diagram 56d shows how the notched turnings can then lie flat inside the curved end of the collar when the seam is turned to the right side and worked to a good shape round the edge.

NOTE: Leave at least $\frac{1}{16}$ inch to spare between stitching and cut, otherwise weakness and fraying will occur.

CURVED SLOT OR CHANNEL SEAMS

From time to time these seams become fashionable decorative features in dressmaking or tailoring.

Straight slot scams require sufficient width of turnings to form the channel stitched to a straight strip of matching fabric (Diagram 57). They are comparatively easy to construct, requiring accuracy for their smart line and finish. The method is described in *Standard Processes in Dressmaking*, page 27.

Curved slot seams are more difficult. Each side of the curve needs a shaped facing to provide flat double material for the curved channel (Diagrams 58a and b). If the garment fabric is thick, use a thinner material matching in colour for the facing. Cut the facings on the same grain as the corresponding part of the garment and of sufficient width to provide the backing required plus turnings. Lay them RS facing RS garment. Pin, tack and stitch on the

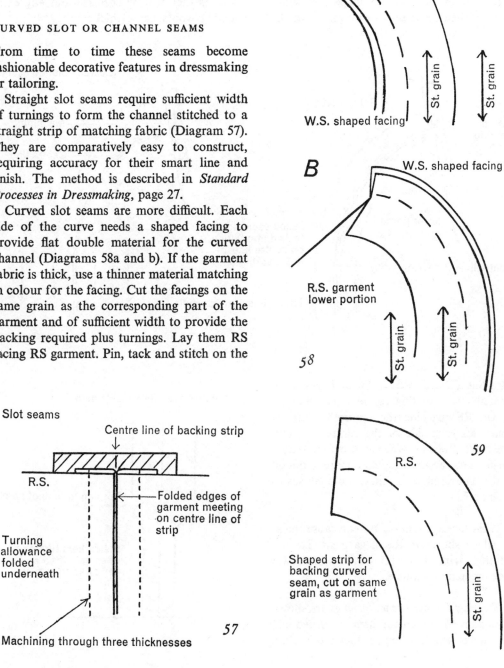

fitting lines. Remove tacks. Trim, snip or notch turnings to ensure a flat finish. Turn each facing to WS. Work the seam edges to the required shape. Tack and press on WS. Refer to Diagram 56 for snipping and notching. The strip for the back of the seam may be of the same fabric as the garment, or of a contrasting colour. It is cut to shape and width of the finished seam plus turnings. Mark the

3. *Treatment of closed seam turnings* is shown in Diagrams 63a and b. Thickness is reduced if the seam turnings are narrowed and pressed open inside the hem. To do this, snip across the seam turnings at the top of the hem. Proceed as shown in Diagrams 63a and b. Do not neaten the edges of turnings inside hems, as they will be enclosed and any extra stitching would cause thickness.

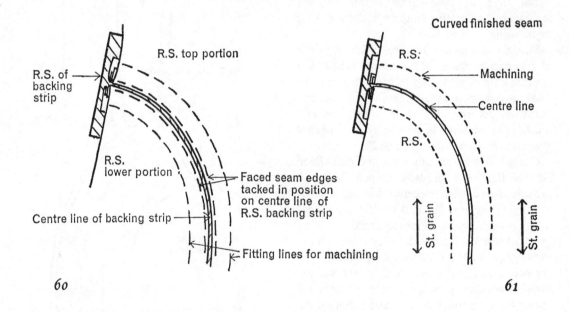

60

61

centre line (Diagram 59). Pin and tack each prepared curve to this centre line (Diagram 60). On RS machine the required width of channel on each side of the centre line. Remove tacks. Press on WS. Good manipulation, pressing and accurate stitching are required for the smart effect of these tailored seams (Diagram 61).

1. *Seam turnings inside hems* can cause thickness which shows on RS of garment. To prevent this, trim the seam turnings narrower inside the hem allowance.

2. *Treatment of open seam turnings* are shown in Diagram 62. When the hem is turned up, the turnings will be layered reducing thickness.

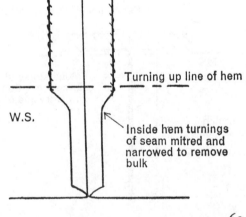

Open seam turnings inside hem

62

Closed seam turnings inside hem

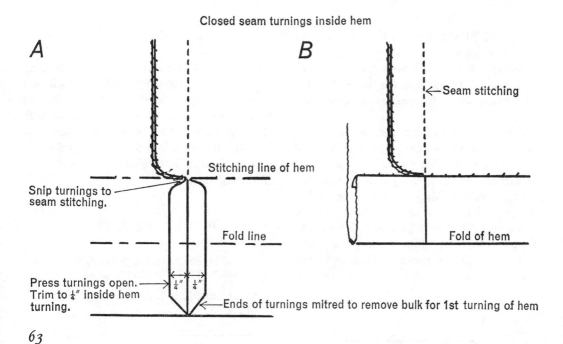

A

Snip turnings to seam stitching.

Stitching line of hem

Fold line

Press turnings open. Trim to ¼" inside hem turning.

Ends of turnings mitred to remove bulk for 1st turning of hem

B

←Seam stitching

Fold of hem

63

Finishing open seam edges

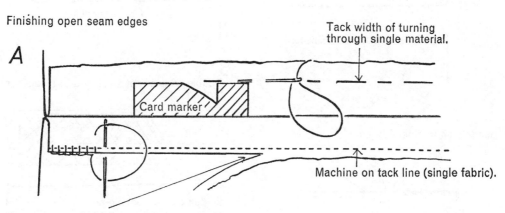

A

Tack width of turning through single material.

Card marker

Machine on tack line (single fabric).

Cut away surplus fabric to machine stitching.

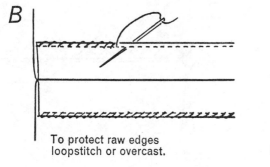

B

To protect raw edges loopstitch or overcast.

64

METHODS OF FINISHING RAW EDGES OF OPEN SEAMS

1. *Fabrics which do not fray* at all may have the seam edges trimmed to the required width with pinking shears for neat quick finish. See Diagram 113.

2. *Fabrics which fray but are too thick to be turned under* may be finished by hand or machine stitching. Decide the finished width of each turning, not less than ½ inch each side of the seam stitching. Mark it with a tack or fine chalk line. Diagram 64 shows a marker cut in card being used as a quick and reliable guide for width. Machine along these guide lines, working on single material of turnings. Trim

away surplus fabric close to machine stitching. Protect the raw edges by overlocking with the machine zigzag attachment, or loopstitch or overcast by hand if no attachment is available (Diagrams 64a and b). Where fabric only frays slightly, the raw edges may be trimmed with pinking shears after machining for quick finish. (See Diagram 113.)

67

Binding raw edges with net

A

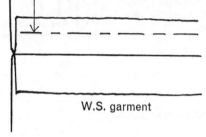

Tacked guide line through single thickness of seam turning for attaching net

W.S. garment

B

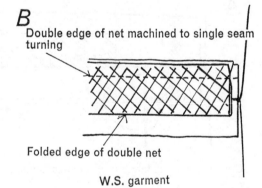

Double edge of net machined to single seam turning

Folded edge of double net

W.S. garment

C

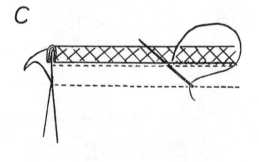

Quick machine finish for thin fabrics

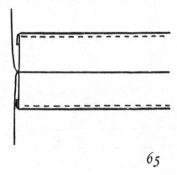

65

Hand finish for finer fabrics

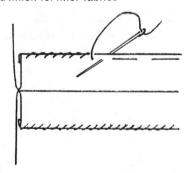

Turn under the raw edge once keeping width of turnings even.
Tack and press.
Finally overcast the folded edge.
This is a softer and more pliable finish than machining.

66

3. *Thinner fabrics may have the raw edges turned under once.* Diagram 65 illustrates the quick machine edgestitch finish used on suitably thin materials. For *pure silk fabrics* a neat and more flexible finish is to overcast the turned edge neatly (Diagram 66).

4. *Binding the raw edges with net* is a particularly neat way of protecting fabrics which fray such as wool georgette or moygashel, because net is very light, easy to manage, and eliminates too much thickness. The finished width of the net binding should be ⅛ or ¼ inch.

Measure from the seam line as shown in Diagram 67a. Mark the line of the finished turning. Cut strips of matching net about 1½ inches wide or slightly less. Fold in half lengthwise with raw edges matching. Tack and machine this double edge to the single seam turning fitting line as shown in Diagram 67b. The distance between the raw edges and the machining should be either ⅛ or ¼ inch whichever is the chosen finished width of binding. Trim away the raw edges to slightly less than the chosen width. Fold over the double net enclosing

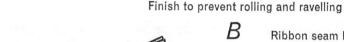
Finish to prevent rolling and ravelling

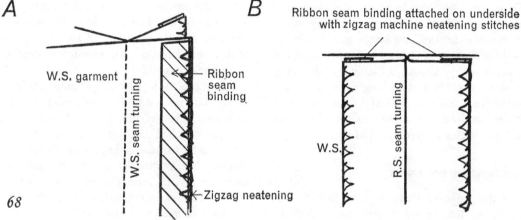

68

Facing raw edges with ribbon seam binding

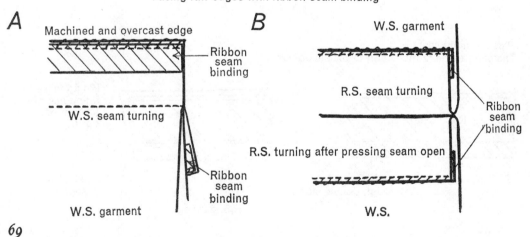

69

these raw edges. Secure the fold to the under-side of the seam turning by felling to the machine stitching (Diagram 67c).

5. *Face the raw edges of very wide seam turnings*, e.g. turnings of equal width to pleat allowance on centre lines of skirts, where above the pleat the fabric is single to eliminate bulk (Diagrams 124 and 127), or where the backing of the pleat is a separate piece of fabric so that the single turning continues from waist to hem (Diagram 129). Use matching seam binding tape on the straight grain. Cut the

tape the required length. Back the edge of the seam turning with the tape. Tack and machine this edge, using the zigzag neatener (Diagram 68), or a straight stitch close to the edge. Then overcast or loopstitch the edges together by hand to prevent ravelling (Diagrams 69a and b). Leave the second edge of tape free. This strengthening and neatening facing will be invisible because it is on the underside of the seam turning (Diagrams 68b and 69b). This method may be helpful in preventing seam turnings of jersey fabrics from rolling under.

PIPED AND CORDED SEAMS

These may be introduced into dressmaking for their decorative effect. Contrasting fabric of suitable texture, thickness and colour is used for the piping strips which are cut on the cross, usually about $1\frac{1}{2}$ inches wide. Any joins, to provide a strip long enough for the purpose, are made on the straight grain of fabric as described on page 82 of *Standard Processes in Dressmaking* (Diagrams 112d and e).

Inserting piping into a seam

Fold the prepared crossway strip in half, WS facing and RS outside. Lightly press. Tack an even fitting line through the double fabric the required distance from the fold, e.g. $\frac{1}{8}$ inch (Diagram 70).

Lay the piping to RS of one seam fitting line on single fabric. Turnings face the same way. Pin and tack in position so the piping fold edge extends the desired amount beyond the seam line (Diagram 71).

Lay the second piece of garment fabric RS facing RS piping and first seam edge. Pin and tack again on the fitting line. The piping is now sandwiched between the two layers of fabric ready for machining on the fitting lines. Diagram 72 shows the machined seam with tacks removed. Trim the raw edges of the piping to about $\frac{1}{4}$ inch, so thickness of turnings can be graduated and they can be between the two seam edges which may be $\frac{1}{2}$ inch wide and can be neatened together after pressing to one side (Diagram 73).

Piped straight seam
The contrasting fabric is part of the decoration.

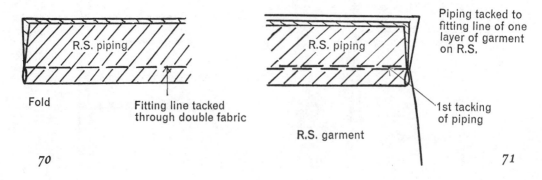

Fold

Fitting line tacked
through double fabric

70

R.S. piping

R.S. garment

Piping tacked to
fitting line of one
layer of garment
on R.S.

1st tacking
of piping

71

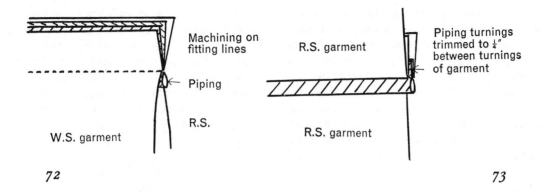

Machining on fitting lines

R.S. garment

Piping turnings trimmed to ¼" between turnings of garment

Piping

R.S.

R.S. garment

W.S. garment

R.S. garment

72

73

Piped curved seam

Note: Where piping is set into a curved seam, as in a collar or princess style, the turnings must be snipped or notched to enable them to lie flat.

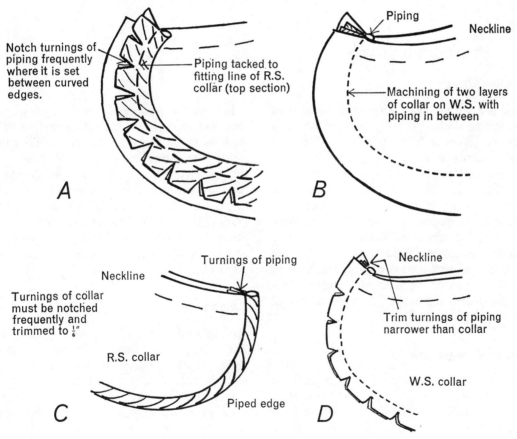

Notch turnings of piping frequently where it is set between curved edges.

Piping tacked to fitting line of R.S. collar (top section)

Piping

Neckline

Machining of two layers of collar on W.S. with piping in between

A

B

Turnings of collar must be notched frequently and trimmed to ⅛"

Neckline

Turnings of piping

R.S. collar

Piped edge

Neckline

Trim turnings of piping narrower than collar

W.S. collar

C

D

74

NOTE: Where piping is set into a curved seam, as in a collar or princess style line, the turnings must be narrower (not more than $\frac{1}{4}$ inch with piping turnings $\frac{1}{8}$ inch inside collar) and snipped or notched to enable them to lie flat. Diagrams 74a, b, c, and d show piping the edge of a collar. Careful manipulation and fixing is needed here to ensure an even width of piping all round the edge, and a flat finish to the collar.

Corded seam

The method is similar to a piped seam. Choose white piping cord of suitable thickness. Shrink it first before inserting by soaking in water and allowing to dry. Lay the cord to WS and between the folds of a crossway strip as shown in Diagram 75. Tack and stitch close to the cord.

For this purpose a one-sided cording foot or zip foot on the machine is advisable and helpful. Insert the cording strip as for piped seam. After careful tacking on the fitting lines machine together, using the cording foot attachment to ensure the stitching is on the fitting lines and holds the cord closely and firmly between the seam edges.

75

R.S. crossway strip

Tacking   Piping cord tacked between folds of crossway strip

TAILORED SEAMS

Machine fell seam

This is a strong, neat, self-finished seam used for sports clothes. It is worked on RS. Lay the two pieces of fabric WS facing. Pin, tack and machine on the fitting line on RS (Diagram 76a). Remove tacks. Press open the seam to flatten it. Then press the turnings flat together facing the back of the garment. Trim the front turning $\frac{1}{2}$ inch wide. Trim the back turning $\frac{1}{4}$ inch wide. Fold the front turning over the back (Diagrams 76b and c). With seam lying flat, pin and tack the folded edge evenly on to the back part of the garment. Machine close to the folded edge on RS. Remove tacks and press (Diagrams 76d).

Seam with lapped finish

This is suitable for centre or raglan seams of softly tailored coats or dressing gowns. Here the first line of machining is on WS and the second one worked on RS (Diagrams 77a, b, c and d).

Lay the two pieces of fabric RS facing. Pin, tack and machine on the fitting line on WS. Remove tacks. Press open the seam. Trim the turnings as shown in Diagram 77b. Close the turnings to one side, so the wider width covers the narrower one. Press flat on WS and tack in position the required finished width (Diagram 77c). On RS machine on the desired fitting line holding the turnings in position, and giving the effect of a lapped seam (Diagram 77d).

Tucked seam

The finished width of this seam (Diagrams 78a, b and c) is influenced by the style and design of the garment. It may be wide or narrow. The under portion requires a normal seam allowance (Diagram 78a). The top section must have twice the width of the tuck plus seam allowance (Diagram 78b). Fold and tack the tuck on its fitting lines and press it on

Machine fell seam

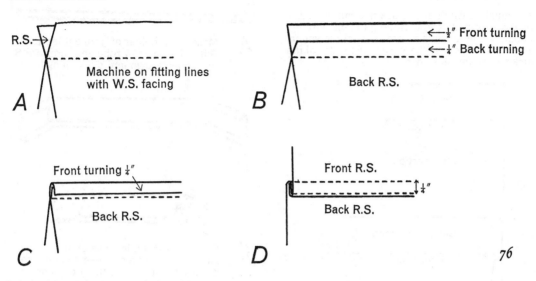

A Machine on fitting lines with W.S. facing

R.S.→

B ←½″ Front turning
←¼″ Back turning
Back R.S.

C Front turning ¼″
Back R.S.

D Front R.S.
¼″
Back R.S.

76

Seam with lapped finish

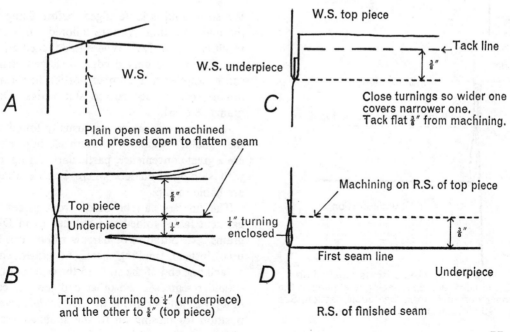

A W.S.
Plain open seam machined and pressed open to flatten seam

B Top piece
Underpiece
⅝″
¼″
¼″ turning enclosed
Trim one turning to ¼″ (underpiece) and the other to ⅝″ (top piece)

C W.S. top piece
W.S. underpiece
←Tack line
⅜″
Close turnings so wider one covers narrower one.
Tack flat ⅜″ from machining.

D Machining on R.S. of top piece
First seam line
⅜″
Underpiece
R.S. of finished seam

77

Tailored tucked seam

The finished width of this seam is influenced by the style and design of the garment. The underportion requires a normal seam allowance. The top section must have twice the width of the tuck and seam allowance.

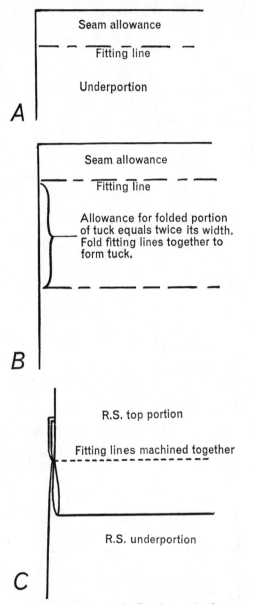

A

Seam allowance

— — — Fitting line — —

Underportion

Seam allowance

— — — Fitting line — —

Allowance for folded portion of tuck equals twice its width. Fold fitting lines together to form tuck.

B

R.S. top portion

Fitting lines machined together

R.S. underportion

C

Where this tucked effect is required on a curved edge, a shaped facing is applied to the upper portion to form the double section. See curved slot seams 1, Diagrams 58–61.

78

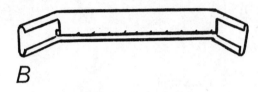

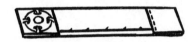

A Make strap holder of garment fabric. Stitch into narrow tube and turn to R.S. or fold as shown and sliphem by hand.

B

C Cut away extra thickness at underlayer and fold raw edges to neaten and form double fabric for attaching one end to shoulder seam and cap of press fastener to opposite end.

79

WS so its fold is knife-edged, before fixing to the under portion. A more tailored finish will result (Diagram 78c). Where this tucked effect is required on a curved edge, a shaped facing can be applied to the upper portion to form a double section. See curved slot seams: Diagrams 58 to 61.

Lingerie strap holders are usually found on the shoulder seams of couture clothes. They are a great convenience, particularly for figures with sloping shoulders where lingerie straps are liable to slip.

The holders can be made from pieces of garment fabric folded and stitched as in Diagrams 79a, b and c, or narrow ribbon can be used instead, making hems at either end. Attach one end of the strap to the centre of the shoulder seam. At the other end sew the cap of a press fastener, fixing the stud in the correct position for closing on to the shoulder seam (Diagrams 80a and b).

Lingerie strap holder on shoulder seam

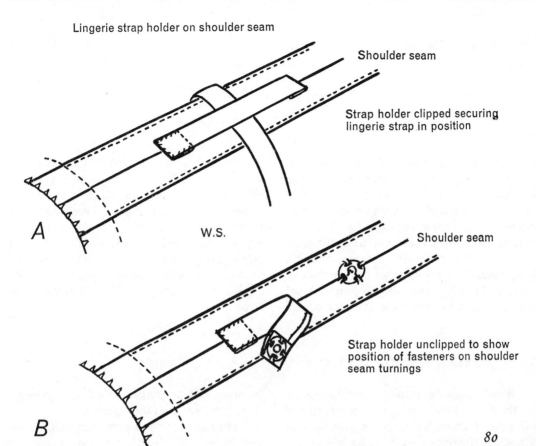

Shoulder seam

Strap holder clipped securing
lingerie strap in position

A

W.S.

Shoulder seam

Strap holder unclipped to show
position of fasteners on shoulder
seam turnings

B

80

Slide fasteners known as zips have become part of our everyday life. They were introduced as clothing fasteners during the First World War, when they were used by the American troops. Production in Britain started after the Armistice of 1918, but it was not until the mid-1920s that zip-fasteners became popular. Development made it possible to manufacture sizes and weights to suit different purposes and fabrics. Coloured zips were introduced and now slide fasteners in both metal and plastic can be bought for most purposes. Some firms will dye zip-fasteners to match a customer's material. An invisible zip-fastener has been invented, so that when it is set into an opening, e.g. CB, the finished appearance on the right side is that of a plain open seam with no stitches visible. The method of inserting this type of zip is explained on pages 85–7, Diagrams 105a to e.

BUYING A ZIP-FASTENER

1.   *Weight* must be suitable; not too heavy for the fabric or too light for the purpose it will serve. *Featherweight* zips are used for thin lightweight fabrics or where there is no great strain, e.g. neck openings. *Lightweight* zips are best for plackets of skirts, slacks and play clothes where the strain will be considerable and where firmer, heavier materials are used. *Open-ended zips* are used for loosely fitting jacket type garments. These are generally of a heavier type of fastener which has a special fitting at the lower end so that the two sides can be separated when the garment is taken off.

NOTE: When inserting open-ended zips the 'semi-concealed' method is advised as being more practical than the 'concealed'.

2.   The *length* of the zip must be suitable for the garment. The length is measured from the top of the slide fastener to the bottom stop when the zip is closed. When the slider tab is at the base of an opened zip, the length is reduced by about $\frac{1}{2}$ inch so a 5-inch zip will be $4\frac{1}{2}$ inches long when it is fully opened. If zips are too short, there will be undue strain in use which may damage both the zip and the garment.

3.   The *finished appearance* is important. If no stitching is to show on RS a special type of invisible fastener must be used. See pages 85–7, Diagrams 105a to e.

PREPARATION OF ZIP BEFORE INSERTION

1.   Where zips fit to curved parts of the body, as in side or long CB openings, the tapes on either side of the zip should be stretched by pulling them from under a moderately hot iron. Plastic zips may be damaged by too great heat, so the iron should not touch the teeth of the zip.

2.   The tape ends of zips must not be cut short or the fastener stops will be weakened. They should lie flat for skirt and dress plackets

72

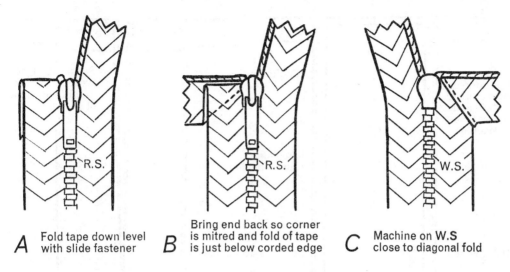

A Fold tape down level
   with slide fastener

B Bring end back so corner
   is mitred and fold of tape
   is just below corded edge

C Machine on **W.S**
   close to diagonal fold

81

and are usually stitched to the seam or facing turnings. Where the slide fastener of a zip comes to the end of an opening as in a collarless neckline, mitre the top tapes as shown in Diagram 81.

3. For semi-concealed zips, tack a guide line for machining ¼ inch from the centre of the teeth on both sides of the zip tape. (See Diagram 82.)

When machining in a zip, use a zip or 'cording' foot (one-sided) on the machine so that the stitching is as close as possible to the zip teeth without touching them.

There are three principal methods of inserting zips: semi-concealed, concealed and invisible.

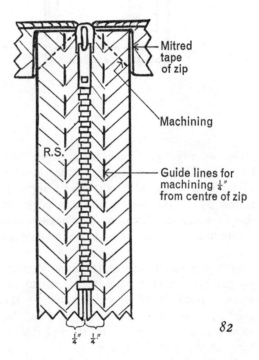

Mitred
tape
of zip

Machining

Guide lines for
machining ¼"
from centre of zip

82

SEMI-CONCEALED ZIPS

These may be inserted into a faced opening, a seam or the centre or side opening of a dress with a waist join.

1. For a *faced opening*, the finished length of the opening should equal the length of the zip. Mark the centre line with tacking and face before cutting the slit to prevent stretching or fraying edges. Cut the facing on the straight

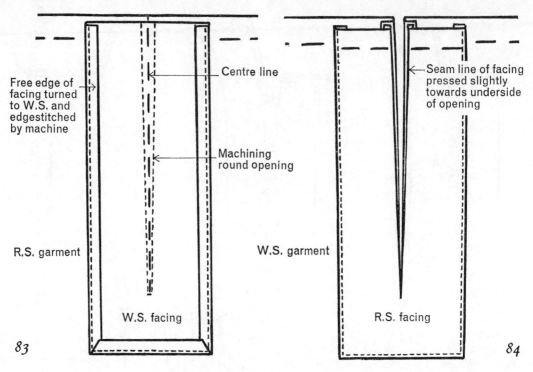

Free edge of facing turned to W.S. and edgestitched by machine

Centre line

Machining round opening

R.S. garment

W.S. facing

Seam line of facing pressed slightly towards underside of opening

W.S. garment

R.S. facing

83

84

grain, selvedge way down if possible. The length should be the length of the slit plus $1\frac{1}{2}$ inches and the width should be approximately $3\frac{1}{2}$ inches. Neaten the raw edges of three sides of the facing by overlocking with the machine zigzagger or as shown in Diagram 83.

With RS facing and centre lines together pin and tack in position. Machine round the marked position of opening, tapering the stitching round the base (Diagram 83). Remove tacks. Cut the centre line through double fabric to the base of the opening.

Turn the facing to WS. Work the seam out, so facing is flat. Tack and press on WS. No seam line should show on RS (Diagram 84). On RS working through double fabric mark the stitching line of zip down both sides, $\frac{1}{4}$ inch from centre of opening and across the base. Hold the two sides of the opening together with diagonal tacking (Diagram 85).

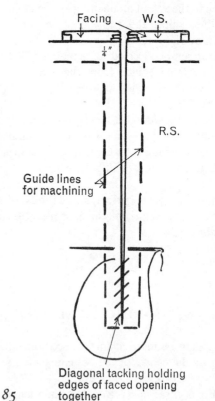

Facing   W.S.

$\frac{1}{4}''$

R.S.

Guide lines for machining

Diagonal tacking holding edges of faced opening together

85

Working bar tack

Attaching zip to opening

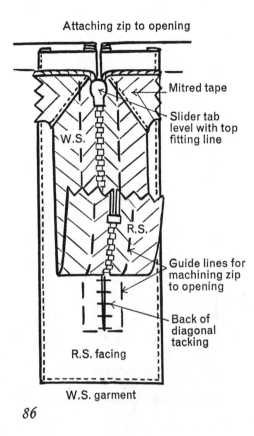

Mitred tape

Slider tab
level with top
fitting line

W.S.

R.S.

Guide lines for
machining zip
to opening

Back of
diagonal
tacking

R.S. facing

W.S. garment

86

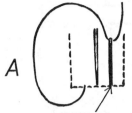

A

Needle stabbed from R.S.
to W.S. to make first strand.
Work three or four strands.

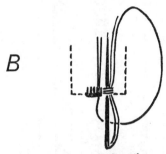

B

Cover and strengthen the
strands by working loopstitch
close together. Note the eye
of the needle passes under
the strands first, to prevent
splitting individual threads.

87

To insert the zip, prepare according to notes 2 and 3 on pages 72–3. With the centre of zip to centre of WS opening, pin and tack the garment to zip tape, matching guide lines. The slider tab and mitred tapes should be level with the top fitting line (Diagram 86). Work on RS and machine exactly on the guide lines. Remove tacks. On RS work a bar tack at the base of the opening for strength (Diagrams 87a and b). On WS fix and neaten the zip tapes to the facing (Diagram 88).

2. A semi-concealed zip may also be inserted *into a seam*, e.g. the centre or side opening of a skirt (Diagrams 89–91). The opening should be prepared so that it equals the length of the zip.

After fitting the garment, pin and tack the opening together on the fitting lines. Enlarge the stitch on the sewing machine (approximately six stitches to the inch for easy removal later) and machine from top to base of opening on the fitting lines. Adjust the stitch to normal length and machine the remainder of the seam (Diagram 90). Remove the hand tacking, press the seam open and neaten the raw edges.

On RS working through double fabric tackmark the stitching line of the zip $\frac{1}{4}$ inch from centre line of the opening and across the base (Diagram 91).

The preparation and insertion of the zip is the same as for the faced opening. Slider tab meets top fitting line and tapes are left flat (Diagrams 86 and 88). After machining the zip remove the tacks and enlarged machine stitches holding the edges of the opening.

NOTE: Many dressmakers prefer to *set zips in by hand*. The opening is prepared in the same way as for machine setting and the tacked guide

75

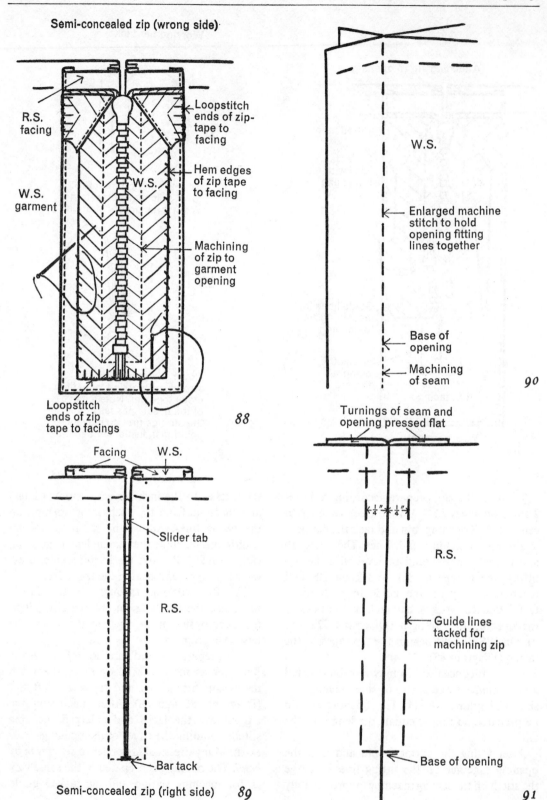

Semi-concealed zip (wrong side)

R.S. facing

Loopstitch ends of zip-tape to facing

Hem edges of zip tape to facing

W.S. garment

W.S.

Machining of zip to garment opening

Loopstitch ends of zip tape to facings

88

W.S.

Enlarged machine stitch to hold opening fitting lines together

Base of opening

Machining of seam

90

Facing   W.S.

Slider tab

R.S.

Bar tack

Semi-concealed zip (right side)   *89*

Turnings of seam and opening pressed flat

$\frac{1}{4}''$ $\frac{1}{4}''$

R.S.

Guide lines tacked for machining zip

Base of opening

91

lines of the opening are machined through double fabric before the zip is attached.

Secure the ends of the machine stitching and press the opening on WS. Pin and tack the zip in position matching guide lines. With matching thread stabstitch backwards and forwards through the machine stitching from RS to back of zip tape to hold it firmly in place. (Stabstitch is illustrated in Diagrams 169 and 170.)

Alternatively, working from WS pick up the zip tape and turning of the seam, and backstitch these two edges together as close to the machine stitching of the opening as possible. On RS strengthen the base of the opening with a bar tack (Diagram 87).

Preparation of opening at waist join

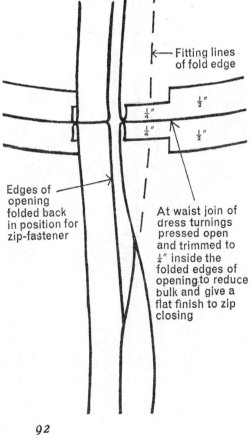

Fitting lines of fold edge

Edges of opening folded back in position for zip-fastener

At waist join of dress turnings pressed open and trimmed to ¼" inside the folded edges of opening to reduce bulk and give a flat finish to zip closing

92

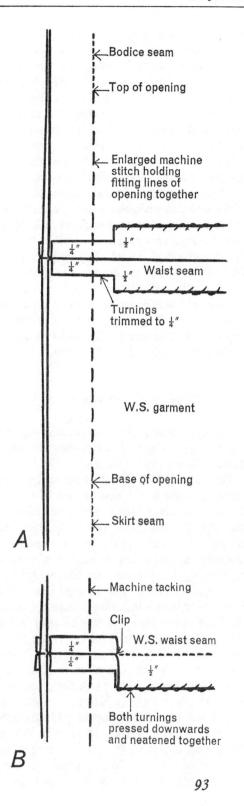

Bodice seam

Top of opening

Enlarged machine stitch holding fitting lines of opening together

Waist seam

Turnings trimmed to ¼"

W.S. garment

Base of opening

Skirt seam

A

Machine tacking

Clip

W.S. waist seam

Both turnings pressed downwards and neatened together

B

93

3. To insert a semi-concealed zip in the *centre or side opening of a dress with a waist join,* fit the dress before inserting the zip. Make sure that the back and front waist seams are level where they meet and that the opening is long enough. Note that the closer the fit of the garment, the longer must be the opening and fastening to avoid undue strain in wear.

Diagrams 92 and 93a and b show the seam turnings pressed open after machining the waist join and reduced to $\frac{1}{4}$ inch on each side of the seam, so when the opening turnings are folded to WS and pressed back on their fitting lines, the layers are as thin as possible. Prepare the opening and insert the zip as before. Diagram 93 shows the dress opening machine tacked on the fitting lines.

Note the shape of the stitching at the closed ends may be triangular as in Diagram 94, or square as in Diagram 89. Bar tacks should be worked at closed ends for strength.

CONCEALED ZIPS

1. If the opening for a concealed zip has *slightly curved edges*, it is strengthened and a guard of fabric fixed at the back.

The seam is stitched to the base of the opening which must be the exact length of the zip. Edges of openings such as those on skirts are often on the bias, and are easily stretched, causing bad fit and finish. To counteract this tendency cut two strengthening strips or stays of lightweight canvas or seam binding tape on the straight grain, or thin bonded interlining, $\frac{1}{2}$ inch wide, and $\frac{1}{2}$ inch longer than the opening. Tack one to the exact fitting line of WS of overlap. Tack the other $\frac{1}{8}$ inch over the fitting line on the turning of WS of underlap. Catch-stitch both these edges in position (Diagrams 95 and 96). For working catchstitch, see Diagrams 36a, b and c. The base of each stay extends $\frac{1}{2}$ inch below base of opening for strength.

For the *overlap* fold seam turning to WS on fitting line, enclosing stay. Tack in position. Press flat on WS. To hold edge firmly, machine close to fold. Measure and tack-mark guide

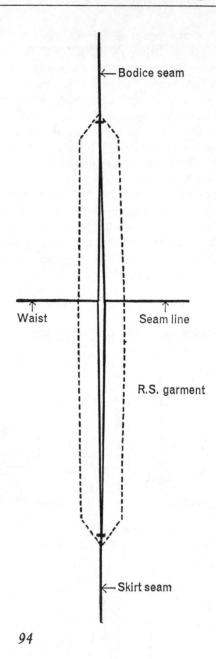

94

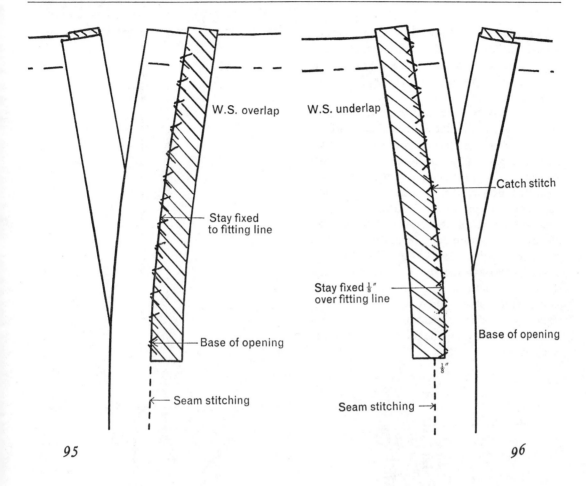

W.S. overlap   W.S. underlap

Catch stitch

Stay fixed
to fitting line

Stay fixed $\frac{1}{8}$"
over fitting line

Base of opening   Base of opening

Seam stitching

$\frac{1}{8}$"

Seam stitching →

95   96

line for machining of zip $\frac{3}{8}$ inch from fold, and across base. (NOTE: The latter can be a square or diagonal line according to taste.) Press again on WS for smooth flat finish (Diagram 97).

For the *underlap* fold seam turning to WS on $\frac{1}{8}$ inch extension line. Tack and press flat on WS. Lay this edge to zip tape, WS to RS zip, edge of fabric $\frac{1}{8}$ inch from zip teeth. The slide fastener of zip must be level with top fitting line. Pin and tack in position. With matching thread fell this edge closely and firmly to the zip tape by hand. From fitting line on underlap measure across zip $\frac{3}{8}$ inch and tack a guide line down zip tape (Diagram 97).

Fold overlap over underlap bringing fitting lines together. Pin into position. The zip is now concealed. Pin and tack the machine guide lines of front opening and zip tape together.

Using a machine cording foot, machine exactly on these lines down the opening and across the base. From RS work a bar tack on the machine line at the base of the opening for strength (Diagrams 87a and b). Finished opening is shown in Diagram 98. NOTE: If the zip is inserted by hand, when preparing the overlap, machine the guide line through double fabric and stay. Remove tacks and press on WS. Pin and tack this line to the zip fitting line as described. Finish with stabstitch or backstitch as described on page 77.

For the *guard*, cut a piece of fabric 1 inch longer than the opening and $1\frac{1}{2}$ inches wide, if single when finished, or 3 inches wide if double. This can be single fabric if firm enough, e.g. cloth, with the free raw edge neatened by seam binding, as in Diagram 99, or a double piece of fabric could be used folded in half lengthwise. Attach one long edge of guard to the seam turning of the underlap, and across the base of the opening. This prevents the zip teeth catching any underclothing.

2. Zips may be concealed *under a knife pleat* because, where the flat unopened seam of two pieces of fabric lies in the position of the underfold of a knife pleat, it is difficult and often impracticable to insert a zip in the actual seam line. By following these directions it is possible to conceal the zip in a flat position. It can be used where knife pleats follow each other round the figure (Diagram 100j) or under one side of an inverted or box pleat. In either case the directions for making the zip opening are similar, since both inverted and box pleats contain single knife pleats. Prepare the opening by carefully marking all pleat lines with thread or chalk. Fold and press the pleat lines in position accurately.

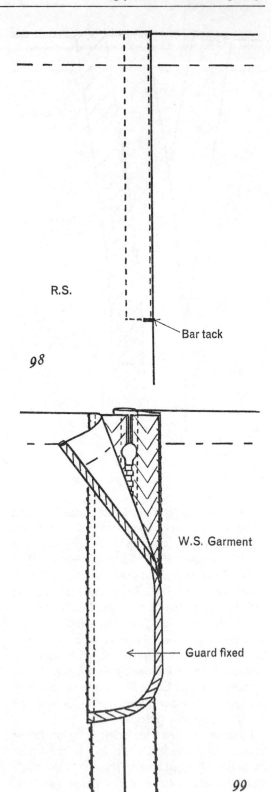

98

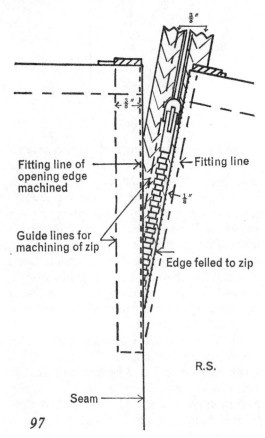

97

80

Machine and neaten the seam on the underside of the pleat as far as ½ inch below the base of the opening. At this position cut across both turnings as far as the seam stitching (Diagram 100a). On *back* of opening *only*, cut in a further ½ inch (Diagram 100b).

Slide the front portion forward ½ inch with WS of front uppermost so that the opening can be tacked together ½ inch from pleat fitting lines. Use small even hand tacking stitches or the largest machine stitch which will be removed later. Press turnings open flat taking

Zip concealed under knife pleat

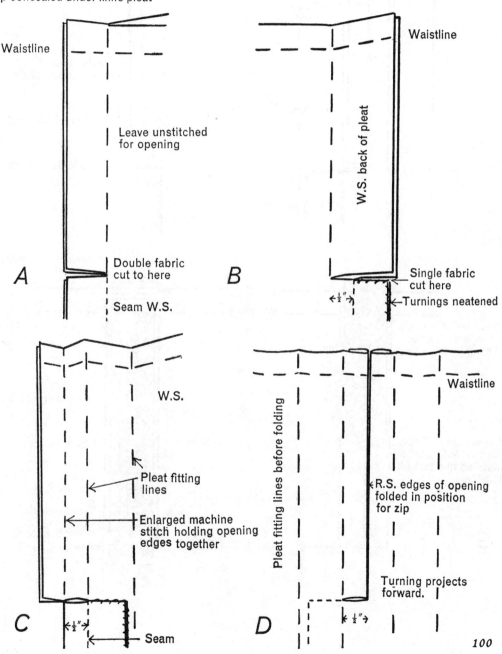

A — Waistline — Leave unstitched for opening — Double fabric cut to here — Seam W.S.

B — Waistline — W.S. back of pleat — Single fabric cut here — ←½″→ — Turnings neatened

C — W.S. — Pleat fitting lines — Enlarged machine stitch holding opening edges together — ←½″→ — Seam

D — Waistline — Pleat fitting lines before folding — R.S. edges of opening folded in position for zip — Turning projects forward. — ←½″→

100

Pleats when folded conceal opening.

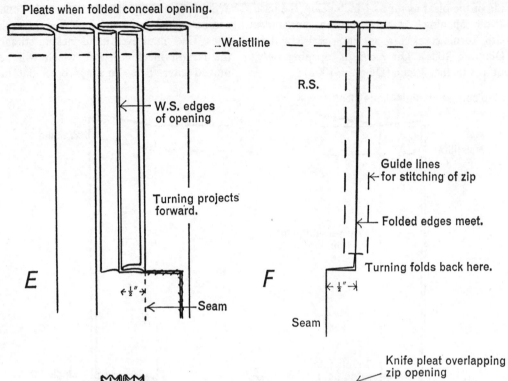

...Waistline

W.S. edges
of opening

Turning projects
forward.

E

←½"→

Seam

R.S.

Guide lines
for stitching of zip

Folded edges meet.

Turning folds back here.

F

←½"→

Seam

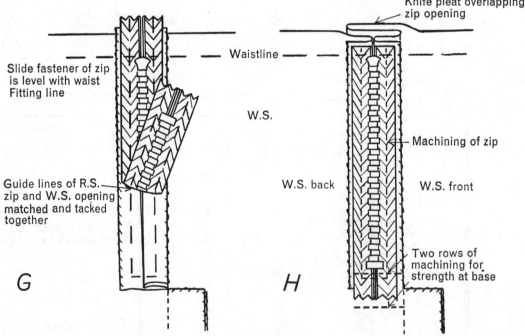

Slide fastener of zip
is level with waist
Fitting line

Waistline

W.S.

Guide lines of R.S.
zip and W.S. opening
matched and tacked
together

G

Knife pleat overlapping
zip opening

Machining of zip

W.S. back   W.S. front

Two rows of
machining for
strength at base

H

100

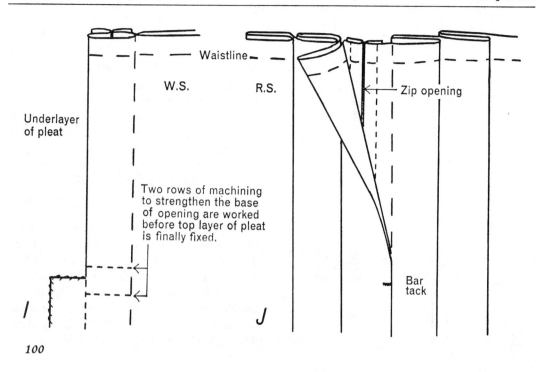

100

care not to spoil the pressed pleat edges (Diagrams 100c, d and e). Insert zip as in the semi-concealed method (Diagrams 100f and g). See notes for faced opening, pages 75–6.

Fold the pleat into position. The zip should lie flat and concealed. In order to strengthen the base of the opening, and to conceal the $\frac{1}{2}$ inch cut made on the back portion, pin, tack and machine or backstitch the two under portions together $\frac{1}{4}$ inch above the cut and $\frac{1}{4}$ inch below (Diagrams 100h and i). Fold the top section of pleat in position. Work a small bar tack on RS at base of placket, stabbing the needle through all thicknesses to back of zip tape (Diagrams 87a and b). Diagram 100j shows the finished opening and Diagram 101 shows a zip set into the back of a box pleat opening.

3. Zips may also be concealed in the *side opening* of a dress with a *waist join*. The method for this opening is similar to that shown for a skirt side placket. See directions for fitting and preparing the waist line join and turnings, page 77, Diagram 92. Both ends of the open-

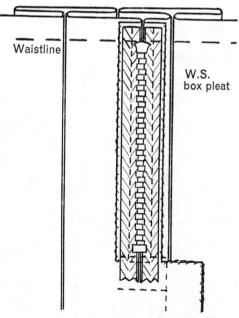

Zip opening concealed behind box pleat

101

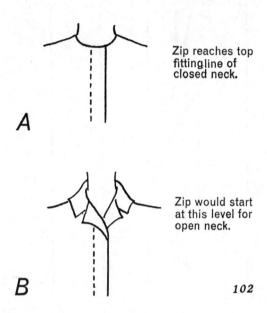

A   Zip reaches top fittingline of closed neck.

B   Zip would start at this level for open neck.

102

ing would be closed. Machining can be finished diagonally or square as desired. Bar tacks should be worked for strength.

4.   A zip concealed *under a fly front* makes a particularly neat opening for the bodice of a tailored blouse or dress. The insertion of the zip is a variation of the semi-concealed method (Diagrams 102a and b).

The right-hand front extends twice the finished width of the fly beyond the centre front line. The left-hand front extends 1 inch beyond the centre line.

To prepare the *right-hand front*, mark the fitting lines and centre line after cutting out. Turn the facing under to WS on the fold line. Tack and press on WS. Tack through the centre line to hold the fabric flat. Through the double fabric tack a fitting line for attaching the additional piece which will hold the right-hand side of the zip (Diagram 103a).

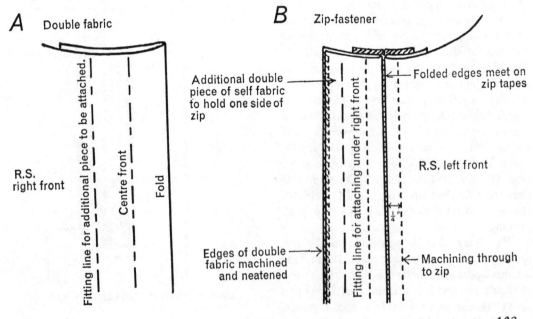

A   Double fabric

Fitting line for additional piece to be attached.

Centre front

Fold

R.S. right front

Additional double piece of self fabric to hold one side of zip

Edges of double fabric machined and neatened

B   Zip-fastener

Folded edges meet on zip tapes

Fitting line for attaching under right front

R.S. left front

$\frac{1}{4}''$

Machining through to zip

103

Prepare the *left-hand side* by folding the turning WS facing on CF line. Tack and press on WS. Measure and tack a fitting line ¼ inch from the fold through the double fabric to act as a guide line for machining zip. (See machine line in Diagram 103b.)

In preparing the *zip*, measure from the centre of the zip ¼ inch on either side and tack guide lines down the length of the tape as shown in Diagram 82. Matching the guide lines, pin and tack the left-hand front of the bodice with WS facing RS of left-hand side of the zip tape, centre lines and guide lines matching. The slide fastener of the zip must be placed to the correct fitting line for the style being made, e.g. for an open neck it will be placed lower than the position for a high closed neckline.

For the right-hand side of the zip cut an additional strip of fabric on the straight grain about 2 inches wide and the length of the zip tape. Fold in half lengthwise, with WS inside, tack and press. From the fold edge measure in ¼ inch and mark through double fabric a guide line for machining the zip. Attach this strip RS uppermost to the right-hand side of the zip by pinning and tacking the guide lines together. The two folded edges of fabric meet in the centre of the zip. Using a zip or cording foot on the machine, stitch the zip in position on the guide lines working on the right side. Remove tacks. Machine and neaten the double raw edges of the strip. Tack in a guide line of similar width from the centre front as that on the right-hand side of the garment (Diagram 103b).

In fixing the two front pieces of garment together, lay the folded edge of the right-hand front WS facing RS of left-hand front, with centre line covering centre of zip (Diagram 104a). The two fitting lines for attaching the additional piece should coincide and are tacked together. Machine through all four thicknesses down the fitting line. Remove tacks.

NOTE: If there is sufficient fabric to extend the right-hand front three times the finished width of the fly, the diagram shows how the material could be folded to form the portion to fix to the right-hand side of the zip, instead of using an additional piece (Diagram 104b).

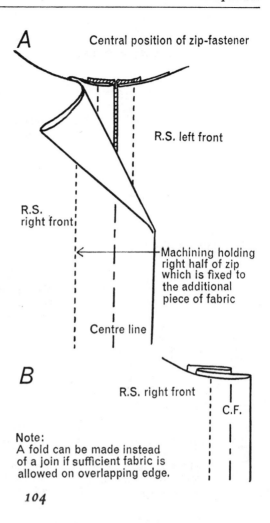

Central position of zip-fastener

A

R.S. left front

R.S. right front

Machining holding right half of zip which is fixed to the additional piece of fabric

Centre line

B

R.S. right front

C.F.

Note:
A fold can be made instead of a join if sufficient fabric is allowed on overlapping edge.

104

INVISIBLE ZIPS

Diagram 105a shows the finished zip set into a plain open seam with *no stitching visible* on RS of the garment.

To prepare the garment, pin, tack and press open the seam on WS. Mark the base of the opening, length from top fitting line equal to length of zip. Set in the zip before machining the lower part of the seam.

When inserting the zip, lay the closed zip RS facing WS of opening, with centre of zip matching the seam line and slide fastener meeting the top fitting line (Diagram 105b). Pin each side of zip tape to *single* thickness of

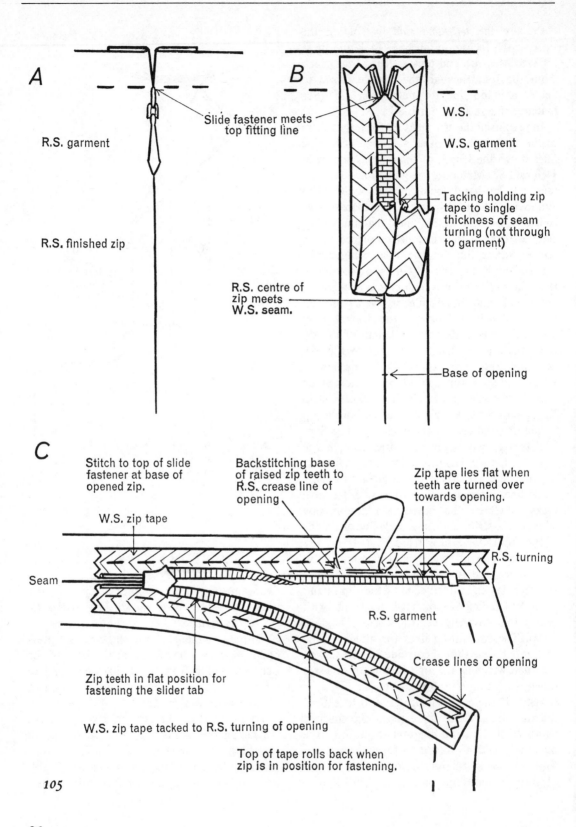

A

Slide fastener meets
top fitting line

R.S. garment

R.S. finished zip

B

W.S.

W.S. garment

Tacking holding zip
tape to single
thickness of seam
turning (not through
to garment)

R.S. centre of
zip meets
W.S. seam.

Base of opening

C

Stitch to top of slide
fastener at base of
opened zip.

Backstitching base
of raised zip teeth to
R.S. crease line of
opening

Zip tape lies flat when
teeth are turned over
towards opening.

W.S. zip tape

R.S. turning

Seam

R.S. garment

Zip teeth in flat position for
fastening the slider tab

Crease lines of opening

W.S. zip tape tacked to R.S. turning of opening

Top of tape rolls back when
zip is in position for fastening.

105

D   With one-sided machine foot needle can stitch close to base of raised zip teeth from lower end to top stop.

E   Rolled back ends and straight edges of zip tape are stitched to single fabric of turnings.

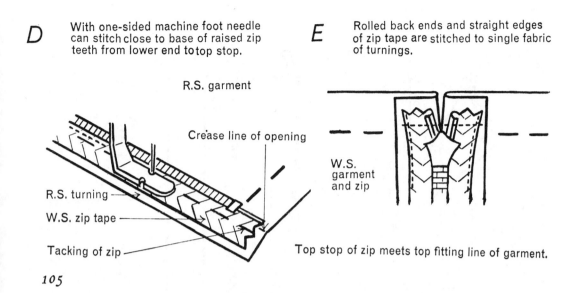

R.S. garment

Crease line of opening

R.S. turning

W.S. zip tape

Tacking of zip

W.S. garment and zip

Top stop of zip meets top fitting line of garment.

105

turnings. Tack close to zip with small stitches so zip is held firmly in position. The zip is opened for permanent stitching, so the first row of tacking which holds the garment opening together must be released from the RS as far as the base of the zip.

To set in the zip *by hand* (Diagram 105c) using matching thread, start at the top stop of one side of zip. Hold zip tape and RS turning together with the teeth turned over towards the opening so the base of the teeth coincides with the RS crease line of opening.

Backstitch the two together from the top stop of zip down the length of one side to the top of the slide fastener. Repeat on the other side, stitching from the top of the fastener (at the base of the opening) to the top stop of zip to ensure smooth fitting.

To set in the zip *by machine* (using a one-sided foot, Diagram 105d) lay the single thickness of the seam turning flat under the machine with WS of zip uppermost. Start at the base of the zip (top of slide fastener). Machine close to the base of the upturned teeth, so the stitching on the underside appears on the crease line of the opening. Stitch to the top stop. Repeat on the second side.

When finishing the garment seam, turn to RS. Close the fastener with care so the zip teeth turn back easily into the 'working position', i.e. flat against the opening.

On WS machine the garment seam on the fitting lines from the lower end of the opening downwards, placing the work in the usual position when stitching a plain open seam. Take care to fold back the zip tapes at the base of the zip so they are not caught into the seam stitching.

NOTE: If the zip is inserted *after* the seam has been machined there will be a slight gap of about $\frac{1}{2}$ inch between the base of the opening and the beginning of the seam when the zip is closed. This is due to the slide fastener being at the lower end of the zip when stitched to the garment. Close this $\frac{1}{2}$ inch space in the seam by hand or machine stitching on the fitting lines. To finish the ends of the zip tape (Diagram 105e), roll the corded edges of the top ends over to WS. Stitch across the top of each side to the single turnings of the garment. Lower edges are neatened on to the seam turnings. The long edges of the tapes on each side can be machined or hemmed to the single turnings of the opening.

Fly front with buttonhole fastening

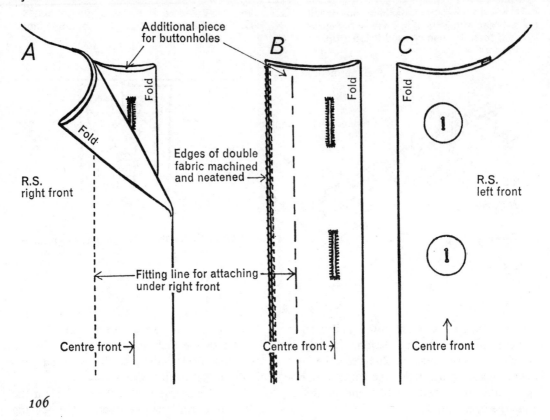

106

BUTTON AND BUTTONHOLE OPENINGS

Fly front opening

Prepare the right-hand front by turning the facing to WS on the fold line (Diagrams 106a and b). Tack and press on WS. Mark the centre line and fitting line for attaching the additional piece on which buttonholes are worked.

Cut a strip of fabric for the buttonhole strip on the straight grain about 3 inches wide. Fold in half lengthwise, with WS facing. Tack and press. From fold edge measure and mark ½ inch from centre line and the desired width for the stitching guide line to attach the strip to the garment.

Measure, mark and work vertical button-holes on the centre line according to the style and number required. Diagram 106b shows these worked with two bar ends.

Pin and tack this buttonhole strip to the right-hand front of the garment, with RS of strip facing WS of garment. The buttonholes should correspond with the centre line. Fix the strip to the garment on the marked fitting lines and machine (Diagram 106a). Neaten the raw edges on WS.

The left-hand side of bodice is prepared as for an ordinary button and buttonhole closing. The buttons must match the buttonholes for position and are sewn on to the centre line, holding the facing in position (Diagram 106c).

Extension opening

For *the centre front of a skirt* (Diagram 107),
there are two methods:

METHOD 1

Here the facings are cut in one with the skirt
front pieces.

Snip the seam turnings diagonally at the
base of the opening on both left and right
front skirt pieces (Diagrams 108a and b). Pin,
tack and stitch the centre seam of the skirt on
the fitting lines as far as the base of the opening.
Remove tacks, press open the seam, and neaten
the raw edges.

Fold the facings of the extensions, RS
facing (Diagram 108c). Pin, tack and machine
on the fitting lines, from the fold to CF line
at the base of the opening (Diagram 108d).
Trim the turnings, and turn to RS working the
free corners of the extension on the upper and
undersides to good sharp angles. Neaten the

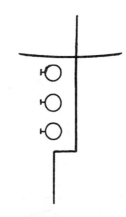

Finished centre front extension opening

107

Extension opening with buttonhole fastening
on centre front of skirt

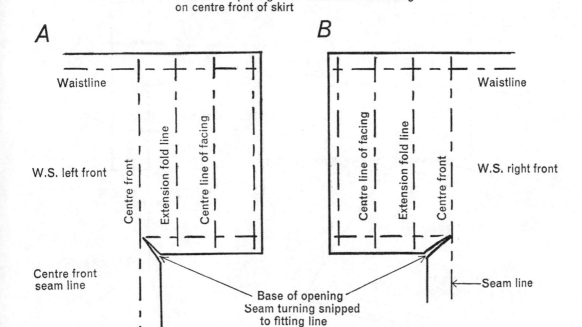

108

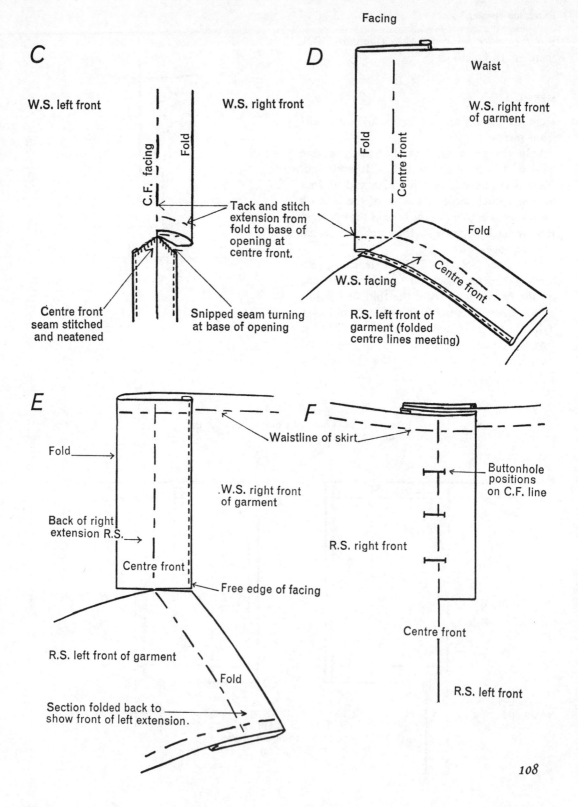

C

W.S. left front   W.S. right front

C.F. facing

Fold

Tack and stitch
extension from
fold to base of
opening at
centre front.

Centre front
seam stitched
and neatened

Snipped seam turning
at base of opening

D

Facing

Waist

W.S. right front
of garment

Fold

Centre front

Fold

Centre front

W.S. facing

R.S. left front of
garment (folded
centre lines meeting)

E

Fold

Back of right
extension R.S.

Centre front

.W.S. right front
of garment

Free edge of facing

R.S. left front of garment

Fold

Section folded back to
show front of left extension.

F

Waistline of skirt

Buttonhole
positions
on C.F. line

R.S. right front

Centre front

R.S. left front

108

Extension opening finished with separate facings

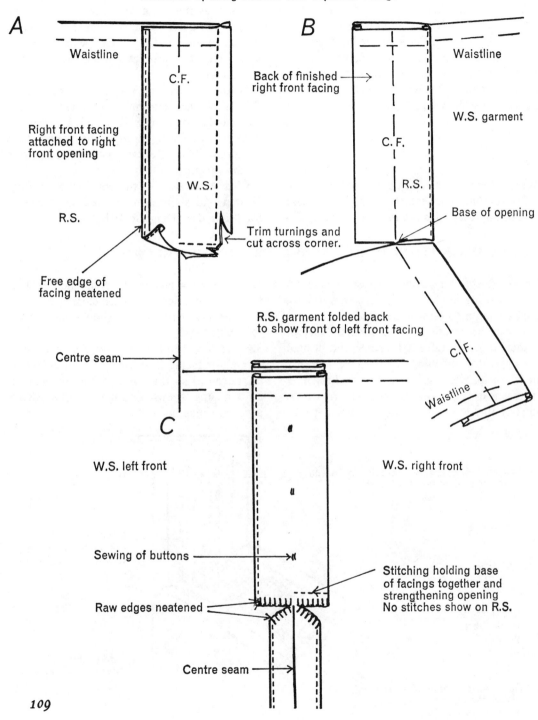

A

Waistline

C.F.

Right front facing
attached to right
front opening

W.S.

R.S.

Free edge of
facing neatened

Centre seam

B

Back of finished
right front facing →

Waistline

W.S. garment

C. F.

R.S.

Base of opening

Trim turnings and
cut across corner.

R.S. garment folded back
to show front of left front facing

C. F.

Waistline

C

W.S. left front

W.S. right front

Sewing of buttons

Stitching holding base
of facings together and
strengthening opening
No stitches show on R.S.

Raw edges neatened

Centre seam

109

free edges of both facings appropriately for the fabric. Press on WS.

Tack the CF lines through double fabric (Diagram 108e). These should meet in alignment with CF seam. Fold the overlap extension over the underlap section. Pin in position. On WS stitch the base of the facings together for added strength. Neaten the raw edges. No stitches must show on RS (Diagram 108f shows finished opening).

METHOD 2

With this method the facings are cut separately. After snipping the seam turnings at the base of opening and constructing CF seam as de-

scribed for Method 1, lay the right front facing to the right front opening with RS facing, and fitting lines matching. Pin, tack and machine down the outside edge and along the base of the extension as far as CF seam. Remove tacks. Trim the turnings and corners as shown in Diagram 109a.

Neaten the free edge of the facing. Turn to RS. Work the seam and corner out to clean edges and a good angle. Tack and press on WS. Tack in position through the centre lines (Diagram 109b). Repeat on the left-hand side of the opening.

Close both sides of the opening in position. Neaten and strengthen the base as described for Method 1 (Diagram 109c).

NYLON 'TOUCH AND CLOSE' FASTENER (VELCRO)

This is useful for many purposes where invisible closing of plackets, bands, pocket flaps, etc., are required on firm fabrics.

It can be bought by the inch in various colours to match fabrics, together with printed directions for attaching. The fastener consists of two strips which grip when pressed together by means of tiny hooks on the firm strip catching into tiny loops on the softer, fluffier strip.

1. The two strips must be planned so that there is exact alignment when closed.
2. The understrip (firm) should be stitched to double fabric.
3. The top strip is best sewn to an interlined turning or facing (to provide double thickness for strength) so that when folded in position no stitching shows through on the RS of garment (Diagram 110).

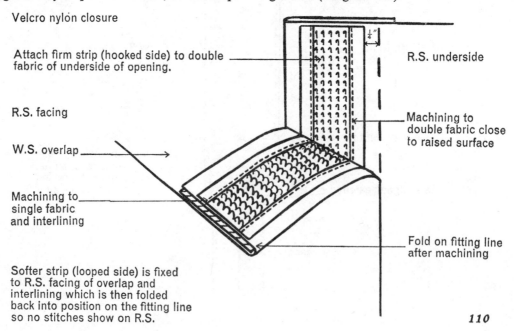

Velcro nylon closure

Attach firm strip (hooked side) to double fabric of underside of opening.

R.S. facing

W.S. overlap

Machining to single fabric and interlining

Softer strip (looped side) is fixed to R.S. facing of overlap and interlining which is then folded back into position on the fitting line so no stitches show on R.S.

R.S. underside

$\frac{1}{4}''$

Machining to double fabric close to raised surface

Fold on fitting line after machining

110

Fabrics vary a great deal and so influence the methods of finishing hems. Tailor treatment in shrinking hems of woollen or worsted fabrics is shown, and appropriate finishes described. Many dresses and skirts are lined and the double fabric is made up as one layer. Diagrams and notes suggest ways of dealing with the hems of these garments so that a professional appearance may be obtained.

Some otherwise smartly finished garments are spoiled by the non-professional look of the hems. One important point is the pressing, before the final attachment to the garment, in order to give the hem a good knife edge whilst preventing any impression of the upper edge showing on the right side. (See Chapter Two, pages 38–42.) Another cause of this impression showing is through the thread being pulled too tightly when the final stitching is worked.

It is important to make sure that the turning-up line of the hem is level when the garment is on the wearer. Methods of levelling the hem are described and illustrated on page 75 of *Standard Processes in Dressmaking*. Assuming that the correct level has been obtained, hems may be finished in a number of ways.

SLIGHTLY SHAPED HEMS FOR THICKER FABRICS

Diagrams 111a and b show the right and wrong side of a finished hem. This can be used for fabrics that will not shrink.

Turn up the hem to WS garment on the fitting line and tack through the folded edge. Measure and mark depth of hem, and trim surplus fabric away evenly all round (Diagram 111c). Any seam turnings inside the hem should be narrowed to ¼ inch to reduce thickness. Diagram 62 shows this. Fold away extra fullness in small darts tapering to nothing at the bottom so the hem lies flat (Diagrams 111d, e).

Protect the raw edge of the hem by (a) using the zigzagger on the machine or (b) machining close to the edge on the single thickness (Diagram 111e). Then overcast or loopstitch the edge to prevent any ravelling. Finally tack the free edge of the hem in position. Press before stitching permanently. Fix with sliphemming to the garment (Diagram 111f). No stitches must show on RS. If only a light stitch is taken it should be invisible on RS.

An alternative method of sliphemming a tailored skirt or coat of cloth or jersey is shown in Diagrams 112a, b and c. After neatening the raw edge of the hem as described above, tack it ¼ inch from the neatened edge and press. The sliphemming is then worked very lightly with the hem folded back.

For fabrics which fray scarcely at all, Diagram 113 shows a quick finish. After edge-stitching the single fabric by machine as shown in Diagram 111e, cut off the surplus raw edge with pinking shears. Then sliphem to garment. Diagram 113 shows both seam turning and hem edge finished in this way.

Diagrams 114a, b and c and notes clearly explain the process of shrinking surplus fullness away from shaped hem turnings.

Seam binding finish

This may be used for the hem of an unlined jacket or skirt of cloth (Diagrams 115a and b).

Slightly shaped hem for unshrinkable thicker fabrics

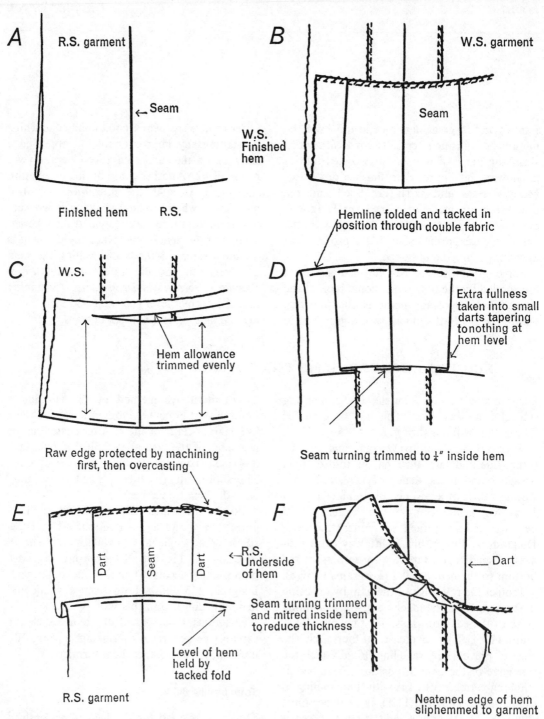

A
R.S. garment
←— Seam
Finished hem   R.S.

B
W.S. garment
Seam
W.S.
Finished
hem

C
W.S.
Hem allowance
trimmed evenly
Raw edge protected by machining
first, then overcasting

D
Hemline folded and tacked in
position through double fabric
Extra fullness
taken into small
darts tapering
to nothing at
hem level
Seam turning trimmed to ¼" inside hem

E
Dart   Seam   Dart
←R.S.
Underside
of hem
Level of hem
held by
tacked fold
R.S. garment

F
Dart
Seam turning trimmed
and mitred inside hem
to reduce thickness
Neatened edge of hem
sliphemmed to garment

111

Hem for cloth or jersey skirt

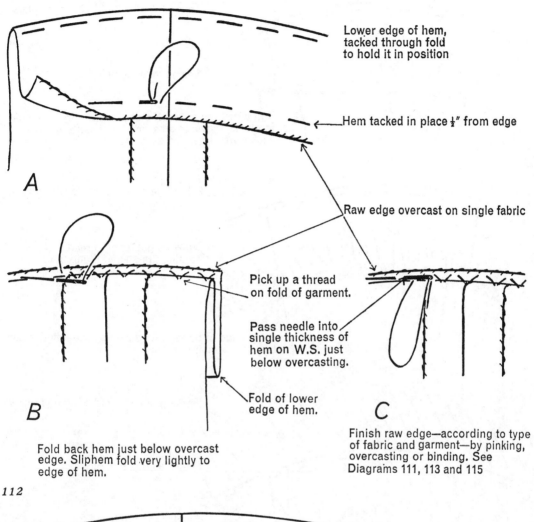

Lower edge of hem, tacked through fold to hold it in position

Hem tacked in place ½" from edge

A

Raw edge overcast on single fabric

Pick up a thread on fold of garment.

Pass needle into single thickness of hem on W.S. just below overcasting.

Fold of lower edge of hem.

B

Fold back hem just below overcast edge. Sliphem fold very lightly to edge of hem.

C

Finish raw edge—according to type of fabric and garment—by pinking, overcasting or binding. See Diagrams 111, 113 and 115

112

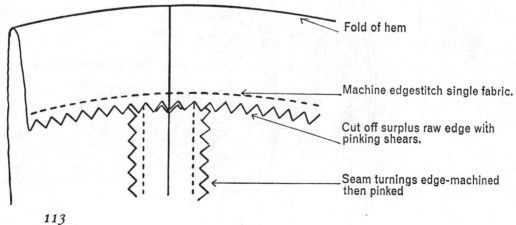

Fold of hem

Machine edgestitch single fabric.

Cut off surplus raw edge with pinking shears.

Seam turnings edge-machined then pinked

113

Shrinking fullness from shaped hem turnings

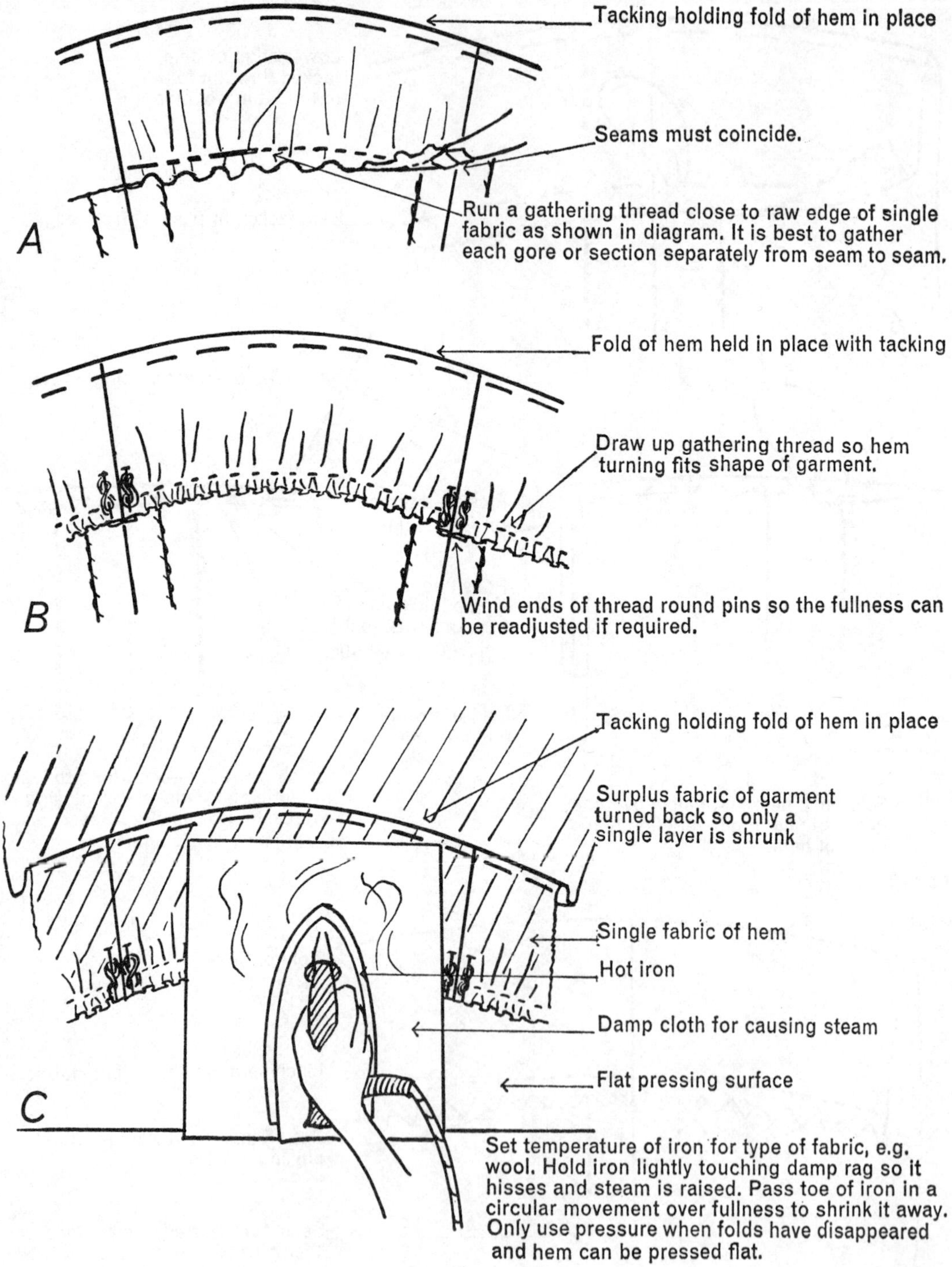

Tacking holding fold of hem in place

Seams must coincide.

A

Run a gathering thread close to raw edge of single fabric as shown in diagram. It is best to gather each gore or section separately from seam to seam.

Fold of hem held in place with tacking

Draw up gathering thread so hem turning fits shape of garment.

B

Wind ends of thread round pins so the fullness can be readjusted if required.

Tacking holding fold of hem in place

Surplus fabric of garment turned back so only a single layer is shrunk

Single fabric of hem

Hot iron

Damp cloth for causing steam

Flat pressing surface

C

Set temperature of iron for type of fabric, e.g. wool. Hold iron lightly touching damp rag so it hisses and steam is raised. Pass toe of iron in a circular movement over fullness to shrink it away. Only use pressure when folds have disappeared and hem can be pressed flat.

114

Hem for unlined cloth coat, jacket or skirt

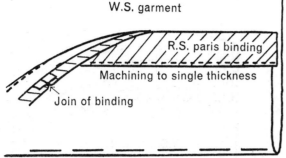

W.S. garment

R.S. paris binding

Machining to single thickness

Join of binding

Tacking holding folded edge in place

A

Use a facing of paris or seam binding to match the fabric in colour. Turn up hem to required level. Tack the folded edge and measure depth of hem. Mark with pins or tailor's chalk. Trim away surplus fabric. Lay W.S. binding to R.S. hem with one edge overlapping raw edge of hem. Pin and tack to single thickness of hem, keeping binding flat. Where a join occurs, use a flat open seam with turnings facing hem. Machine close to edge as shown in diagram. Sliphem free edge of paris binding to garment, so no stitches show on R.S.

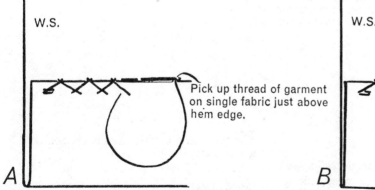

Match seam of hem to seam of garment.

Sliphem free edge of paris binding to garment.

W.S. garment

B

115

116

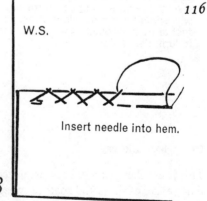

W.S.

Pick up thread of garment on single fabric just above hem edge.

A

W.S.

Insert needle into hem.

B

Hems on lined coats or jackets are often kept in place by herringbone stitch worked so the raw edges are protected, but no stitching shows on R.S.

Turn up hem to W.S. Tack. Measure and trim turning to equal depth throughout. Press so fold of hem is sharp. Using matching sewing thread, hold and protect raw edge of hem with herringbone stitch

Hems finished with decorative machine stitching
Used on circular skirts or coats of heavier fabrics,
e.g. sailcloth, wool, or wool blended cloths, etc.

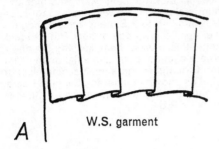

A   W.S. garment

Turn under raw edge to W.S. on fitting line.
Tack through double fabric close to fold
Either shrink surplus fullness in hem turnings
if woollen (see Diagram 114) or dart if unable
to shrink (Diagram 111). Press flat, and tack
in position.

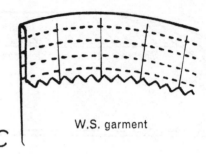

C   W.S. garment

After machining, trim away the raw edge on
W.S. with pinking shears. If fabric frays
easily, trim raw edge close to machining and
overcast on W.S. without showing stitches
on R.S.

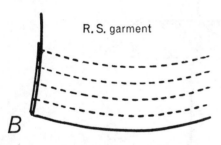

B   R.S. garment

On R.S. stitch hem on extreme edge or an
equal distance from edge by machine. Then
machine required number of rows, spacing as
wished, either by the width of machine presser
foot or by individually spaced and tacked lines
to form decoration.

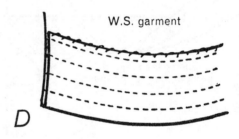

D   W.S. garment

117

Herringbone stitching

This is another popular way of protecting and
fixing edges of skirts and coats of tweed, suiting,
double jersey and other thick materials (Diagrams 116a and b). In addition to this hand-
stitching, hems are sometimes finished decora-
tively with several rows of machine stitching
with planned spacing. This also stiffens the

hem edge to a certain extent (Diagrams 117a,
b, c and d).

Bound hems

Note that, when it is turned over, the binding
is only one layer of fabric facing the underside
of the hem in order to retain a flat finish
(Diagrams 118a, b, c and d).

Bound hem

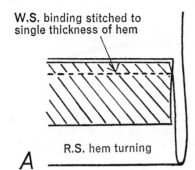

W.S. binding stitched to
single thickness of hem

R.S. hem turning

A

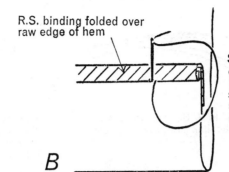

R.S. binding folded over
raw edge of hem

Single thickness
of binding held
in place by stab-
stitching through
single thickness
of hem

B

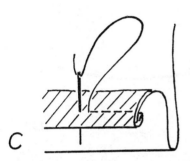

C

Underside of hem showing longer stitches
holding single fabric of binding in place

A bound hem is used on thicker materials
which may fray easily. The binding may be of
thin crossway fabric such as silk, rayon,
mercerised cotton or net, matching the
garment fabric in colour. Although taking
more time, this finish when neatly and skilfully
done gives an expensive look to a garment,
and is recommended for advanced examinations.

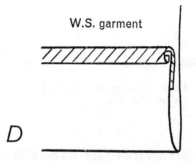

W.S. garment

D

Bound edge of hem fixed to garment with light
sliphemming　Press before stitching.

118

Roll hem used for edges of thin or
transparent fabrics

A

To prevent raw edges stretching, machine on
fitting line.　Trim raw edges close to
machining.　Press lightly on W.S.

119

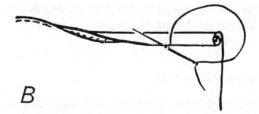

B

Roll edge to W.S. with finger and thumb.
Use fine needle and thread to hold roll in
position with sliphemming.

Narrow machine stitched hems—
used on curved edges of thin fabrics

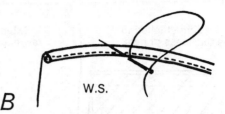

A

Turn raw edge ¼″ to W.S. Tack and press.
Edgestitch by machine. Trim raw edge close
to stitching.

B

Fold over to W.S. again to make a narrow hem.
Tack and press. Fix in position by either:
sliphemming by hand to give invisible finish on
R.S. or D

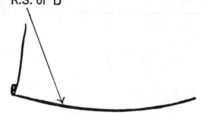

D

machine on R.S. close to fold (edgestitching);
quick method, but shows on R.S.

C

120

HEMS FOR THINNER FABRICS

The edges of drapery or loose sashes of thin or
transparent fabrics may be finished in a number
of ways. A *roll hem* is illustrated in Diagrams
119a and b. A narrow *machine stitched* hem
is shown in Diagrams 120a, b, c and d or, by
using the machine attachment, the hem may
be given a *picot edge*. With transparent material
double hems may be used. These can be any
width according to purpose (Diagram 121).

The hems of thinner fabrics may be stiffened
using horsehair or crinoline braid. This is used
to give support to the hems of evening dresses
and to hold their shape. See Diagrams 44a,
b and c.

Hems of lined skirts

Where the garment fabric and the lining are
made up together as one, Diagrams 122a and b
may be followed for thin fabrics such as silk,
when the lining is of similar kind and thickness, and Diagrams 123a and b for thicker
fabrics like jersey or dressweight wool.

Raw edge meets fold of hem.

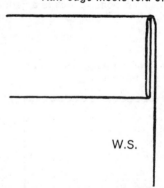

W.S.

Hem for transparent material, where the
garment needs a deeper or heavier hem.
Make the first turning as deep as the depth
of hem to give an opaque appearance.

121

Hems for lined skirts—used with thin fabrics
such as silk, lined with jap silk, where the two
materials are made up as one

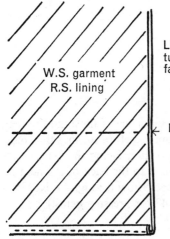

W.S. garment
R.S. lining

Fitting line of hem

A

Single turning on edge of hem
machined close to fold

122

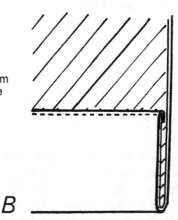

Lining on inside of hem
turning making double
fabric

B

W.S. garment showing R.S. lining

Neatened edge of hem is lightly
sliphemmed to single thickness of
lining only, so no impression shows
on R.S. garment.

Hems for thicker fabrics

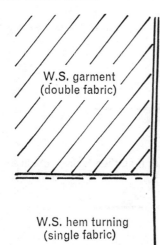

W.S. garment
(double fabric)

W.S. hem turning
(single fabric)

A

Raw edge is edge machined
and overcast or overlocked.

123

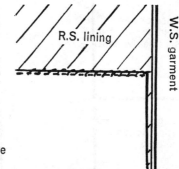

B

R.S. lining

W.S. garment

Edge of lining reaches the
hem fitting line only.

Neatened edge of hem is lightly
sliphemmed to lining only
(single thickness).

In some cases the hems of garments and
linings are made separately, so that the lining
is slightly shorter than the garment edge and
hangs loose. In this case each hem is made
according to type of fabric.

SLITS

So as to give freedom of movement, yet maintaining a slim line and an even hang to the lower edge of a garment, slits are sometimes left open at the ends of seams. These occur for instance at the lower edge of slim fitting skirts or slacks, and in overblouses. Diagram 124 shows the sequence of finishing the hem edges of the garment before turning the folds of the slits into position facing the hem. Catch these edges in place to the back of the hem turnings, so no stitches show through on RS. Press well. (See page 42 for pressing hems.)

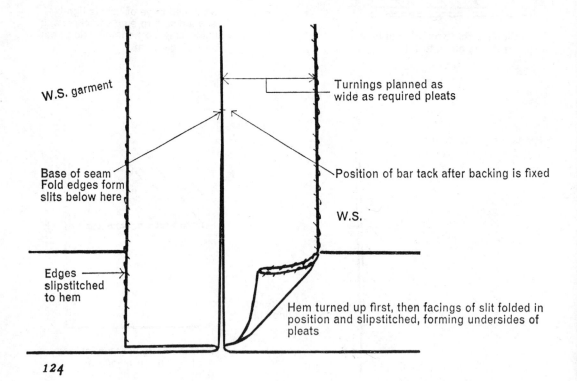

W.S. garment

Turnings planned as wide as required pleats

Base of seam
Fold edges form slits below here

Position of bar tack after backing is fixed

W.S.

Edges slipstitched to hem

Hem turned up first, then facings of slit folded in position and slipstitched, forming undersides of pleats

124

VENTS

A vent is a slit in the lower edge of a garment to give freedom of movement. It is usually at the base of a seam and is constructed with an underlay to cover the back of the opening (Diagrams 125, 126 and 127).

The facing of the underlay can be cut in one

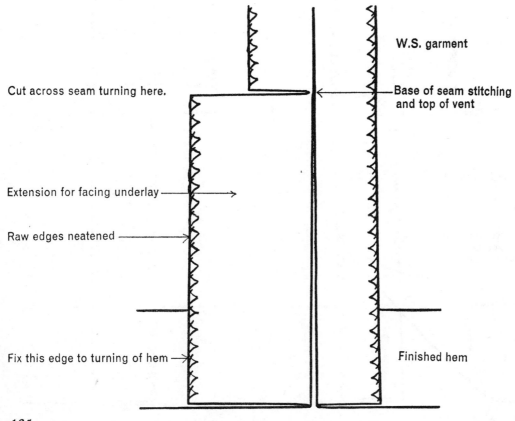

Cut across seam turning here.

W.S. garment

Base of seam stitching and top of vent

Extension for facing underlay

Raw edges neatened

Fix this edge to turning of hem

Finished hem

125

with the main turnings as shown in Diagram 125. Otherwise a separate piece would be required for the backing.

Stitch the seam of the garment to the top of the slit. Press the turnings and neaten the raw edges. Turn up, press, and finish the hem. Fold over the top side of the vent as described for slits fixing the lower edge to the single turning of the hem (Diagrams 124 and 125).

Cut across the turning of the underside to the seam stitching to release it, so as to fold over and face the top part of the slit (Diagrams 125 and 126). Attach the lower edge to hem as for a slit and the top edges to seam turning.

Neaten the raw edges of the top of the vent on WS with a piece of ribbon seam binding hemmed to the turnings as shown in Diagram 127.

SIMULATED PLEATS

Inverted pleats

When an inverted pleat effect is required, e.g. CB of a slim fitting skirt, the turnings of the seam may be planned as wide as required for each single pleat, as shown in Diagram 129. Neaten and finish as described for slits (Diagram 124). (See also strengthening and finishing wide seam turnings of fabric such as jersey, page 65, Diagrams 68 and 69.)

If *double fabric* is used with a fold at the lower edge as shown in Diagram 128 cut the backing on the straight grain twice the length of the slits plus 3 inches by the width of inverted

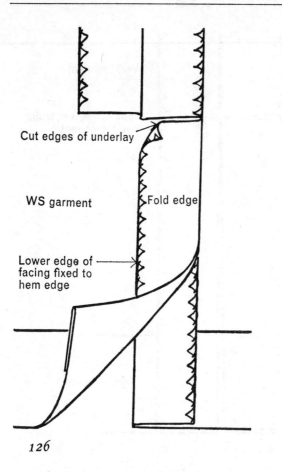

Cut edges of underlay

WS garment

Fold edge

Lower edge of facing fixed to hem edge

126

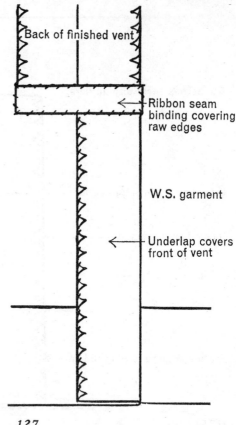

Back of finished vent

Ribbon seam binding covering raw edges

W.S. garment

Underlap covers front of vent

127

pleat plus 2½ inches. Fold backing RS facing. Stitch ¼ inch from raw edges down the two sides. Turn to RS. Neaten top edges together. Press.

If the backing is of *two materials*, e.g. garment fabric and lining, cut both on the straight grain, length of slits plus 1½ inches by width of inverted pleat plus 2½ inches. Lay fabric and lining RS facing. Stitch down the two sides and across the base, ¼ inch from the raw edges, leaving the top edges open. Trim the lower corners of the seam turnings. Turn to RS. Work out the seam edges. Tack and press on WS. Neaten the top edges together.

Attach the top edge of the backing, RS facing WS of garment, to the single thickness of the pleat turnings so no stitches show through on RS. The lower edges must be level when the garment is worn (Diagram 129). For strength at the base of the seam and top of slit, work a bar tack from RS through to backing. Diagrams 87a and b show method of working bar tack.

If the garment has a loose lining at the lower edge, the pleat backing may be attached to the lining instead of the turnings of the garment. In this case, it can if desired be considerably wider than the slit turnings as it is attached separately. The final level of the backing at the hem edge must be watched carefully for the smart look of the garment when on the wearer.

For freedom of movement in the lining itself, leave slits in seams other than the one holding the pleat backing. (See notes on fully lined skirts, page 164.)

Knife pleats

When these are in the slit at the lower edge of a garment seam, e.g. CB of skirt, cut the CB turnings of the skirt so that the back or under

W.S. Backing for slit to simulate pleat

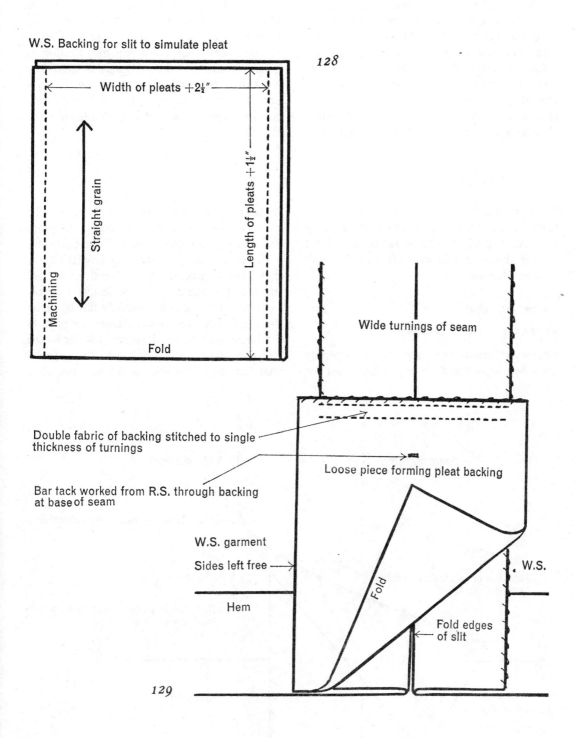

128

Width of pleats +2½″

Straight grain

Length of pleats +1½″

Machining

Fold

Wide turnings of seam

Double fabric of backing stitched to single
thickness of turnings

Loose piece forming pleat backing

Bar tack worked from R.S. through backing
at base of seam

W.S. garment

Sides left free →

Hem

Fold

W.S.

Fold edges
← of slit

129

turning is wider than the other, e.g. 3½ inches widest turning to back the other turning of 2½ inches (pleat width). Allow these widths from the hem edge to the waist (Diagram 130).

Construct the seam on the fitting lines as far as the top of the slit. Neaten both raw edges separately for flat finish. (See also Diagrams 68 and 69 for strengthening single raw edges of wide seam turnings.) Turn up, press and stitch the hem. Fold back the first layer of the pleat as described for slits. Leave the under layer quite flat. Fix the two layers together at the top of the slit on WS by stitching the double fabric across the width (Diagram 130). The third or outside skirt layer must not be connected so no stitches show on RS. This process is suitable for fabrics such as double jersey or similar thickness.

INSET PLEATS

The pleated section is constructed and pressed before it is set into the prepared opening in the garment, e.g. CF or CB of skirts. The front view is shown in Diagram 131 and the back view in Diagram 132.

Straight inset pleat

PREPARING THE GARMENT

For smart results the shape of the opening must be proportionate, e.g. not too short for its width, and accurately marked out on the garment before construction begins. Diagram 133 shows the shaped opening slit up the centre with corners snipped, showing how the turnings must be released to enable them to fold under to the fitting line of the design. The corners are thus weakened. Remedy this by lining out the shaped portion as described on page 49 for lining out corners. Diagram 134 shows the lining RS facing and stitched to the required shape on the fitting lines of the garment, after

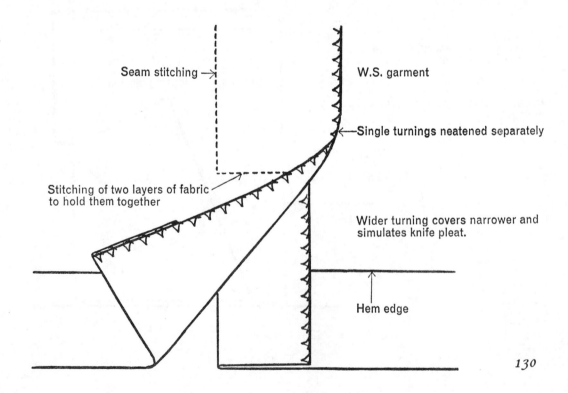

Seam stitching →

W.S. garment

←—Single turnings neatened separately

Stitching of two layers of fabric
to hold them together

Wider turning covers narrower and
simulates knife pleat.

Hem edge

130

Finished inset pleats   R.S.

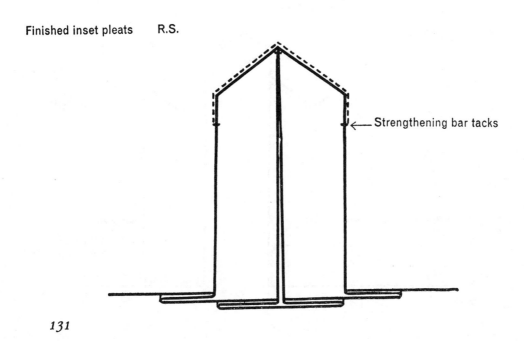

Strengthening bar tacks

131

Finished inset pleats   W.S.

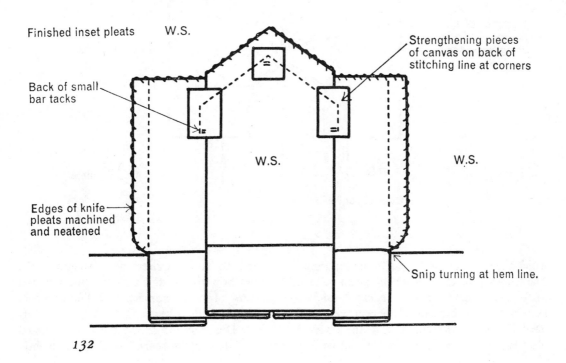

Strengthening pieces
of canvas on back of
stitching line at corners

Back of small
bar tacks

W.S.

W.S.

Edges of knife
pleats machined
and neatened

Snip turning at hem line.

132

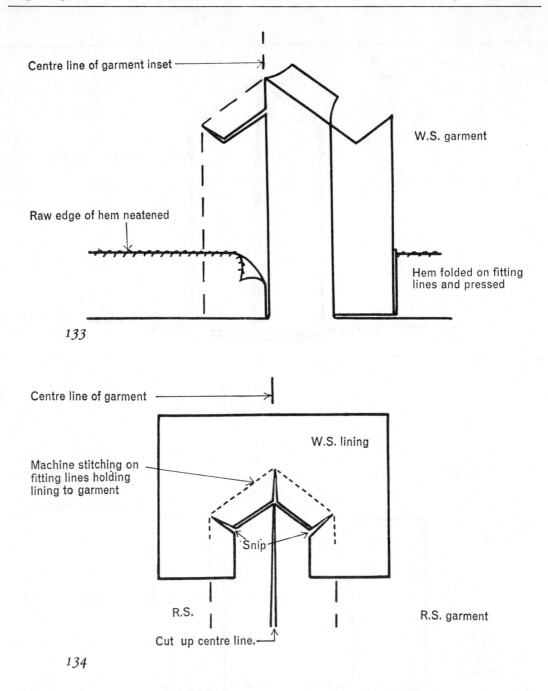

Centre line of garment inset ──────→

W.S. garment

Raw edge of hem neatened

Hem folded on fitting lines and pressed

133

Centre line of garment ──────→

W.S. lining

Machine stitching on fitting lines holding lining to garment

Snip

R.S.

R.S. garment

Cut up centre line.──↑

134

which the opening can be cut to the top point. The two long edges of the opening can be used to fold under and form the backing for two knife pleats at either side of the centre inverted pleat if desired. (NOTE: If only the inverted pleat is planned, these turnings would be nar-rowed to suit requirements.) Diagram 134 shows how to cut and snip the turnings and corners of both garment and lining before turning the lining through to WS of the gar-ment. Diagram 135 shows the lining pressed back flat with the seam line showing slightly

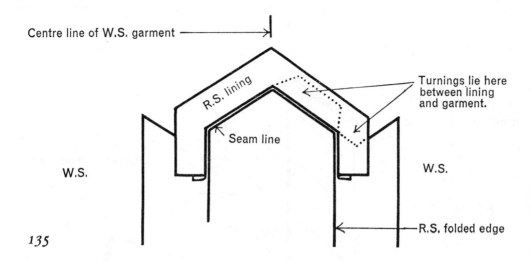

135

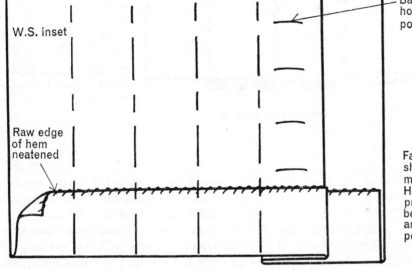

136

on WS. The dotted line indicates the position of the turnings folded back and lying in between the lining and the garment. Tack the shaped opening in position and press the folded edges well on WS. For best results the hemlines of both garment and pleated inset should be levelled, raw edges neatened by overcasting or with a zigzag machine attachment, and turned under on their respective fitting lines. Press the lower edges of both portions into

position before folding and pressing the pleats, but do not permanently stitch either hem until after the inset has been attached to the garment as the hem must be let down again to join the side edges together.

PLEATED INSET

All pleat lines must be carefully measured and marked after cutting out the inset. Prepare and

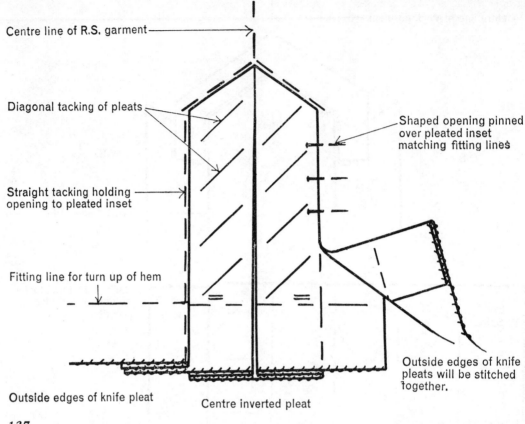

Centre line of R.S. garment

Diagonal tacking of pleats

Shaped opening pinned over pleated inset matching fitting lines

Straight tacking holding opening to pleated inset

Fitting line for turn up of hem

Outside edges of knife pleats will be stitched together.

Outside edges of knife pleat

Centre inverted pleat

137

press the hem as described above. Then fold and tack the pleats in position as shown in Diagram 136. On the WS press this inset well and carefully. Then release the hem to free the side edges (Diagram 137). Note the diagonal tacking on the front of the pleats and horizontal tacks at the back to hold them in position.

ATTACHING INSET TO GARMENT

Lay the prepared opening over the pleated section after releasing the hem. Match the centre folds of the inverted pleat to the centre line of the garment, and the side folds of the opening to the fitting lines of the side pleats. Pin and tack in position (Diagram 137). Turn to WS. Pin, tack and machine the outside edges of the knife pleats together. Clip the turnings at the hemline. Trim and neaten them together

above the hem. Open and press the turnings inside the hem for flat finish. Turn up the hem to its final position. Tack and sliphem.

Cut three pieces of strengthening canvas or bonded fabric to attach to the back of the pleat tops on WS where the machine stitching will be worked round the corners of the opening (Diagram 132).

On RS machine round the top of the opening and about $\frac{1}{2}$ inch down each side, leaving the lower folds of the pleats free. Fasten off the machine stitching securely on WS. For additional strength work bar tacks from RS through to the back of the strengthening stays at the top of the inverted pleat and at the lower edges of the machine stitching at each side. Finally press the inset pleats again from WS (Diagram 132). See Diagrams 87a and b for working bar tacks.

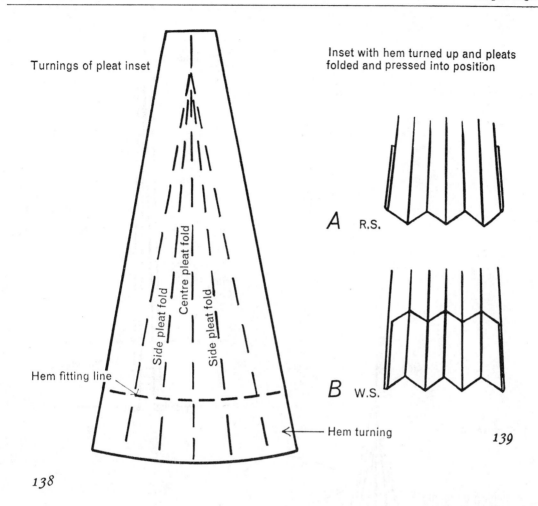

Turnings of pleat inset

Side pleat fold

Centre pleat fold

Side pleat fold

Hem fitting line

138

Inset with hem turned up and pleats folded and pressed into position

A R.S.

B W.S.

Hem turning

139

Fan pleated inset in a seam

PREPARATION OF INSET

Fan pleating is based on a circular principle so the inset is the segment of a circle, with the pleats converging together at a central point. Turnings of at least $\frac{1}{2}$ inch must be allowed at the sides and top, with the hem allowance similar to that of the rest of the garment. Diagram 138 illustrates this. Mark out the pleat lines and hemline with single tacking. Accuracy is the keynote of success.

Turn the hem allowance to WS on the fitting line and tack the folded edge. Because it is slightly circular the free edge of the hem will be larger than the fitting line to which it must be connected. If the fabric is wool the fullness can

be shrunk away. (See Diagrams 114a, b, and c.

Press the fold of the hem on WS so the turning lies flat. Then fold and tack the pleats in position (still with the hem turned up so the creases will be correct) starting with the central one. It is most important at this stage to press each individual pleat fold in order to obtain sharp edges both back and front otherwise the 'fan' arrangement will not close smartly when in wear.

Diagrams 139a and b show the lower hem edge of the folded pressed pleats. The direction of the pleats will be reversed on the underside, converging inwards again to fit and back the top pleats. Diagram 141 shows this by dotted lines. The hem allowance is let down again when the inset is attached to the garment.

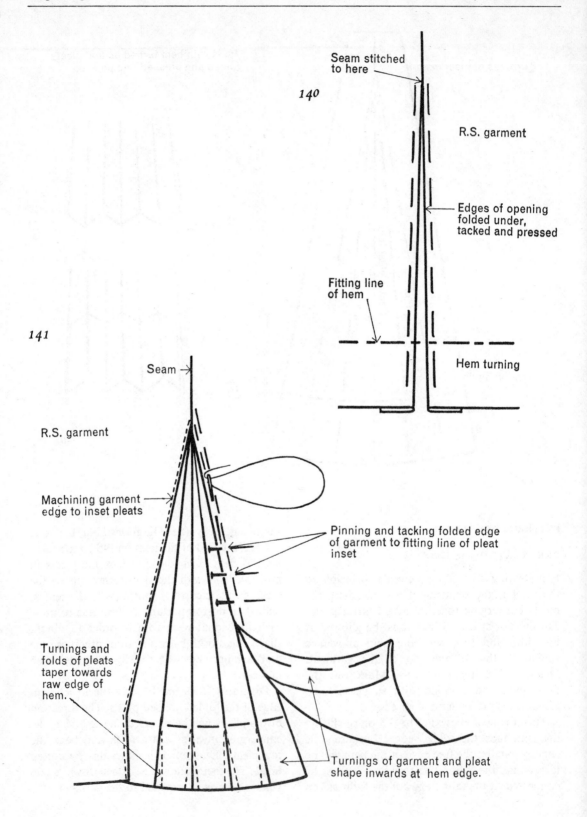

140

Seam stitched
to here

R.S. garment

Edges of opening
folded under,
tacked and pressed

Fitting line
of hem

Hem turning

141

Seam →

R.S. garment

Machining garment
edge to inset pleats

Pinning and tacking folded edge
of garment to fitting line of pleat
inset

Turnings and
folds of pleats
taper towards
raw edge of
hem.

Turnings of garment and pleat
shape inwards at hem edge.

A   B

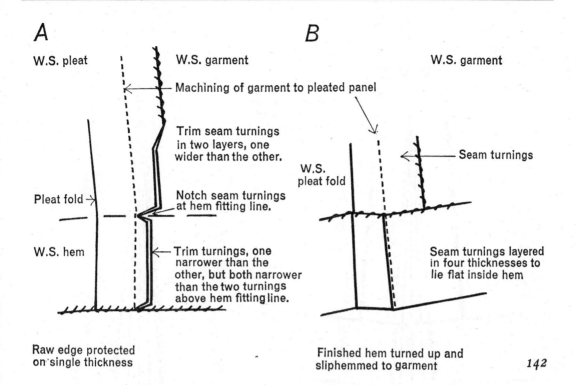

W.S. pleat   W.S. garment   W.S. garment

Machining of garment to pleated panel

Trim seam turnings in two layers, one wider than the other.

W.S. pleat fold

Seam turnings

Pleat fold →

Notch seam turnings at hem fitting line.

W.S. hem

Trim turnings, one narrower than the other, but both narrower than the two turnings above hem fitting line.

Seam turnings layered in four thicknesses to lie flat inside hem

Raw edge protected on single thickness

Finished hem turned up and sliphemmed to garment   *142*

PREPARATION OF GARMENT

On WS stitch the seam of the garment to the top of the opening. Fasten off the machine ends securely. Press open the seam. Fold under the turnings on the fitting lines each side of the opening. Tack the folded edges and press on WS (Diagram 140).

ATTACHING INSET TO GARMENT

Lay the garment RS uppermost with WS facing RS of pleated inset and the top of the opening to the top of the centre pleat. Pin the centre point. Lay one edge of the opening over the corresponding fold edge of the pleat, so that the turnings are in alignment. Pin and tack. Repeat on the other side (Diagram 141). At the hem edge the garment portion can be shaped inwards, so as to counteract the extra fullness of the circular turning. When fixed in position machine close to the folded edge. Take care to maintain an accurate point at the apex, with turnings kept flat underneath.

FINISHING THE HEM

After topstitching the panel, but before final turning up of the hem, the turnings of the inset and skirt must be clipped at the hem fold level, and layered inside the hem for flat finish. See Diagrams 142a and b enlarged to show this.

NOTE: The turnings fold back on to the garment section, not the pleated portion, to allow the 'fan' to close in tightly, thus maintaining the smart line of the design. Turn up the hem finally. Tack the folded edge. Level the turnings. Neaten the single raw edge. Then tack and sliphem this edge to the garment so no stitches show on RS. Neaten the turnings of the inset and attach the top edge to the seam turnings, shown as herringboned in Diagram 143. On RS work a bar tack (Diagrams 87a and b) at the top of the inset panel for strength. Finally press the pleated hem and inset from the WS. The finished pleat is shown in Diagrams 143 WS and 144 RS.

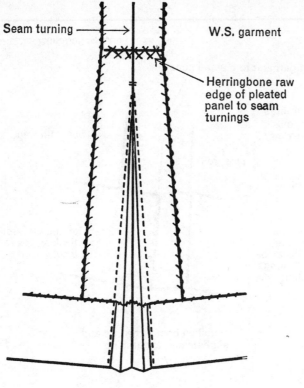

Seam turning

W.S. garment

Herringbone raw
edge of pleated
panel to seam
turnings

W.S. fan pleated inset

143

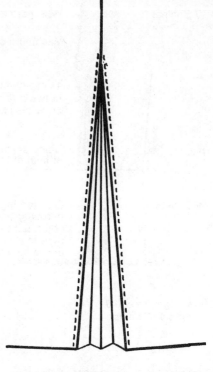

Finished fan pleated inset   R.S.

144

Fashion may influence pockets in so far as position, purpose, and shape are concerned, but the fundamental construction remains much the same through the varying periods of time. Basic horizontal pockets were described in *Standard Processes in Dressmaking*. In this chapter more difficult positions, such as diagonal or curved, are shown, together with tailor treatment using strengthening strips and linings. An invisible pocket set into a seam is also shown. This is particularly useful, as the method could be used to insert a pocket, if desired, into the seam of a ready-made garment. An interesting feature of this pocket is its adaptability, such as a welt finish on the outside.

INVISIBLE INSET POCKET

This is shown in Diagrams 145–151. If the fabric of the garment is suitably thin it may be used to construct the whole pocket, as shown in Diagram 146.

With RS facing, pin, tack, and machine the front pocket bag to the corresponding seam turning of the front of the garment, stitching $\frac{1}{8}$ inch from the fitting line. Repeat the process with the back pocket bag to the back portion of the garment. Stitch this piece a second time about $\frac{1}{2}$ inch from the first row to keep the turnings flat (Diagrams 146a and b). Fold the front pocket completely over to WS on the seam fitting line (Diagram 147). Fold the back pocket seam and turnings to the WS letting RS of the pocket project forward (Diagram 148).

Construct the garment seam to the top and base of the pocket. Press the turnings open (Diagram 149). Lay the front and back pocket bags RS facing together towards the front of the garment. Pin, tack, and machine round the bag on the fitting lines. Trim the turnings evenly to about $\frac{3}{8}$ inch and neaten the raw edges (Diagram 150). On RS work strengthening bar tacks (Diagrams 87a and b) at the top and base of the pocket mouth to prevent the

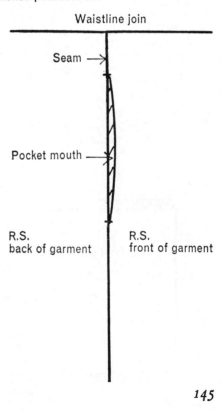

R.S. finished pocket in slit

Waistline join

Seam →

Pocket mouth →

R.S.
back of garment

R.S.
front of garment

145

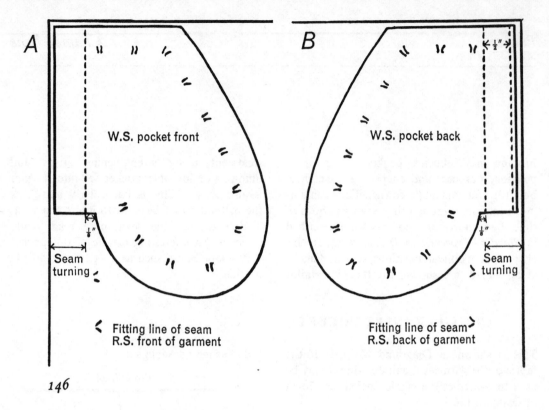

A

W.S. pocket front

⅛"

Seam
turning

Fitting line of seam
R.S. front of garment

B

W.S. pocket back

½"

⅛"

Seam
turning

Fitting line of seam
R.S. back of garment

146

Turning folded back and
front pocket bag folded
forward

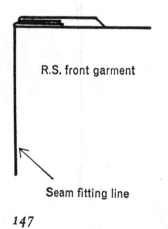

R.S. front garment

Seam fitting line

147

seam stitching from splitting when the pocket
is in use (Diagram 145).

NOTE: If the fabric of the garment is too
thick for the construction of the whole pocket,
e.g. suiting or tweed, use a strip of the garment
fabric to face the seam turnings and act as
half the pocket. To each strip attach thinner
lining fabric to form the rest of the pocket bag
(Diagram 151).

If a welt effect is required on RS make and
press the welt first. Apply it with RS facing
RS garment and fitting lines matching, sandwiched between the front pocket bag and the
garment. When the pocket bag is turned under
to WS and the garment seam is constructed,
the welt will fold up into position covering the
pocket mouth. The ends of the welt can then
be attached firmly to the garment either by
hand or machine stitching.

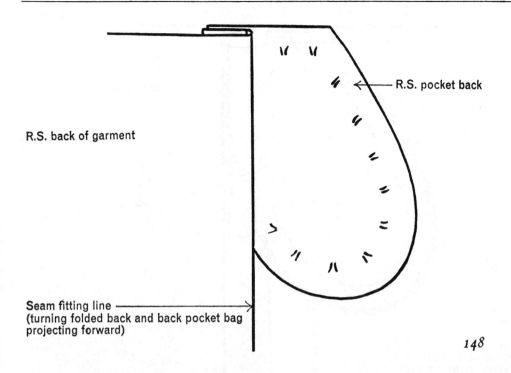

R.S. back of garment

R.S. pocket back

Seam fitting line
(turning folded back and back pocket bag
projecting forward)

148

The two pieces of pocket bag being pinned
together on fitting lines before tacking and
machining

Garment seam stitched to here

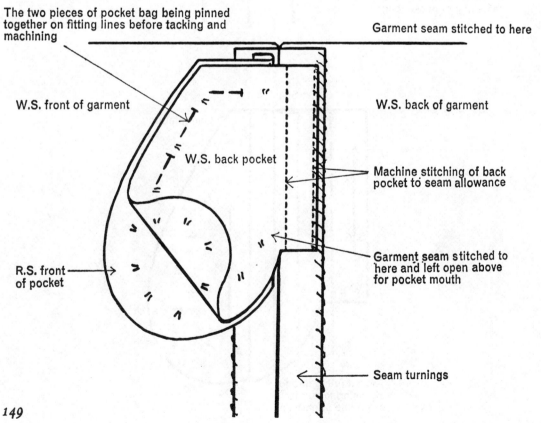

W.S. front of garment

W.S. back pocket

W.S. back of garment

Machine stitching of back
pocket to seam allowance

R.S. front
of pocket

Garment seam stitched to
here and left open above
for pocket mouth

Seam turnings

149

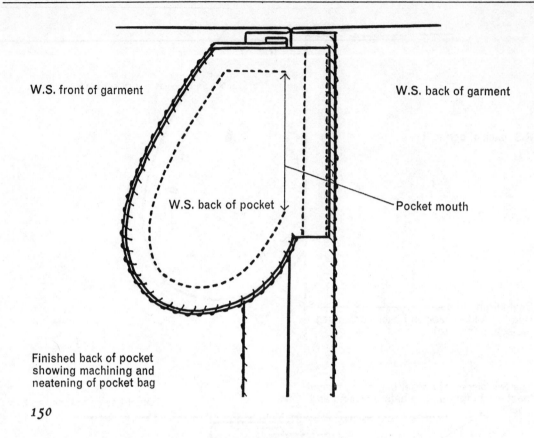

W.S. front of garment

W.S. back of garment

W.S. back of pocket

Pocket mouth

Finished back of pocket
showing machining and
neatening of pocket bag

150

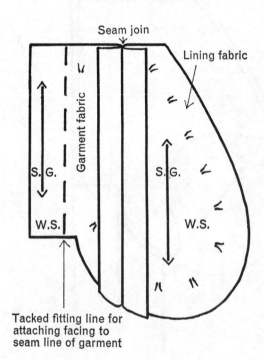

Seam join

Lining fabric

Garment fabric

S. G.

S. G.

W.S.

W.S.

Tacked fitting line for
attaching facing to
seam line of garment

151

TAILORED DIAGONAL POCKET

Test the position of the stitching lines of pocket mouths when the garment is fitted on the wearer. Use cut out paper shapes of welt or flap for both right and left sides. Pin them in position and mark RS and WS to save mistakes or confusion when cutting out or applying. Welts turn upwards and flaps hang downwards from their stitched positions and may appear too high or too low when finished unless this precaution is taken. Weave or design of fabric can be matched in pocket and garment at this stage for right and left hand sides as suggested in cutting out a suit jacket, page 173. Whether welt, flap, or straight bound pockets are being made, the garment is prepared in the same way. After marking the position of the

pocket mouth on the garment, cut and attach to WS a firm piece of fabric to act as a strengthening stay. If this is of canvas or similar woven material, the position of the straight grain should be on the longer sides of the stay running parallel to the pocket mouth (Diagrams 152a and b). If bonded fabric is used, there will be no grain.

The pocket bags may be made partly of garment fabric and partly of lining or thinner materials. In the welt pocket, the back pocket piece is shown as garment fabric and the front as lining. In the flap pocket each portion is shown as part garment fabric and part lining. The craftsman learns to choose according to circumstances.

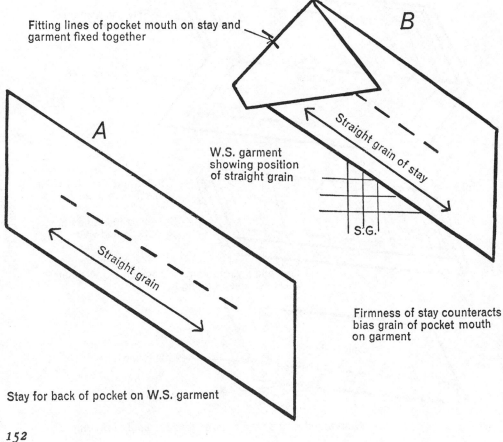

Fitting lines of pocket mouth on stay and garment fixed together

B

Straight grain of stay

W.S. garment showing position of straight grain

S.G.

A

Straight grain

Firmness of stay counteracts bias grain of pocket mouth on garment

Stay for back of pocket on W.S. garment

152

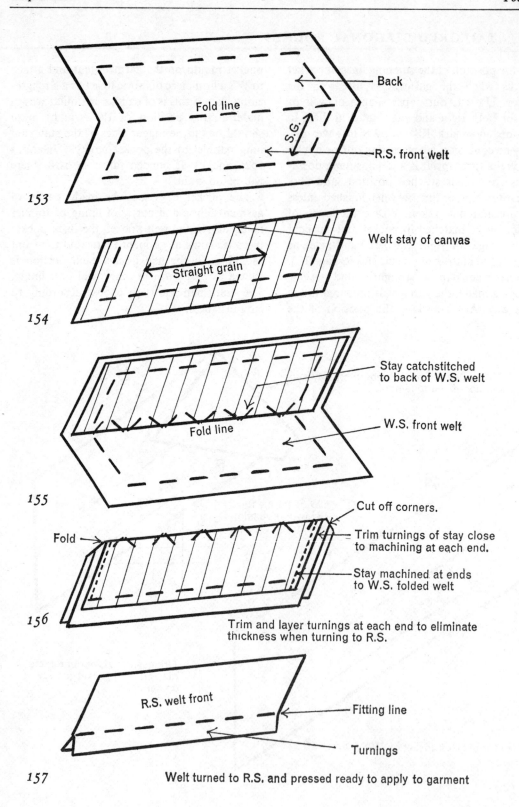

153   Back / Fold line / S.G. / R.S. front welt

154   Welt stay of canvas / Straight grain

155   Stay catchstitched to back of W.S. welt / Fold line / W.S. front welt

156   Cut off corners. / Fold / Trim turnings of stay close to machining at each end. / Stay machined at ends to W.S. folded welt

Trim and layer turnings at each end to eliminate thickness when turning to R.S.

157   R.S. welt front / Fitting line / Turnings

Welt turned to R.S. and pressed ready to apply to garment

Diagonal welt pocket

The shapes of welt and stay are shown in Diagrams 153 and 154. NOTE: The position of the straight grain on the stay will counteract any bias stretch on the welt.

On the back of the welt catchstitch the stay to the WS of the fold line (Diagram 155). Fold the welt RS facing with the stay uppermost on one side. Pin, baste, and machine the ends on the fitting lines. Remove basting, trim the turnings and corners as shown in Diagram 156 to eliminate thickness. Turn to RS and work the welt to a good shape. Press on WS (Diagram 157).

Lay the welt with RS facing RS of garment, lower raw edges uppermost and fitting lines matching. Pin, baste and machine in position through garment and stay.

Lay the back of the pocket bag upside down, with RS facing RS of garment as shown in Diagram 158. Pin, baste and machine. The stitching line should be approximately $\frac{1}{2}$ inch from that of the welt, and $\frac{1}{4}$ inch shorter at each end when the welt is turned up, so the mouth of the pocket is hidden. Remove basting. (NOTE: The length of the pocket stitching may appear peculiar in the diagram, but in actual making up this was found to be correct.)

Cut the pocket mouth evenly through both garment and stay between the two rows of stitching to the exact length of the pocket stitching. (NOTE: This is shorter at each end than the welt.) Snip straight up to the pocket. Snip diagonally to the welt (Diagram 159). Turn the pocket piece through to WS. Press the turnings of both sides of the mouth open on WS to flatten the seams.

On RS fold the welt up into position, pressing the turnings downwards on WS. Baste and press well on WS before attaching the front of

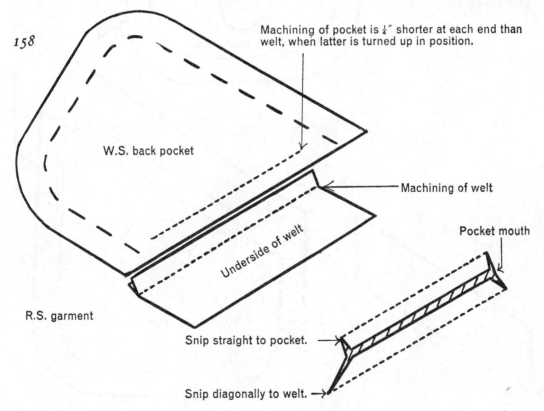

158

Machining of pocket is $\frac{1}{4}$" shorter at each end than welt, when latter is turned up in position.

W.S. back pocket

Machining of welt

Underside of welt

Pocket mouth

R.S. garment

Snip straight to pocket.

Snip diagonally to welt.

Cut mouth through garment and stay only. *159*

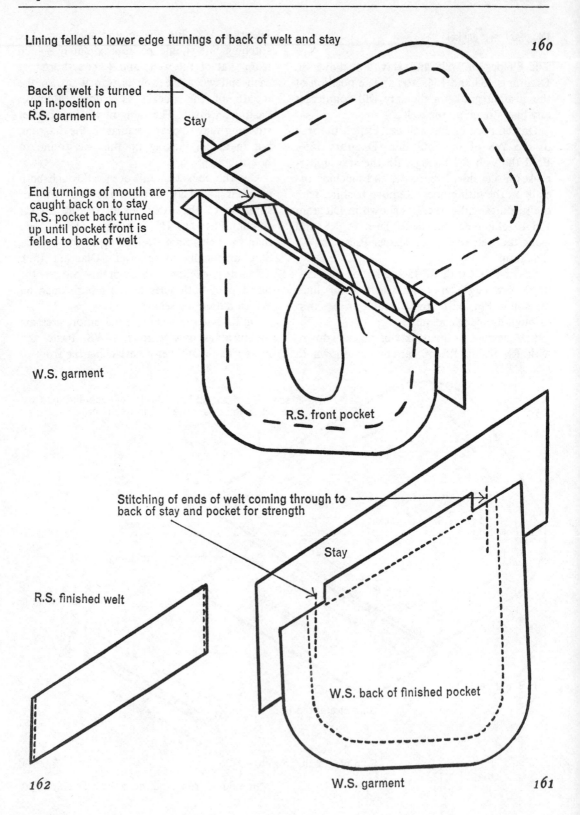

Lining felled to lower edge turnings of back of welt and stay

160

Back of welt is turned
up in position on
R.S. garment

Stay

End turnings of mouth are
caught back on to stay
R.S. pocket back turned
up until pocket front is
felled to back of welt

W.S. garment

R.S. front pocket

Stitching of ends of welt coming through to
back of stay and pocket for strength

Stay

R.S. finished welt

W.S. back of finished pocket

162

W.S. garment

161

the pocket bag. Fold back the ends of the mouth turnings on WS and catch on to the stay.

Keep the back pocket folded up (Diagram 160), until the front of the pocket is fixed to the turnings of the welt. This part of the pocket can be of lining. Turn in the upper edge to WS and fell by hand WS facing WS of garment. Turn down the back pocket in position over the front portion. Pin, baste, and machine together on the fitting lines round the three sides. Remove bastings. Trim turnings (Diagram 161). If unlined, neaten raw edges.

Turn to RS and stabstitch or machine the ends of the welt in position, stitching through to the back of the pocket and stay for strength (Diagrams 161 and 162). Press on WS.

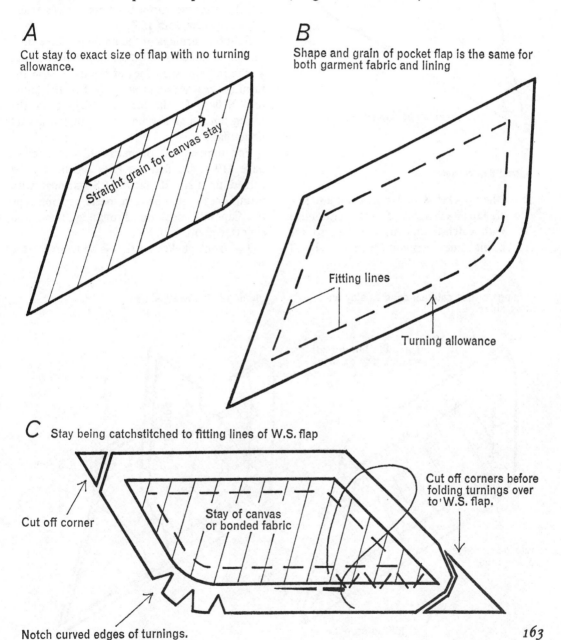

A

Cut stay to exact size of flap with no turning allowance.

Straight grain for canvas stay

B

Shape and grain of pocket flap is the same for both garment fabric and lining

Fitting lines

Turning allowance

C Stay being catchstitched to fitting lines of W.S. flap

Cut off corner

Stay of canvas or bonded fabric

Cut off corners before folding turnings over to W.S. flap.

Notch curved edges of turnings.

163

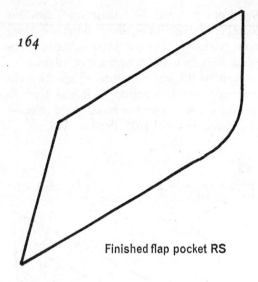

164

Finished flap pocket RS

Diagonal flap pocket

The finished pocket is shown in Diagram 164.

On WS flap attach a stay of canvas or bonded fabric with catchstitch. Cut the stay to the exact fitting lines without turnings. If of woven fabric, the straight grain must be parallel to the long edges (Diagram 163). Notch the turnings of the flap on the curved edge and trim away the corners so when turned over on the fitting lines thickness is eliminated and corners mitred neatly. Catchstitch the turning edges on three sides to the stay on WS leaving the upper edge turning flat for attaching to the garment. Press on WS ready for lining (Diagram 165).

Fold the turnings of the lining on three sides to WS so the edges of the lining will be about ⅛ inch in from the edges of the flap. Trim the turnings neatly (Diagram 166). Fell the lining to WS flap. At the top raw edges baste the fitting lines together holding both fabric and lining flat.

For preparation of garment, see note on page 119 and Diagrams 152a and b. Lay the turned up flap RS facing RS garment with fitting lines matching. Pin, baste and machine the flap into position through garment and stay (Diagram 167).

The front pocket portion is shown with the

Turnings of flap catchstitched to stay on three sides

Lining felled to W.S. flap

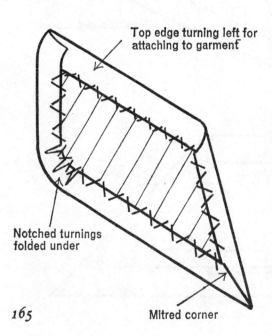

Top edge turning left for attaching to garment

Notched turnings folded under

165

Mitred corner

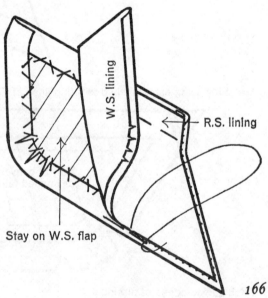

W.S. lining

R.S. lining

Stay on W.S. flap

166

124

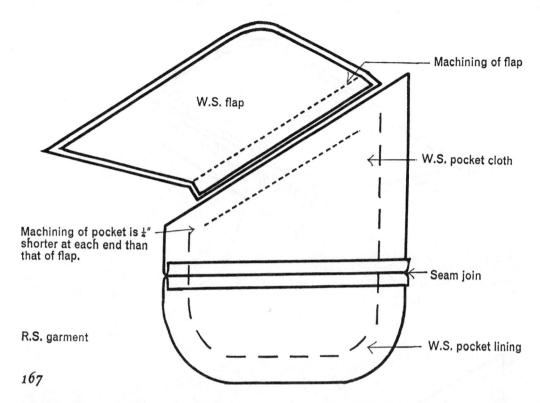

W.S. flap

Machining of flap

W.S. pocket cloth

Machining of pocket is ¼"
shorter at each end than
that of flap.

Seam join

R.S. garment

W.S. pocket lining

167

upper part of garment fabric, and the lower part of lining. The seam of the join is pressed open for flatness. Lay the front pocket with RS facing RS of garment, and upper edge close to the raw edges of the flap. Baste and stitch this portion parallel to, and about ½ inch below, that of the flap, ¼ inch shorter at each end, so when the flap folds down into position it covers the ends of the pocket mouth (Diagram 167). Remove basting.

Cut the mouth of the pocket through garment and stay to the length of the lower stitching of pocket bag. Snip diagonally up to the corners of the flap. Snip straight down to the pocket stitching (Diagram 168).

Turn the pocket piece through to WS. Press open the turnings. Bind the lower lip of the mouth evenly (single turning only to avoid bulk). Baste in position. Stabstitch through the seam line with matching thread to hold the binding and pocket piece in position (Diagrams 169 and 170).

Turn the flap down into position on the RS garment. The turnings of the flap will project

upwards on WS. Catch the triangular ends of the mouth turnings to the stay on WS (Diagram 171).

On WS garment lay the back of the pocket bag with RS facing RS of front pocket. Baste and machine the top edge to the turnings of the flap (Diagrams 171 and 172).

Connect the other three edges of the pocket

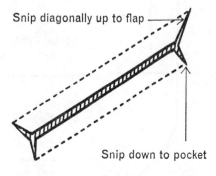

Snip diagonally up to flap

Snip down to pocket

Cutting the mouth through
garment and stay only

168

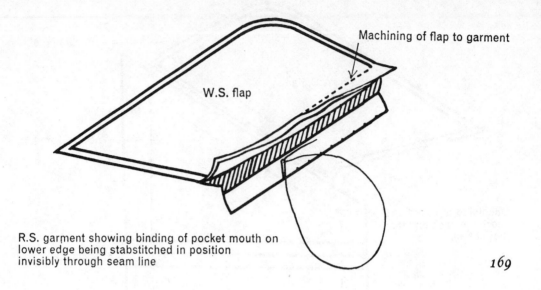

Machining of flap to garment

W.S. flap

R.S. garment showing binding of pocket mouth on
lower edge being stabstitched in position
invisibly through seam line

169

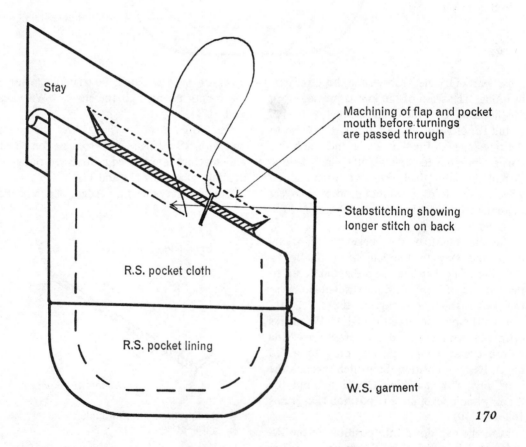

Stay

Machining of flap and pocket
mouth before turnings
are passed through

Stabstitching showing
longer stitch on back

R.S. pocket cloth

R.S. pocket lining

W.S. garment

170

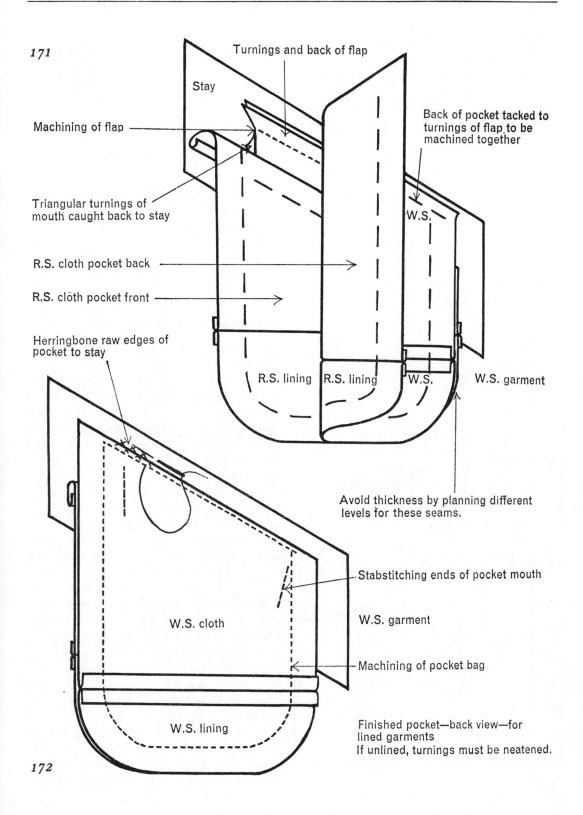

171

Turnings and back of flap

Stay

Machining of flap

Back of pocket tacked to turnings of flap to be machined together

Triangular turnings of mouth caught back to stay

W.S.

R.S. cloth pocket back

R.S. cloth pocket front

Herringbone raw edges of pocket to stay

R.S. lining   R.S. lining   W.S.   W.S. garment

Avoid thickness by planning different levels for these seams.

Stabstitching ends of pocket mouth

W.S. cloth

W.S. garment

Machining of pocket bag

W.S. lining

Finished pocket—back view—for lined garments
If unlined, turnings must be neatened.

172

bag together with the stay for firmness, but not through to the garment. Machine. Trim the turnings. Neaten if garment is unlined.

From RS under the flap, stabstitch the ends of the mouth through to the back of the pocket for strength and firmness (Diagram 172). Some tailors work fine bar tacks across these ends.

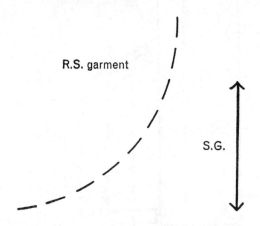

R.S. garment

S.G.

Mark position of pocket on R.S. garment with tacks

173

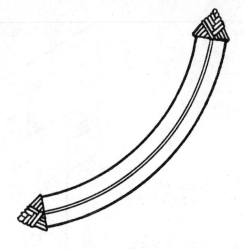

Pocket mouth finished at each end with arrowhead tacks *175*

Curved bound or jetted pocket

The finished pockets are shown in Diagrams 175, 180–1.

Mark the position and shape of the curve on the RS garment (Diagram 173). Cut a stay of canvas, tailor's linen or bonded fabric. See straight grain position on Diagram 174. Pin this to the back of the garment, and from RS baste it into position through the marked curve (Diagram 174).

On RS baste a piece of self fabric, cut on the same grain as the garment. Match the curved fitting line exactly (Diagram 176). This piece will form the front pocket as well as binding the mouth, so it must be cut deep enough. This is the reason for cutting it on the straight grain.

On RS machine about $\frac{1}{4}$ inch each side of the curved pocket mouth line (Diagram 177). Cut the mouth through the centre line of the binding and garment and stay to within $\frac{1}{4}$ inch of each end. Snip to each corner (Diagram 177).

Turn the binding piece through to WS. Open the seams and press the turnings, snipping or notching as shown in Diagram 178 so they lie flat and open.

Wrap the binding piece round each lip of the mouth evenly (single turning only to avoid bulk). Stabstitch through the seam line from RS to the back of the binding to hold it

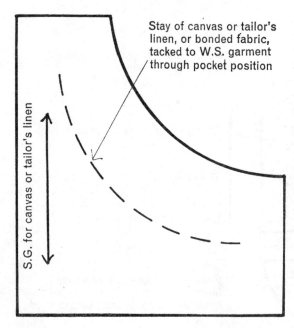

Stay of canvas or tailor's linen, or bonded fabric, tacked to W.S. garment through pocket position

S.G. for canvas or tailor's linen

174

R.S. garment

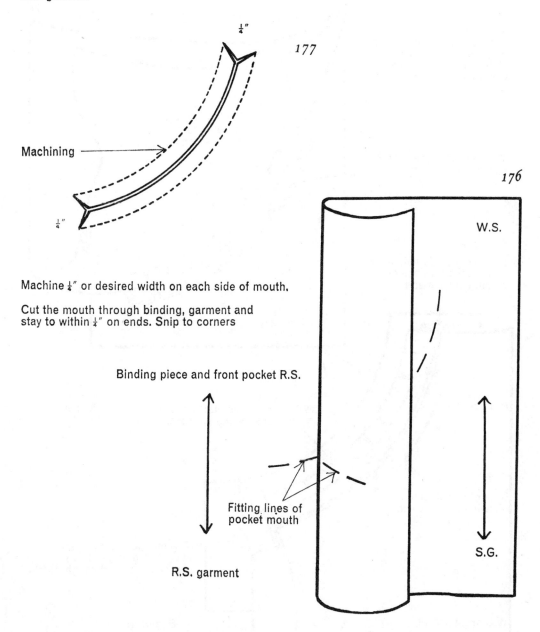

177

Machining

$\frac{1}{4}''$

$\frac{1}{4}''$

Machine $\frac{1}{4}''$ or desired width on each side of mouth.

Cut the mouth through binding, garment and stay to within $\frac{1}{4}''$ on ends. Snip to corners

Binding piece and front pocket R.S.

176

W.S.

Fitting lines of pocket mouth

S.G.

R.S. garment

in position (Diagrams 179 and 180). Fold back the triangular tabs on WS at each end of the mouth and catch them to the stay. The ends of the binding will form inverted pleats. Hold these folds together with two or three over-sewn stitches (Diagram 179). Press the mouth well on WS.

The upper part of the pocket must be of garment fabric to back the pocket mouth, but the lower section can be of thinner material, e.g. lining. The illustration shows a curved seam join with turnings pressed downwards for flat finish on a convex curve (Diagram 181). Attach the top edge of the pocket to the turn-

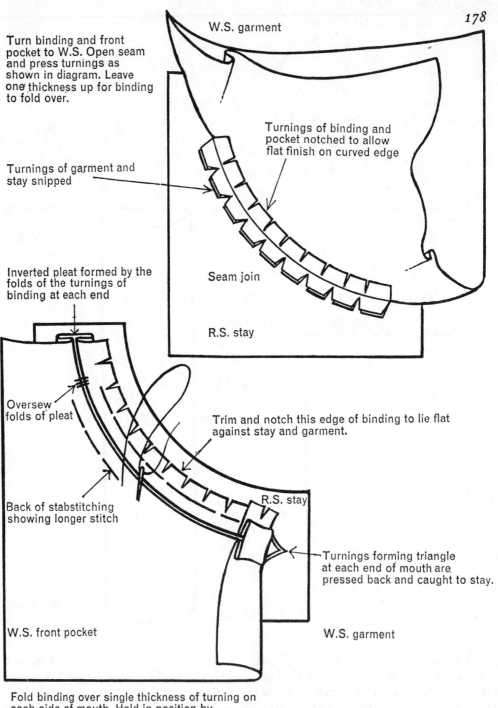

178

W.S. garment

Turn binding and front
pocket to W.S. Open seam
and press turnings as
shown in diagram. Leave
one thickness up for binding
to fold over.

Turnings of binding and
pocket notched to allow
flat finish on curved edge

Turnings of garment and
stay snipped

Inverted pleat formed by the
folds of the turnings of
binding at each end

Seam join

R.S. stay

Oversew
folds of pleat

Trim and notch this edge of binding to lie flat
against stay and garment.

Back of stabstitching
showing longer stitch

R.S. stay

Turnings forming triangle
at each end of mouth are
pressed back and caught to stay.

W.S. front pocket

W.S. garment

Fold binding over single thickness of turning on
each side of mouth. Hold in position by
stabstitching through each seam line, to back of
binding. Ends of inverted pleat are held together by
several oversewn stitches.

179

Binding folded over each lip of mouth evenly
and stabstitched in position with invisible
stitches on R.S. through seam line

R.S. garment

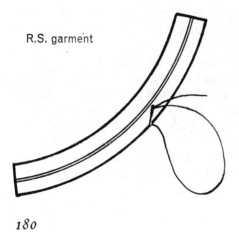

180

Stitching of back and front pocket bag

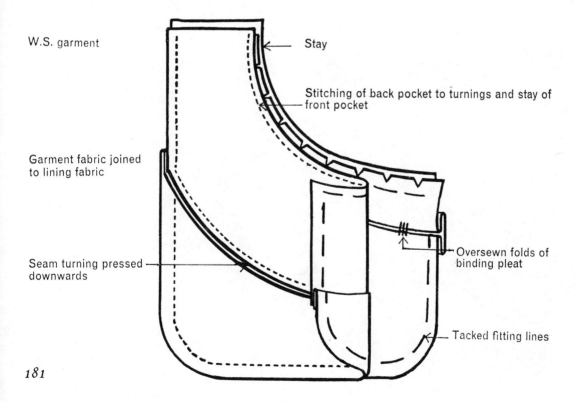

W.S. garment   Stay

Stitching of back pocket to turnings and stay of
front pocket

Garment fabric joined
to lining fabric

Seam turning pressed
downwards

Oversewn folds of
binding pleat

Tacked fitting lines

181

ings of the binding and stay. Trim and layer the turnings for flat finish. Pin, baste and stitch round the remaining three sides of the pocket bag. Trim the turnings and neaten if the garment is unlined (Diagram 181).

On RS strengthen each end of the pocket mouth by either stabstitching through to the back of the pocket or by working arrowhead tacks (Diagram 175). (Stages of working arrowhead tacks are shown on page 39 of *Standard Processes in Dressmaking*.)

NOTE: If crossway material is preferred for binding the pocket mouth, both the binding and the front pocket bag should be cut and attached separately since the latter will be on the straight grain. The method of binding is the same. Attach the front pocket bag to WS of the lower lip, as for welt pocket (see Diagram 160).

Piped pocket

The making of this pocket is similar to the bound or jetted pocket. Stitch the two sides of the mouth about $\frac{1}{8}$ inch from the marked line, so the lips are narrower. After cutting the mouth, turn the piping to WS. Press the turnings on both sides of the mouth back into the garment. This will enable the strips to be folded as pipings (double material only) meeting in the centre of the pocket mouth. Stabstitch through the seam line (Diagrams 170 and 180) and finish as for bound pocket.

CLOSE-FITTING ROUND NECK

This may have a short opening either back or front finished with shaped facings. See Diagrams 182 and 186.

To prepare the bodice lay the bodice shoulders of back and front together with RS facing. Pin, tack and machine on the fitting lines. Remove tacks. Press open and neaten the turnings. The neck and centre front lines, length of opening, and centre back must be clearly marked. If possible do not cut the opening until the facing has been applied and stitched (Diagram 183). This will avoid unnecessary stretching and dangerous fraying of raw edges.

NOTE: The length of this type of opening, whether at front or back of neck, must be sufficient to pass over the wearer's head without strain. The circumference of an adult's head is approximately from 21 to 23 inches. Therefore the neckline plus opening must be not less than 24 inches, i.e. if the neckline measures 14 inches the opening must be at least 5 inches deep, giving 10 inches when the two sides are opened. If interlinings are required to give support they should be inserted at this stage. (See Chapter Four, pages 54 and 55.)

If of suitable thickness the facings may be of the same fabric as the garment, or use thinner lining material, matching in colour if the bodice fabric is too thick. They should be cut to the shape of (a) the back neck of the bodice, and (b) the front neckline, extending to below the length of the opening by approximately 2 to 2½ inches.

Pin, tack and machine the shoulder seams together with RS facing. Remove tacks. Press

open the turnings. Trim them a little narrower than those of the bodice, and leave the edges raw to avoid thickness when placed together. Handling is easier if the outer edges of the facing are neatened before it is fixed to the bodice. Diagram 184 shows these edges turned to WS on the fitting lines after notching curves and snipping or mitring corners to ensure flatness. Remove tacks and press after edge-stitching.

To attach the facing to neckline and opening lay RS facing to RS bodice matching centre and neck fitting lines as well as shoulder seams. Pin, tack and machine round the neck and both sides of the opening on the fitting lines, working one stitch across the base. Remove tacks. Trim the turnings of the neck to ¼ inch and snip frequently to facilitate turning (Diagram 185). If necessary, mitre the shoulder

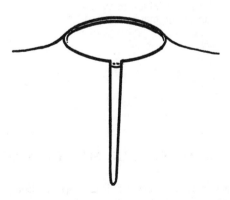

Close-fitting round neck with short front opening

182

seam turnings at the neck edge. (See Diagrams 51a and b on page 59 for crossed seams.) Cut through the centre line of opening to the base. Turn the facing to WS of the bodice. Tack round the neck and opening, working the seam line slightly to WS so it does not show on RS (Diagram 186). Press lightly. Remove tacks and press firmly again. Catch the turnings of the facing on the shoulder seams to hold it in place.

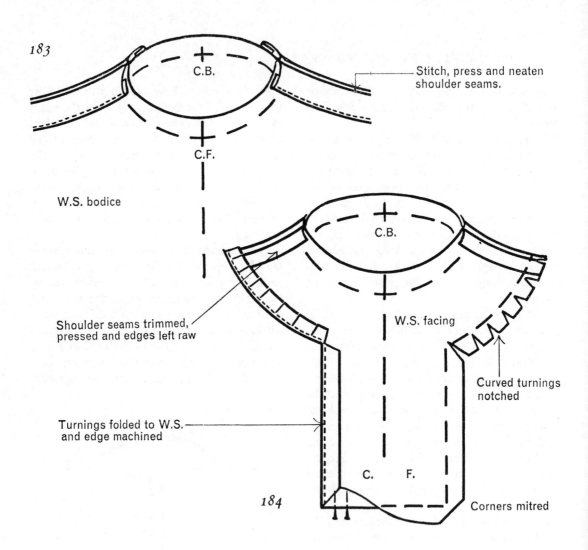

MANDARIN, MILITARY OR UPRIGHT COLLAR

This can be interlined for support (Diagram 187). A well fitting collar of this type must be slightly shorter (approximately ½ inch) than the neckline it has to fit to give a professional finish. Tack the interlining to WS of the top section of collar, CB and fitting lines matching. Lay the two pieces of collar RS facing with CB and CF matching and interlining on top of one side. Pin, tack and machine together on the fitting lines round the top edges leaving

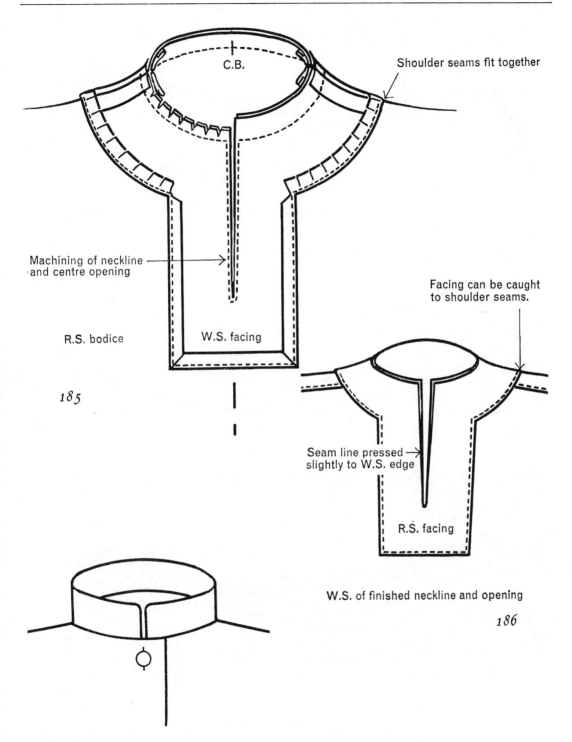

C.B.

Shoulder seams fit together

Machining of neckline and centre opening

R.S. bodice

W.S. facing

185

Facing can be caught to shoulder seams.

Seam line pressed → slightly to W.S. edge

R.S. facing

W.S. of finished neckline and opening

186

Finished mandarin, military or upright collar RS

187

Turnings notched and trimmed in three layers
Interlining is cut close to stitching.

Machining of collar

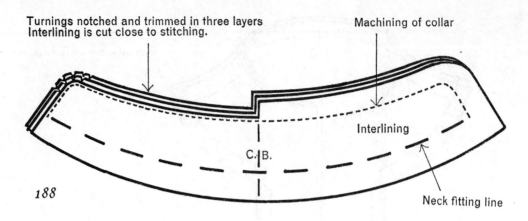

Interlining

C.B.

Neck fitting line

188

Machine to neck fitting line only,
leaving neck turnings free.

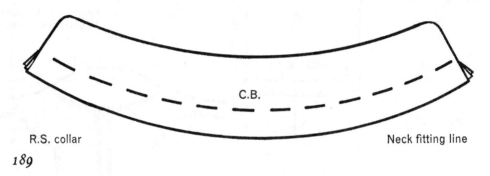

C.B.

R.S. collar

Neck fitting line

189

Extension beyond C.F. line   W.S. collar and interfacing   Ends of collar touch
centre line

Machining of collar to
neckline of garment

Turnings trimmed in layers

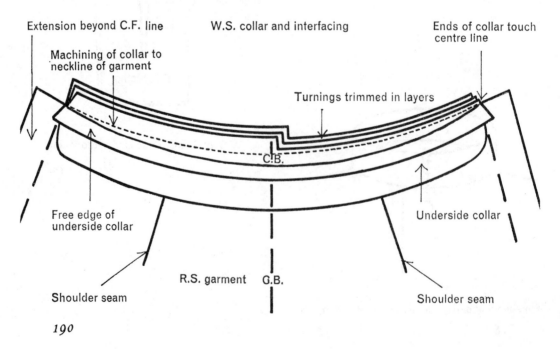

C.B.

Free edge of
underside collar

Underside collar

Shoulder seam   R.S. garment   C.B.   Shoulder seam

190

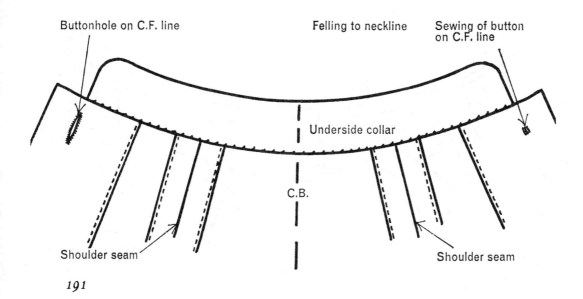

Buttonhole on C.F. line   Felling to neckline   Sewing of button on C.F. line

Underside collar

C.B.

Shoulder seam   Shoulder seam

191

the neck edge free. Remove tacks from machined sections. Trim, layer and notch the turnings (Diagram 188). Turn to RS. Work the seam line to the correct shape. Press on WS. Diagram 189 shows the collar ready for setting on to the neck edge of bodice.

METHOD 1

Stitch and neaten the shoulder seams of the bodice. Prepare the small extensions (over and underlaps for fastening) on the front neck edges as far as the centre lines. Snip the neck turnings at CF before turning the extensions and facings to RS. This frees them for attaching the collar. CF and CB lines should be marked as well as neck fitting lines and balance marks, and the facings tacked in position on the neck edge.

To set on the collar lay the top collar upside down, RS facing RS of bodice and neck fitting lines together. Pin CB through interlining and top collar to CB neck of bodice. Pin front ends of collar to CF bodice neck. Pin and tack the rest of the collar in position leaving the under collar free. Fit before machining. Machine on the fitting lines through interlining, top collar, and bodice neck. Remove tacks. Trim the interlining edge close to the stitching. Press the

seam open carefully to flatten it. Layer the turnings to remove thickness (Diagram 190). Turn the collar up and press the turnings into the collar on WS.

Fold under the raw edge of the under collar. Bring the fold to meet the machining on WS bodice matching CB and front edges. Pin and test for fit. This side should be slightly tighter than the top collar to avoid bulging and to prevent the top seam of the collar showing on RS when worn. When the fitting line has been adjusted, unpin and trim the turnings of the under collar to $\frac{1}{8}$ or $\frac{1}{4}$ inch. Tack and fell this edge to the machined neckline enclosing the turnings. No stitches should show on RS of bodice (Diagram 191). The two edges of the collar meet at CF above the button and buttonhole fastening (Diagram 187). The overwrap extension should fit neatly under the seam of the collar when fastened.

METHOD 2

Machine, press and neaten the shoulder seams of the bodice. Neaten the free edges of the facings (Diagram 192). Mark the neck edge fitting line as well as CB, CF and balance marks.

Lay the collar upside down with RS facing RS of bodice. Match CB and pin through all

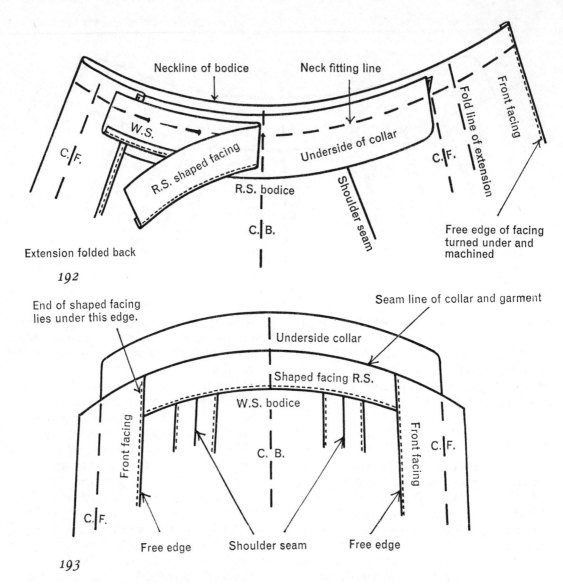

Neckline of bodice   Neck fitting line

W.S.

C. F.

R.S. shaped facing

Underside of collar

Fold line of extension

Front facing

C. F.

R.S. bodice

C. B.

Shoulder seam

Free edge of facing
turned under and
machined

Extension folded back

192

End of shaped facing
lies under this edge.

Seam line of collar and garment

Underside collar

Shaped facing R.S.

Front facing

W.S. bodice

Front facing

C. F.

C. B.

C. F.

Free edge   Shoulder seam   Free edge

193

thicknesses. Pin CF collar ends to CF lines. Pin in between these points. Tack the collar to the fitting line of the neck edge. Fold over the facings of the bodice on the front extension lines with RS together and neck fitting lines matching. Tack in position covering the ends of the collar. Cut and prepare a shaped facing to fit the rest of the neckline at the back and sufficiently long to project about ¾ inch over the facings. Neaten the lower raw edges as shown in the diagram (or overlock with the machine zigzagger). Pin the upper edge of the shaped facing to the collar neckline across the back and tack in position (Diagram 192). Machine along the neck fitting line through all thicknesses. Remove tacks. Trim the interlining turnings close to the machine stitching. Layer the rest of the turnings to prevent thick edges. Turn up the collar, turning the front facings through to RS at the same time. The shaped neck facing will turn downwards, neatening the raw edges underneath and can be caught on to the shoulder turnings at each side (Diagram 193).

SHAWL OR ROLL COLLAR

METHOD 1

This method, where the collar is cut in one with the front bodice and interlined, is often used for blouses or dress bodices and sometimes for jackets or coats. It differs from the method for collars set on to necklines. The shape of the outer edge can be styled according to fashion and may be different from the classic style illustrated in Diagram 194.

In preparing the bodice, note that some commercial patterns give a small dart which runs into the neckline, usually ending where the corner slit occurs at the shoulder end of the neck. This should be stitched and pressed first as well as any shoulder darts.

As the under collar is cut in one with the bodice, there is a sharp corner at the neck end of the shoulder Staystitch this angle after marking out fitting lines and before completing the shoulder seam. (See Diagram 28c.) Snip diagonally almost to the stitching as shown in Diagram 195. NOTE: If a pin is inserted on the exact corner over the stitching an accident in

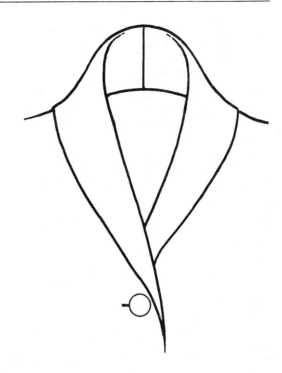

Finished shawl or roll collar   *194*

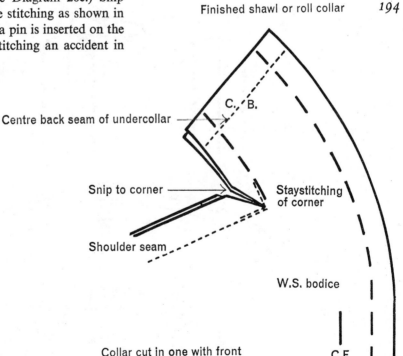

Centre back seam of undercollar

C. B.

Snip to corner

Staystitching of corner

Shoulder seam

W.S. bodice

Collar cut in one with front   C.F.

195

overcutting is avoided. Press open and neaten the shoulder seam. Join CB of under collar RS facing (Diagram 195). Press open and trim the turnings to ⅜ inch (Diagram 196).

If an interlining is required for added firmness, it is attached at this stage. It is cut to the same shape as the top collar and front facings. All fitting and centre lines should be marked. Join the CB seam with the flat overlaid join (Diagram 197). See Chapter Four, Interlinings, page 51, Diagram 35. Lay the interlining on WS of bodice and under collar. Pin at CB. Matching the fitting lines and balance marks, pin and tack together round the outer edges of the collar and facings, then to the neck edge

keeping interlining flat. Join the neck edges of the under collar, interlining and bodice together. RS facing (Diagram 197). Trim the turnings of the interlining to the stitching. Press the neck seam open and trim the turnings to ⅜ inch (Diagrams 196 and 197).

When the fitting lines on the top collar and front facings have been marked, staystitch the sharp inner corners of neck and shoulder lines as described for bodice, as these will be snipped at a later stage. Join CB seam with RS facing. Press open the turnings. Trim them to ¼ inch (Diagram 198).

Lay the top collar to the under collar RS facing and CB seams matching. Pin together

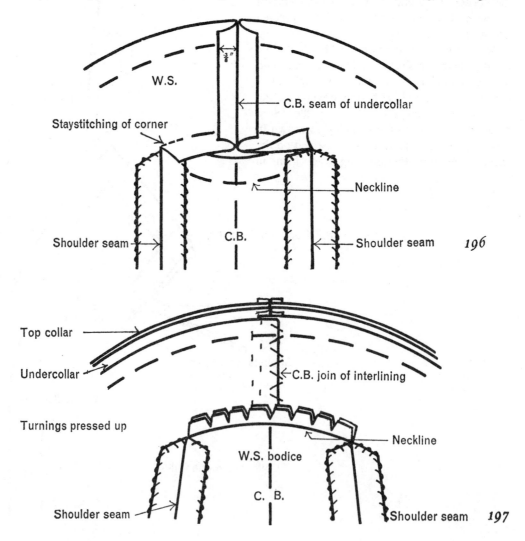

Preparation of top collar

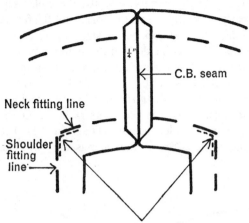

Staystitch corners of neck and shoulder where turning needs snipping before final fixing

198

on the outer fitting lines working from the centre round the outer edges of the collar and down the front facings of both right and left-hand sides of the garment. Tack in position, then machine on the exact fitting lines through three layers, top collar, under collar and inter-lining. Remove tacks. Trim and layer the turnings as described in Chapter Four, Inter-linings, page 54 and Diagram 199. When turning the top collar and facings over, it will be easier to work out the seam line if the turn-ings have previously been pressed open on WS before trimming and layering. Use a thin padded roll held in the hand under RS of the seam, or lay it on the edge of a sleeve board to press. On RS work the seam line slightly under

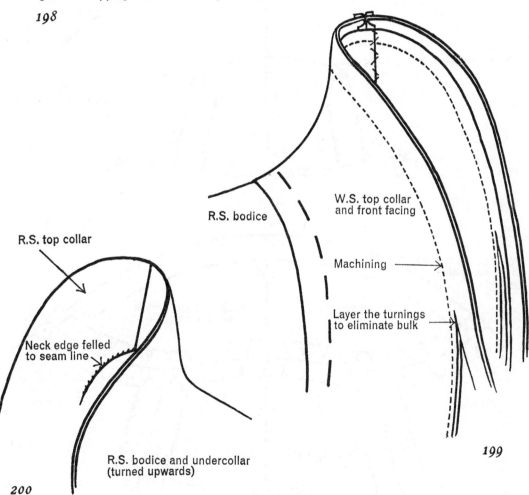

199

200

the extreme edge of the collar as shown in Diagram 200. Tack in position. On the front facings roll the seam line so it lies slightly under the garment edges, to avoid showing when the garment is worn. Tack and press the collar and facings on WS.

Turn under to WS the free edge of the top collar, bring this to meet the machined neckline and pin at CB. Allow enough width here so that when the collar rolls over into the wearing position there is sufficient fabric to enable the

seam on the outer edge to remain invisible and slightly to the underside whilst the collar sets neatly in position. Test the corners of the facing at shoulder and neck before snipping, to ensure the positions coincide with those on the bodice. Fit the neck and shoulder lines, turning under the raw edges of the latter. Tack in position and fell by hand, thus enclosing the neckline turnings, whilst the shoulders face and fit the garment shoulder turnings (Diagram 201). The long front edges of the facings are left free.

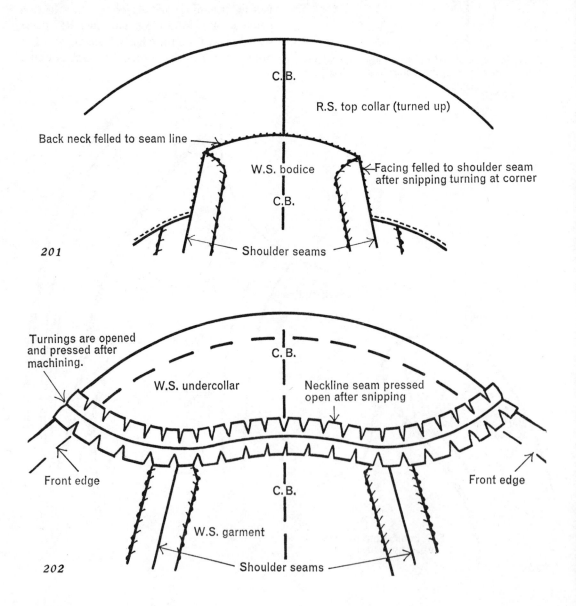

201　Back neck felled to seam line — R.S. top collar (turned up) — C.B. — W.S. bodice — C.B. — Facing felled to shoulder seam after snipping turning at corner — Shoulder seams

202　Turnings are opened and pressed after machining. — W.S. undercollar — C.B. — Neckline seam pressed open after snipping — Front edge — Front edge — W.S. garment — C.B. — Shoulder seams

Neaten the raw edges appropriately for the fabric (unless the garment is lined). Fix the lower edge to the inside edge of the hem.

METHOD 2

In some patterns the under collar is cut separately and joined to the neck edge of bodice or jacket after the shoulder seams have been finished. Lay the under collar RS facing RS bodice with CB necklines matching. Pin together. Pin the front edges and balance marks. Pin in between on the fitting lines. Tack and machine. Remove tacks. Trim and snip the turnings as shown in Diagram 202. Press them open for flat finish. Allow the turnings to remain open from the front edges to the shoulder lines. Across the back between the shoulders press the turnings up into the neck, so the top collar edge can be felled to the seam line and enclose the turnings (Diagram 203).

If the garment is lined, the turnings of the under collar can remain pressed open all round the neck edge. In this case allow the top collar turnings to lie flat down, covering the under-collar neck seam. Catch the raw edges lightly in position to jacket turnings. No stitches must show on RS garment. The lining will cover all raw edges when it is felled to the back neckline.

Diagram 204 shows the join on RS.

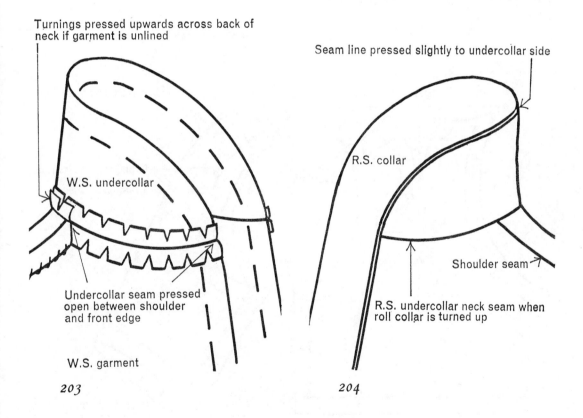

203

Turnings pressed upwards across back of neck if garment is unlined

W.S. undercollar

Undercollar seam pressed open between shoulder and front edge

W.S. garment

204

Seam line pressed slightly to undercollar side

R.S. collar

Shoulder seam

R.S. undercollar neck seam when roll collar is turned up

This classic style varies from that of sleeves set into armholes. In the cutting of raglan patterns the shoulder section of the bodice is transferred to the top or head of the sleeve. The resulting line curves from neckline to underarm at both back and front sections of the garment.

Two versions are shown here. The one-piece raglan sleeve is usually used in dressmaking styles, and two-piece raglan for more tailored jackets.

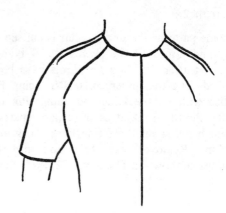

One-piece raglan sleeve with shoulder dart

205

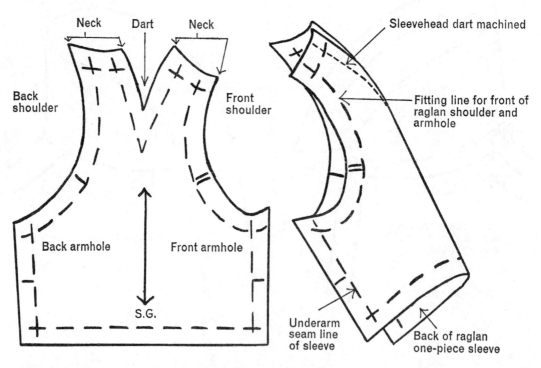

Neck   Dart   Neck

Back shoulder

Front shoulder

Back armhole   Front armhole

S.G.

Shape of one-piece raglan sleeve before making up

206

Sleevehead dart machined

Fitting line for front of raglan shoulder and armhole

Underarm seam line of sleeve

Back of raglan one-piece sleeve

207

144

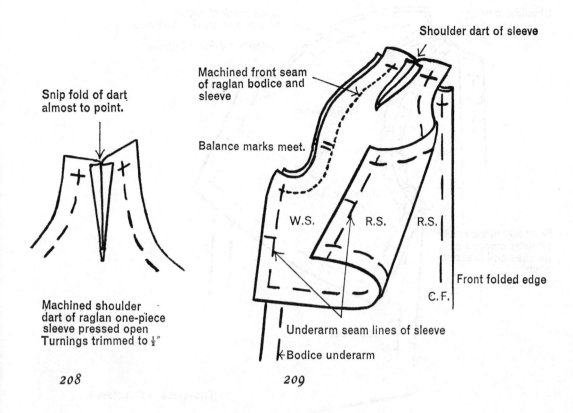

Shoulder dart of sleeve

Machined front seam
of raglan bodice and
sleeve

Snip fold of dart
almost to point.

Balance marks meet.

W.S.   R.S.   R.S.

Front folded edge

C.F.

Machined shoulder
dart of raglan one-piece
sleeve pressed open
Turnings trimmed to ½″

Underarm seam lines of sleeve

Bodice underarm

208   209

ONE-PIECE RAGLAN SLEEVE

The finished sleeve is shown in Diagram 205 and the shape of the sleeve in Diagram 206. Note the fitting lines and balance marks. The shoulder sections appear like two 'horns' when added to the sleevehead. In constructing this style, the seaming of a dart brings the back and front shoulder pieces together, causing a curved shape to fit the shoulder and arm joint (Diagram 207). After stitching, split open the remaining fold of the dart, cutting nearly to the point. Press the dart flat and trim the turnings to ½ inch on each side (Diagram 208). Next join the front raglan edge of the sleeve to the corresponding edge of the bodice. Match the balance marks and pin together on the fitting lines. Pin the neck edges, then the armhole points. Then pin in between. Tack and machine

on the fitting lines maintaining a smoothly curving line (Diagram 209). Remove tacks, and press the seam open after snipping or notching the turnings to enable them to lie flat, as shown in Diagram 210. Trim both turning edges to ½ inch.

Repeat this process with the back raglan edge of sleeve and bodice as shown in Diagram 210.

Lastly, construct the underarm seam of sleeve and bodice, matching the back and front raglan seams together first, then pinning the balance marks of the sleeve together, and those of the bodice. Tack and machine on the fitting lines (Diagram 211). Remove tacks. Press and neaten the seam edges as for the rest of the garment.

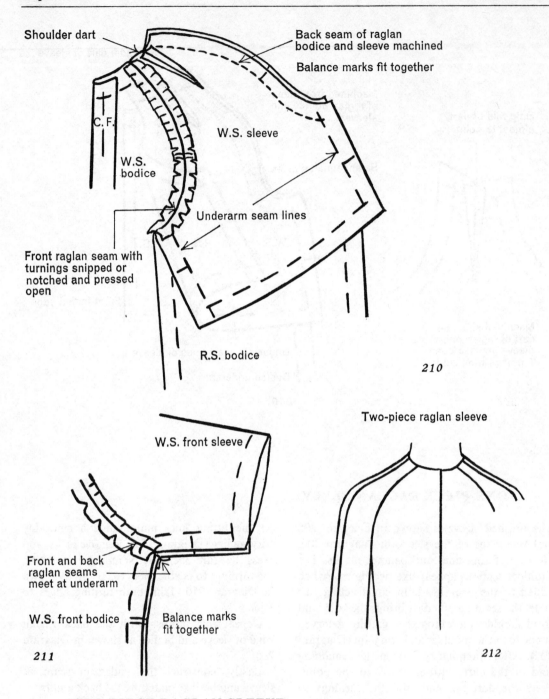

Shoulder dart

Back seam of raglan
bodice and sleeve machined

Balance marks fit together

C.F.

W.S. sleeve

W.S.
bodice

Underarm seam lines

Front raglan seam with
turnings snipped or
notched and pressed
open

R.S. bodice

210

W.S. front sleeve

Two-piece raglan sleeve

Front and back
raglan seams
meet at underarm

W.S. front bodice

Balance marks
fit together

211

212

TWO-PIECE RAGLAN SLEEVE

Diagram 212 shows the finished sleeve. In this case the sleeve itself is in two portions, as well as the bodice or top part of the garment.

Take the front sleeve and front of garment.

Matching balance marks, also neck and underarm points of both sleeve and garment, pin, tack and machine the raglan line on the curved fitting lines (Diagram 213). Remove tacks.

Snip or notch the turnings so the seam can be pressed open with a neat flat finish. Trim each turning edge to ½ inch. Repeat this procedure fixing the raglan edge of the back sleeve to the corresponding edge of the back of the garment (Diagram 214).

The outer seam lines of the back and front sleeves are matched together next (Diagram 215). Pin together balance marks, then neck points, and lastly lower edges. Tack and machine on the fitting lines from neck, through shoulder and sleeve. Remove tacks. Press open the turnings. Trim each edge to ½ inch.

Lastly, construct the underarm seam of garment and sleeve. Match and pin together the raglan seams of back and front on the fitting lines at the underarm ends. Pin balance marks together matching them first on the sleeve and then on the garment. Next pin the lower ends of the sleeve, then the lower ends of the bodice or jacket underarm. Tack and machine on the fitting lines through the underarm seam of sleeve and garment (Diagram 216). Remove tacks. Press open the turnings, snipping or notching where necessary on any curved parts to obtain a flat finish.

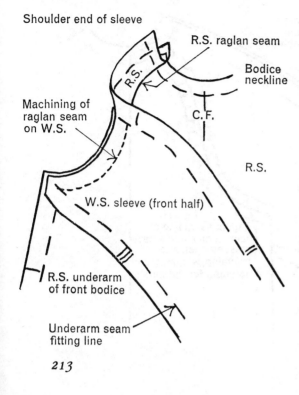

Shoulder end of sleeve

R.S. raglan seam

Bodice neckline

Machining of raglan seam on W.S.

C.F.

R.S.

W.S. sleeve (front half)

R.S. underarm of front bodice

Underarm seam fitting line

213

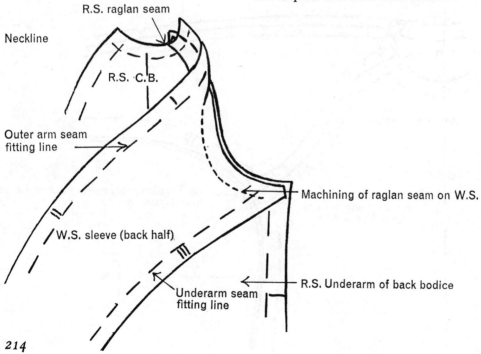

R.S. raglan seam

Neckline

R.S. C.B.

Outer arm seam fitting line

Machining of raglan seam on W.S.

W.S. sleeve (back half)

Underarm seam fitting line

R.S. Underarm of back bodice

214

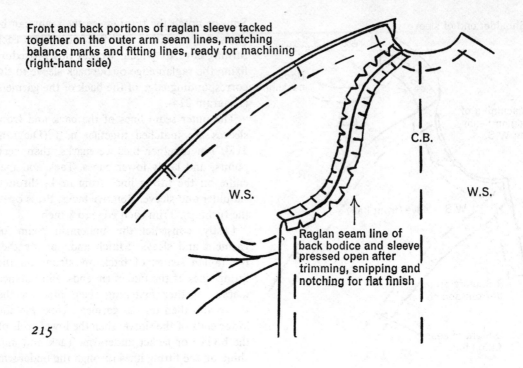

Front and back portions of raglan sleeve tacked together on the outer arm seam lines, matching balance marks and fitting lines, ready for machining (right-hand side)

C.B.

W.S.

W.S.

Raglan seam line of back bodice and sleeve pressed open after trimming, snipping and notching for flat finish

215

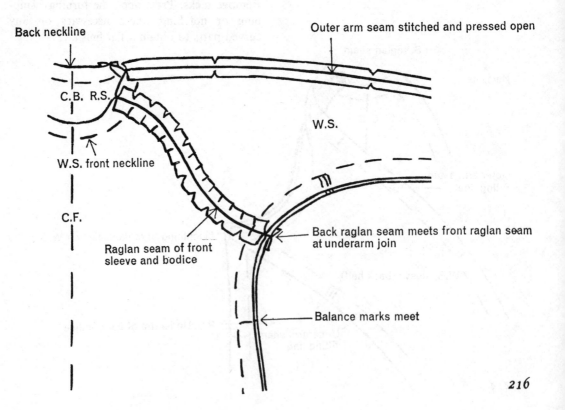

Outer arm seam stitched and pressed open

Back neckline

C.B. R.S.

W.S.

W.S. front neckline

C.F.

Raglan seam of front sleeve and bodice

Back raglan seam meets front raglan seam at underarm join

Balance marks meet

216

A gusset is a strengthening piece of material inserted into a garment to give added freedom of movement while retaining a close fit. Basic shapes are triangles, squares or diamonds. Two methods are given here for underarms of sleeves cut in one with the bodice.

A *triangular gusset* (Diagram 218) is set into one half of a sleeve and bodice underarm, e.g. garment front, whilst the back of the sleeve is set into a back armhole (Diagram 217).

A *diamond-shaped gusset* is set into slits at both back and front of kimono or magyar shaped sleeves. Where these types of sleeves are below elbow, either three quarter or full length, gussets are essential to avoid strain and seam splitting, and to give comfortable, closer, and therefore smarter fit.

Gussets are often set into shorter sleeves, above elbow length, where a neat close fit is required.

A

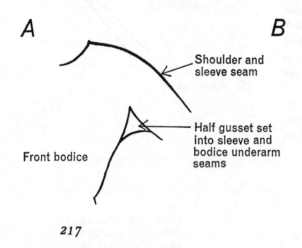

B

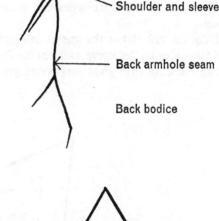

217

METHOD 1

Here a *triangular or half gusset* is used.

Mark the position of the slit on the garment. Strengthen the point by staystitching before cutting the slit, either by machining, or backstitching by hand round the point as shown in Diagram 219a.

Cut the slit as far as the marked point (Diagram 219b). Two sides of the gusset triangle correspond in length with the two sides of the slit. The third side will continue and give extra length to the underarm seam of the sleeve

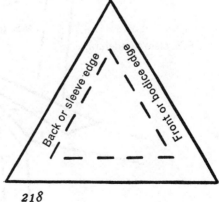

218

and bodice. (See Diagram 217 for the finished gusset.)

Lay one side of the gusset RS facing RS slit on the sleeve side. The fitting line of the point of the gusset should meet the strengthening stitches at the point of the slit so that no stitches will show on RS when the gusset is set in and stitched on its fitting lines (Diagram 220). The turnings of the slit will gradually widen from the point to about ¼ inch at the open end. Pin, tack and machine this side starting at the exact point. Fasten off the stitching at the point end securely. Remove tacks. Press the seam.

Diagram 221 shows RS of the first seam of the gusset and sleeve, and the second seam of the triangular gusset being pinned to the bodice side of the slit, with RS facing, from the point to the bodice end. (The bodice is shown only partly folded back.) Tack and stitch this side from the exact point of the slit to the underarm seam edge. Note that the stitching of the two sides must meet at the point. Secure the threads at the point. Remove the tacks and press the seam.

Diagram 222 shows the gusset inserted on the two sides to the sleeve and bodice fronts, whilst the third edge gives length and gradual

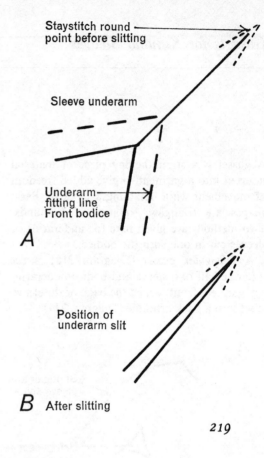

Staystitch round point before slitting

Sleeve underarm

Underarm fitting line
Front bodice

A

Position of underarm slit

B   After slitting

219

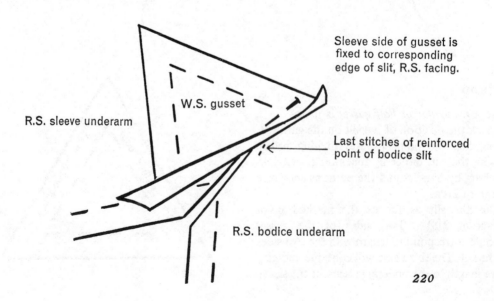

R.S. sleeve underarm

W.S. gusset

Sleeve side of gusset is fixed to corresponding edge of slit, R.S. facing.

Last stitches of reinforced point of bodice slit

R.S. bodice underarm

220

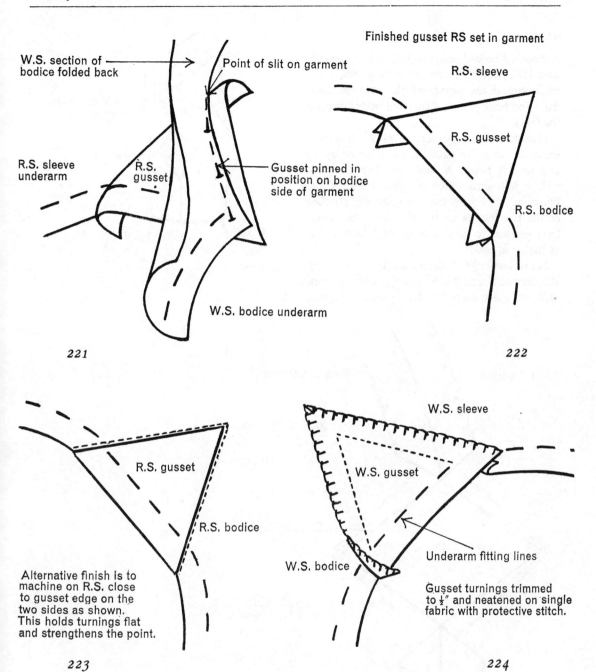

221

Finished gusset RS set in garment

W.S. section of bodice folded back

Point of slit on garment

R.S. sleeve

R.S. gusset

R.S. sleeve underarm

R.S. gusset

Gusset pinned in position on bodice side of garment

R.S. bodice

W.S. bodice underarm

222

R.S. gusset

R.S. bodice

Alternative finish is to machine on R.S. close to gusset edge on the two sides as shown. This holds turnings flat and strengthens the point.

223

W.S. sleeve

W.S. gusset

W.S. bodice

Underarm fitting lines

Gusset turnings trimmed to ½″ and neatened on single fabric with protective stitch.

224

curve to the underarm line instead of the sharp angle seen before the slit was cut. On some garments both back and front gussets are inserted as halves in this way, the underarms being finally joined through sleeve and bodice in one operation.

As further strengthening, topstitching by machining close to the edge of the gusset seams may be worked from the RS. This is optional (Diagram 223). On WS neaten the raw edges with some appropriate protective stitch (Diagram 224).

METHOD 2

A *diamond-shaped gusset* (*whole or one-piece*) is
used (Diagram 225). As for half gusset, staystitch round the points of the slits on both
front and back pieces of garment before cutting
the fabric.

Machine the sleeve and bodice underarm
seams as far as the slits. Press the seams open,
and neaten them. A diamond-shaped cavity
will be left, into which the gusset should fit.
Diagram 226 shows the strengthening stitches
at the two points of the slits and the fitting
lines marked to give turnings of $\frac{1}{4}$ inch width
at the seam ends.

Set in one edge of the gusset first, RS facing
RS garment, and fitting lines matching. Pin,
tack and machine on the fitting lines (Diagram

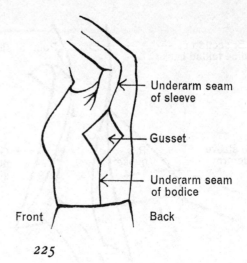

Underarm seam
of sleeve

Gusset

Underarm seam
of bodice

Front   Back

225

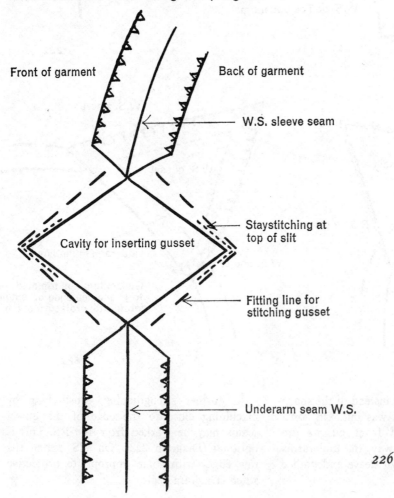

Front of garment   Back of garment

W.S. sleeve seam

Cavity for inserting gusset

Staystitching at
top of slit

Fitting line for
stitching gusset

Underarm seam W.S.

226

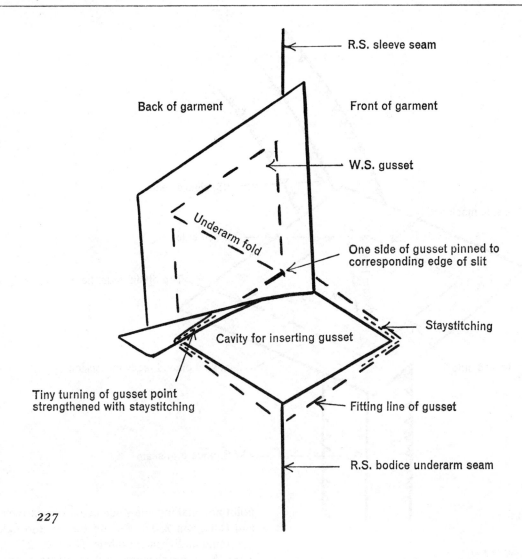

R.S. sleeve seam

Back of garment

Front of garment

W.S. gusset

Underarm fold

One side of gusset pinned to
corresponding edge of slit

Staystitching

Cavity for inserting gusset

Tiny turning of gusset point
strengthened with staystitching

Fitting line of gusset

R.S. bodice underarm seam

227

227). Remove tacks. Fold the gusset turning through to WS and press the seam.

With WS of garment facing the worker, set the other three sides of the gusset, RS facing RS of garment fitting lines and points matching as for the first side. See Diagram 228 to make sure the stitching lines coincide at the points of the slits and at seam ends.

Diagram 229 shows the finished gusset.

METHOD 3

Either shaped gusset may be used here. For extra strength, and to counteract fraying at the points in wear, the following method of lining out each slit, and then top stitching the garment edges to the gusset from the RS is recommended.

Use thin material for the lining, matching the garment fabric as nearly as possible in colour. Cut each strip on the straight grain about 2 inches wide and 1½ inches longer than the slit. Before cutting the slit, lay the strip of lining RS facing RS of garment, and centre of strip over position of slit. Tack. Machine about ⅛ inch each side of tack line, tapering to the

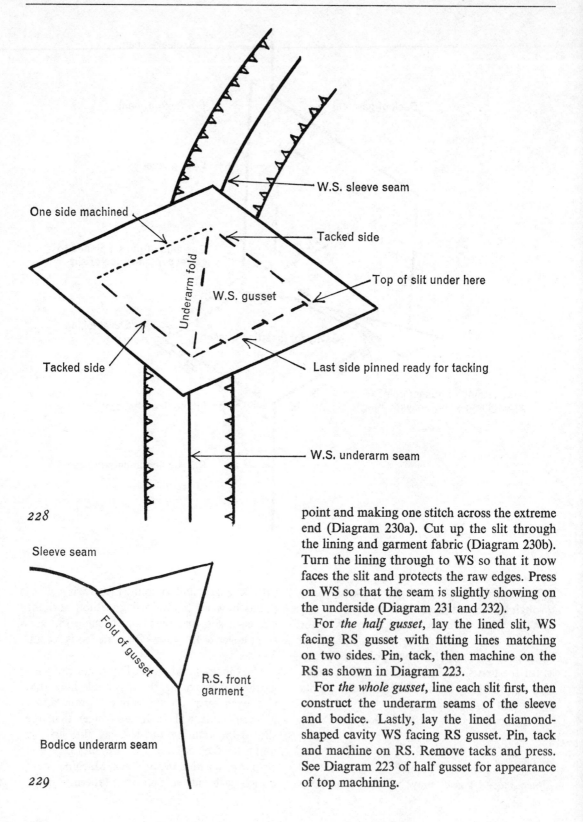

W.S. sleeve seam

One side machined

Tacked side

Underarm fold

Top of slit under here

W.S. gusset

Tacked side

Last side pinned ready for tacking

W.S. underarm seam

228

Sleeve seam

Fold of gusset

R.S. front garment

Bodice underarm seam

229

point and making one stitch across the extreme end (Diagram 230a). Cut up the slit through the lining and garment fabric (Diagram 230b). Turn the lining through to WS so that it now faces the slit and protects the raw edges. Press on WS so that the seam is slightly showing on the underside (Diagram 231 and 232).

For *the half gusset*, lay the lined slit, WS facing RS gusset with fitting lines matching on two sides. Pin, tack, then machine on the RS as shown in Diagram 223.

For *the whole gusset*, line each slit first, then construct the underarm seams of the sleeve and bodice. Lastly, lay the lined diamond-shaped cavity WS facing RS gusset. Pin, tack and machine on RS. Remove tacks and press. See Diagram 223 of half gusset for appearance of top machining.

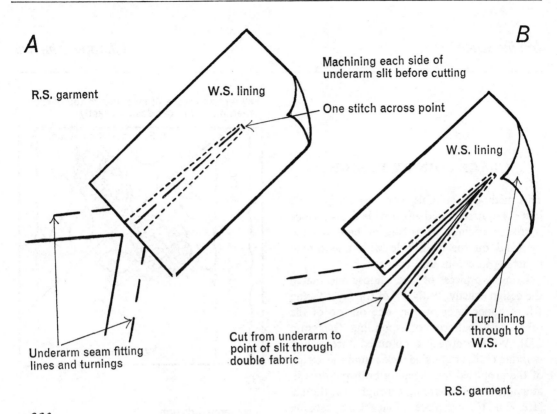

A

R.S. garment

W.S. lining

Machining each side of
underarm slit before cutting

One stitch across point

W.S. lining

B

Underarm seam fitting
lines and turnings

Cut from underarm to
point of slit through
double fabric

Turn lining
through to
W.S.

R.S. garment

230

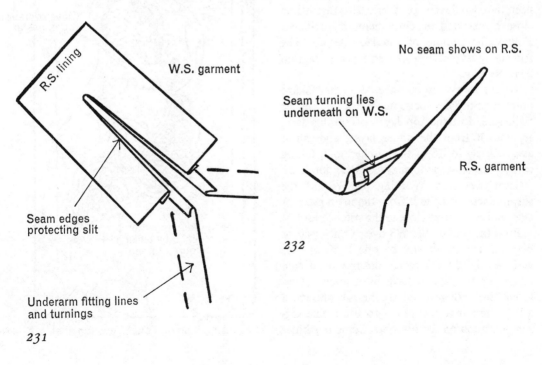

R.S. lining

W.S. garment

No seam shows on R.S.

Seam turning lies
underneath on W.S.

R.S. garment

Seam edges
protecting slit

232

Underarm fitting lines
and turnings

231

LACE JOIN BY DESIGN

This method is suitable wherever an invisible
join is required, whether on wide dress lace or
narrower edgings. It is shown here worked
by hand on the right side with fine thread
matching in colour and texture.

Using two pieces of lace, choose and match
the design exactly. With WS of top layer facing
RS of under layer overlay one on top of the
other with pattern corresponding (Diagram
233). With contrasting coloured thread and
working on the right side tack round the design
of the proposed join keeping both patterns in
alignment and stitching through the double
lace. Hold the two pieces of lace flat by tacking
near the raw edges (Diagram 234).

With matching thread and fine needle connect the two layers of fabric together using
close oversewing or close hemming stitches.
Follow the outline of the lace design. The
stitches must be close for strength (Diagram
234). Remove tacks.

To cut away surplus lace, use small sharp
pointed embroidery scissors. Work first on the
right side. Lift the top layer of surplus lace,
separate it from the under layer, and cut it
away closely to RS of the stitched join, taking
care not to snip the lower lace (Diagram 235).

Turn over lace. Working on WS lift the
surplus lace, separate it from the main piece of
lace, and cut it away close to the stitched join.

Press the join on the WS over a thick pad or
blanket. The result will be one layer of lace
with a slightly thickened outline of design
where the two pieces have been joined (Diagram 236). Where hand stitching is shown, a
quick alternative method is to use a fine zig-
zagging stitch on the machine. Some machines

Laying two pieces of lace one on top of the
other, matching the design exactly

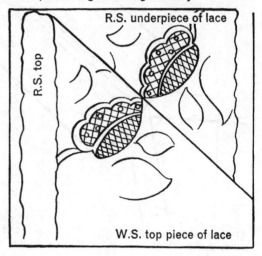

R.S. underpiece of lace

R.S. top

W.S. top piece of lace

233

Overlapped design   Underpiece

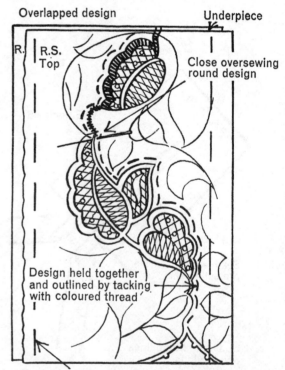

R.S.
Top

Close oversewing
round design

Design held together
and outlined by tacking
with coloured thread

Tacking holding double lace together   *234*

Cutting away top layer from join

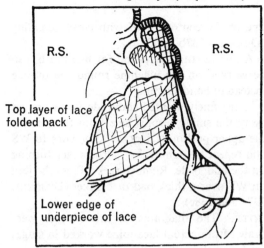

R.S.   R.S.

Top layer of lace folded back

Lower edge of underpiece of lace

235

Cut away underpiece of lace on W.S.

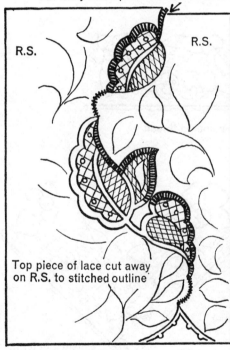

R.S.   R.S.

Top piece of lace cut away on R.S. to stitched outline

236

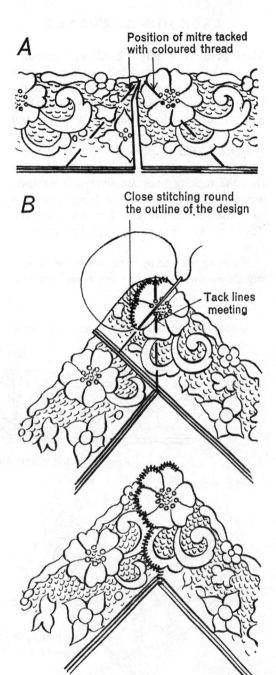

A   Position of mitre tacked with coloured thread

B   Close stitching round the outline of the design

Tack lines meeting

C   Finished outer corner mitred and joined by the design
Surplus lace has been trimmed away close to the stitching on both sides of join.

237

have the zigzagger as a built-in device. For others, an attachment can be obtained through sewing machine agencies.

LACE JOIN AT CORNER

Mark position of mitre on RS with coloured thread. On outer corners the two sides form a Λ shape, whilst inner corners form a V. Cut the lace through the centre of either shape taking care to cut round the outline of the central motif. Cut almost to the point, but do not sever (Diagrams 237a or 238a).

With RS uppermost fold over the lace so that the tacking lines are over one another, and the central motif is on top, lying in position over the second portion. Pin into position. Tack the two pieces through the coloured lines.

If joining the lace by hand, use a fine matching thread and needle to work round the out-line of the central motif with close hemming (Diagrams 237b or 238b).

A zigzag stitch, adjusted for fine finish, can be worked on the machine round the outline instead of hand stitching.

Using finely pointed embroidery scissors cut away the single surplus lace from the join on the upper portion (Diagram 235). Turn to WS and repeat the removal of surplus lace turning on the underside. Remove tacks. Press the join on WS over a thick pad or blanket (Diagrams 237c and 238c).

NOTE: The diagrams in this chapter were drawn from actual lace joins worked in stages for 'self help' visual aids.

Mitring lace with invisible join on inner corner

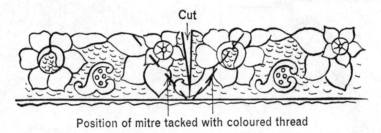

Cut

A

Position of mitre tacked with coloured thread

B

Tack lines of mitre folded over each other

close stitching round outline of design

C

Finished outer corner mitred and joined by the design

Surplus lace has been trimmed away close to stitching on both sides of join.

238

GARMENT AND LINING MADE UP AS ONE FABRIC

This method is used extensively for skirts and dresses of silk, jersey, wool crepe, lace, etc. Linings are usually of silk or similar fabric of man-made fibres. For cutting out, see page 36, *Cutting out: Lace*. Make up the two layers as one fabric. The advantage of this method is that more substance is given to the garment without much extra bulk. The lining helps to preserve good shape and prevent sagging. Turnings of seams do not show through on the right side if carefully pressed. Hems and facings may be fixed to linings alone so avoiding stitches showing through on RS (Diagrams 122 and 123). Pleats may be backed with floating pieces, giving ease of movement with good hanging qualities (Diagrams 128 and 129).

GARMENTS WITH SEPARATE LININGS

Sleeveless bodice

This is finished with a shaped half-lining (Diagram 239).

Machine and press the darts and underarm seams on the fitting lines of the bodice leaving an opening on the left side. Neaten the seam turnings. Leave the shoulder seams unstitched (Diagram 240).

Machine underarm seams of the lining on the fitting lines and press open. Trim the turnings a little narrower than the corresponding ones of the bodice and leave the edges raw to avoid thickness. Turn up and fix the hem at the lower edge. Press (Diagram 241).

Place lining over bodice, RS facing with centre and fitting lines matching. Pin, tack and machine together on the fitting lines round neck and armholes, beginning and ending exactly at the shoulder seam fitting lines which are left open. Remove tacks from the machining (Diagram 242). Trim the turnings to $\frac{1}{4}$ inch and snip to within a fraction of the stitching lines (Diagram 243). Turn the lining through to WS. Work each seam line to a good shape.

Finished neck and armholes

239

Tack and press (Diagram 244). Join the shoulder seams of the bodice by turning them inwards and stitching RS facing (Diagrams 244 and 245). Trim the turnings to $\frac{1}{2}$ inch and press open. NOTE: The join must allow the neck and armhole lines to continue smoothly. Finish the

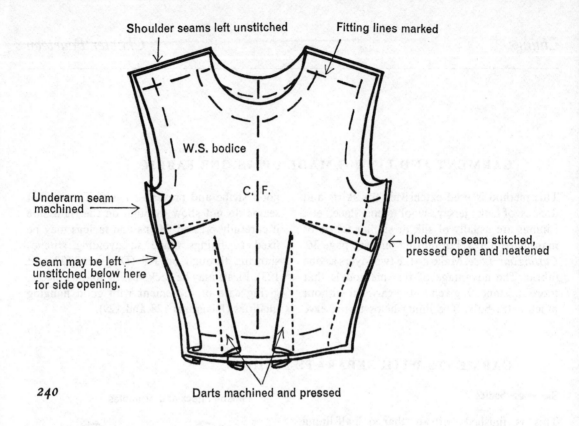

Shoulder seams left unstitched   Fitting lines marked

W.S. bodice

C. F.

Underarm seam machined

Underarm seam stitched, pressed open and neatened

Seam may be left unstitched below here for side opening.

240   Darts machined and pressed

shoulder seams of the lining by folding the turnings inwards to face and coincide with the bodice seams. Slipstitch the two folded edges together (Diagram 246).

Some commercial patterns show the lining portions with shaped lower edges, forming shaped facings, instead of straight as given here, but the method of attaching at neck and armholes is the same, except that neckline shapes vary in design.

Half-linings for skirts

These linings extend below the hip line and are often inserted into the back portion only to prevent 'seating' and to support pleats. Suitable fabrics are silk or satin type materials sold as 'coat linings' with a slippery surface.

Cut the lining from the back pattern of the

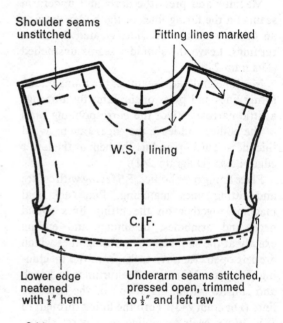

Shoulder seams unstitched   Fitting lines marked

W.S. lining

C. F.

Lower edge neatened with ½" hem

Underarm seams stitched, pressed open, trimmed to ½" and left raw

241

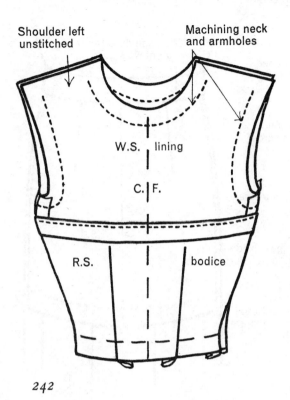

Shoulder left unstitched

Machining neck and armholes

W.S. lining

C. F.

R.S.   bodice

242

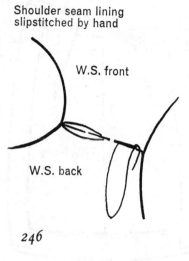

Shoulder seam lining slipstitched by hand

W.S. front

W.S. back

246

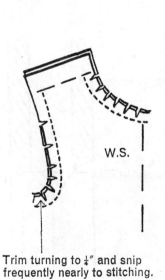

W.S.

Trim turning to ¼" and snip frequently nearly to stitching.

243

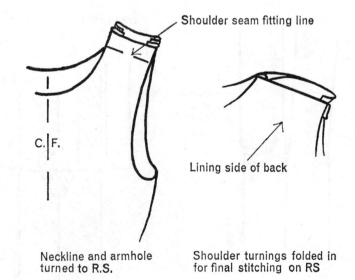

Shoulder seam fitting line

C. F.

Lining side of back

Neckline and armhole turned to R.S.

244

Shoulder turnings folded in for final stitching on RS

245

Half-lining for back of skirt prepared ready for stitching

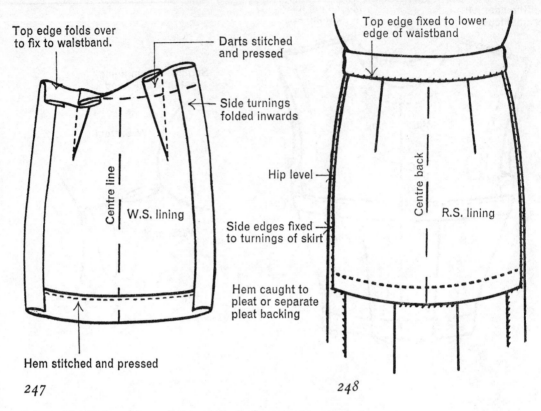

247

Top edge folds over to fix to waistband.

Darts stitched and pressed

Side turnings folded inwards

Centre line

W.S. lining

Hem stitched and pressed

248

Top edge fixed to lower edge of waistband

Hip level

Centre back

R.S. lining

Side edges fixed to turnings of skirt

Hem caught to pleat or separate pleat backing

Snip and fold lining at base of zip opening before attaching to zip tape.

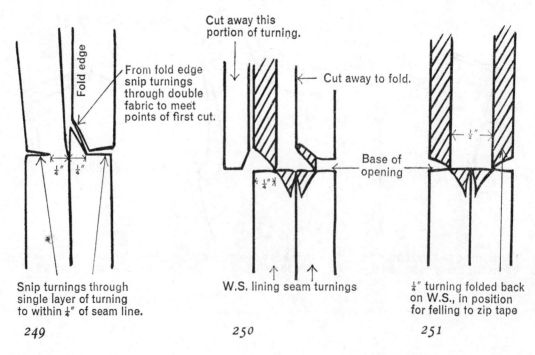

249

Fold edge

From fold edge snip turnings through double fabric to meet points of first cut.

¼" ¼"

Snip turnings through single layer of turning to within ¼" of seam line.

250

Cut away this portion of turning.

Cut away to fold.

Base of opening

¼"

W.S. lining seam turnings

251

½"

¼" turning folded back on W.S., in position for felling to zip tape

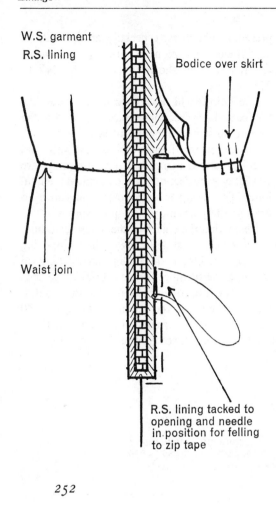

W.S. garment
R.S. lining

Bodice over skirt

Waist join

R.S. lining tacked to
opening and needle
in position for felling
to zip tape

252

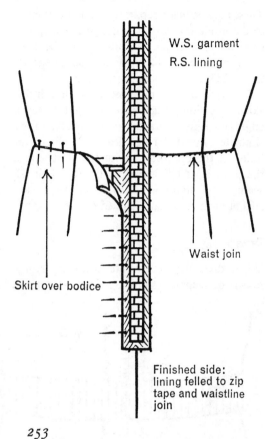

R.S. lining edges folded once and pinned in
position at opening and waistline

W.S. garment

R.S. lining

Skirt over bodice

Waist join

Finished side:
lining felled to zip
tape and waistline
join

253

skirt allowing approximately 1 inch turnings all round because of the fraying tendency of the fabric. The length should extend to about 6 inches below hipline, approximately 14 inches below waist when finished. Tack in the centre line. Stitch and press any darts to correspond with the skirt in shape. Mark, stitch and press the hemline at the base of the lining as this will be a free edge. Turn over the raw edge of the waist to WS. Tack and press (Diagram 247). The skirt is made up, pressed and finished except for lining.

Turn the skirt to WS. Matching centres and darts, pin the lining at the waist. Fit and pin the side edges to the turnings of the skirt side seams. Make sure it does not drag in any way,

but fits smoothly. If hand stitching is used to fix the lining, it can easily be readjusted. Attach the top edge to the lower edge of the waistband or petersham (Diagram 248). An alternative way would be to fix the top raw edge of lining flat inside the waistband, finishing the back of the waistband by hemming the folded edge to the waist fitting line of the lining. Hem the lower edge of the lining to the backs of any pleats to support them.

Straight skirts with pleats all round are improved with half linings inserted in both front and back, supporting all the pleats from the waistline.

Panel linings are used to support separate groups of pleats in a similar way.

Whole linings for skirts

These may be made separately and are attached to the inside of waistlines, hanging freely, with separate hem edges. Turnings must be fixed neatly to the back of zip plackets. See Diagrams 249 to 253 for skirt portion of lining.

For freedom of movement in slim fitting skirts, the lining may have slits left at lower edges of seams. If it supports the backing for a simulated inverted pleat, leave the slit in the lining at the opposite side of the skirt, e.g. if the pleat is at CB leave the lining slit in CF seam. If CF lining is cut to a fold, then leave slits at each side seam instead of the centre.

Dress linings

When dress styles indicate waist joins, the finish of separate lining edges sometimes presents difficulties, especially at the ends of zip-fasteners where neat corner arrangements are required as shown in Diagrams 249 to 253.

The linings will have been inserted into the bodice and skirt sections separately, leaving the join at waist and opening till last.

Pin and fit the lining to the bodice waist and opening to make sure that the fitting lines are correct at each section, as these will be the final joins. The lining must be easy and cause no drag to the garment yet fit quite smoothly.

Check that the length of the lining seam lines which reach the closed ends of the zip opening are correct. Unpin the lining and working on WS snip the turnings (single fabric) at the ends of the opening to within $\frac{1}{4}$ inch of the seam at the exact end of the stitching. Diagram 249 shows the lower corners being prepared. From the fold edges, through double fabric approxi-

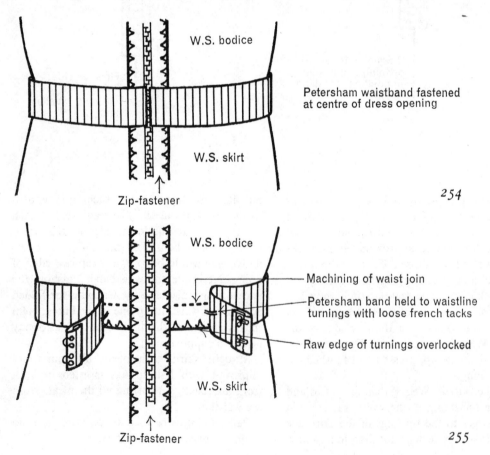

W.S. bodice

Petersham waistband fastened at centre of dress opening

W.S. skirt

Zip-fastener

254

W.S. bodice

— Machining of waist join

— Petersham band held to waistline turnings with loose french tacks

— Raw edge of turnings overlocked

W.S. skirt

Zip-fastener

255

mately ½ inch above the seam stitching, snip the turnings diagonally to meet the points of the previous cuts. Diagram 249 shows one side being snipped. Repeat this cut on the opposite turning. Turn the triangular points of the lining under to WS (Diagram 250). Fold back the long side edges evenly, leaving ½ inch distance between the two folds. Trim these turnings on WS to ¼ inch (Diagram 251). Pin the prepared lining edges to the zip tape, WS of lining facing WS of garment, as shown in Diagram 253. Fell the folded edges to the zip tape, stitching the corners neatly. If the top end of the zip opening is closed also, as in a side dress placket, prepare the bodice lining similarly to fit the top corner.

Two ways are shown of joining the lining at the waist: (a) bodice over skirt (Diagram 252), or (b) skirt over bodice (Diagram 253). According to the style of the dress choose the one more suited to the rest of the construction to give a neat flat finish.

In (a) Diagram 252 the waist fitting line of the skirt lining is tacked to the fitting line of the dress waist with turnings left flat, darts, centre and seam lines matching. The waist turnings of the bodice lining are folded under to WS and pinned, overlapping the skirt lining, again matching the waistline, darts, centre and side lines. Make sure the lining is sufficiently easy and does not drag at all, so tack and fit the garment, making any necessary alterations *before* finally felling the lining at the waist.

In (b) Diagram 253 the bodice lining is fixed first, with turnings flat, and the skirt laid over the bodice with turnings folded under to WS at waistline. Proceed as for method (a) and fell the lining at the waistline.

NOTE: Waistlines of dresses can be held firmly with a *petersham band* set inside. Use petersham (for skirt mounting) about 1 inch wide. Terylene petersham will not shrink or stretch, and will retain its firmness after washing or dry cleaning. Cotton petersham should be shrunk before using.

Cut the petersham to measure size of waist plus 2 inches for hems at either end. Fix and stitch hems and sew on hooks and eyes. Finished

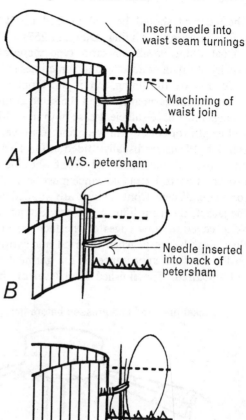

Working loose french tacks

Insert needle into waist seam turnings

Machining of waist join

A   W.S. petersham

Needle inserted into back of petersham

B

C

Cover and strengthen strands with loopstitch passing eye of needle under strands as shown.

256

petersham when fastened edge to edge should be the exact size of the wearer's waist (Diagrams 254 and 255). Attach WS petersham to WS waistline turnings of the dress at suitable intervals with loose french tacks. Diagrams 256a, b and c show the working of french tacks, which is similar to working bar tacks. The petersham holds the garment firmly to the waistline of the wearer, while the loose french tacks allow the slightly slacker waist turnings of the dress to keep their position without dragging.

Lining a jacket

The garment should be well pressed on WS before inserting the lining (Diagram 257).

Coat lining is silk or satin type material, usually of rayon or acetate, and sometimes silk.

To prepare the lining, cut it out from the pattern of the garment, and on the same grain. Linings must have sufficient ease both in width and length for comfort in wear and to prevent splitting. Pleats are usually folded at CB neck, and often at the centre of front shoulders instead of darts. Extra allowance must be made for these. Where front facings are applied to the jacket, the front linings will only extend so as to cover the raw edges of the facings, but they must be 'easy' when inserted and worn, so the outward appearance of the garment is not impaired. The finished hem level of the lining will be shorter than that of the jacket, so the pattern can be cut to the jacket fitting line without extra hem turnings.

After cutting out threadmark all fitting lines and balance marks. Stitch and press any darts if required. Then stitch the seams about $\frac{1}{8}$ inch outside the fitting lines to allow the extra ease required in the lining. Where shaped, snip or notch the turnings as required and press open on WS. The shoulder seams may be left open until the lining has been inserted into the rest of the jacket. This will allow any shoulder pads to be pinned in for fitting the sleeves, and then removed until the machining of the sleeves has been completed.

To insert the lining, turn the jacket to WS. If possible, place on a dress stand. This facilitates slipping the lining into place with WS facing WS of garment. Match seams and darts

Jacket prepared and pressed before lining

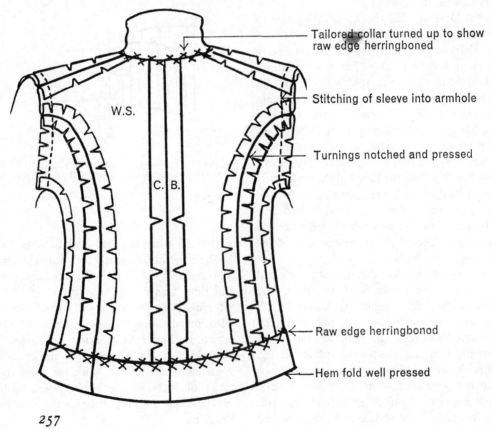

Tailored collar turned up to show raw edge herringboned

Stitching of sleeve into armhole

Turnings notched and pressed

W.S.

C. B.

Raw edge herringbonod

Hem fold well pressed

257

and pin in position. Fold a ½ inch pleat at CB neckline and pin in place. Keeping the lining 'easy' turn it upwards from the lower edge so the turnings of both garment and lining seams can be caught together lightly at underarm and waist levels on WS. These stitches will hold the lining in place during wear, and can be inserted before the lower edge is finally fixed. The CB pleat is best folded down its length and diagonally tacked (flashbasted) to hold it in place until the lining is finished (Diagram 258).

Fold under the *neck turnings* of the lining to WS snipping slightly if necessary to keep a smooth line. Pin in position to the back neck of the jacket covering the raw edges of the collar turnings (Diagram 258).

Fold under the raw edges of the *front lining*. Handle carefully for the curves are on the bias and will stretch easily. Maintaining a smooth

line pin and baste the lining in position over the facing edges (Diagram 259).

NOTE: As the jacket front facings extend at the shoulder beyond the seam line of the collar, the front lining need not be as wide as the back lining at the neck end of the shoulder. In this case the shoulder turning can be left flat, and the turning of the back lining folded under on the fitting line and felled to the fitting line of the front shoulder, after inserting shoulder pads between WS jacket and lining. These are caught to shoulder and armhole sleeve turnings after sleeves have been inserted (Diagram 260).

Armhole edges of lining and garment should be flashbasted together before sleeves are inserted and sleevehead linings are felled in position (Diagram 258).

The sleeves can be lined separately before being inserted into the jacket armholes. Dia-

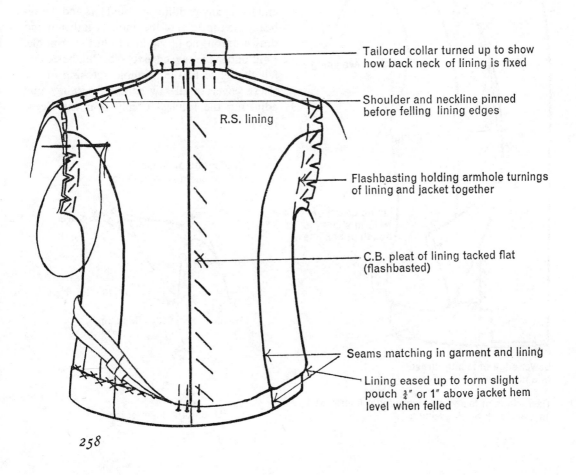

Tailored collar turned up to show how back neck of lining is fixed

Shoulder and neckline pinned before felling lining edges

R.S. lining

Flashbasting holding armhole turnings of lining and jacket together

C.B. pleat of lining tacked flat (flashbasted)

Seams matching in garment and lining

Lining eased up to form slight pouch ¾" or 1" above jacket hem level when felled

258

grams 261 and 262 show this in two stages. After making and pressing the sleeve turn it to WS. Stitch and press the two seams of the corresponding lining in the same way as the sleeve was constructed.

Lay WS of sleeve lining to WS of sleeve with the forearm (front) seam turnings matching together. Flashbaste the open turnings facing together on one edge from just above elbow level to the lower end, keeping the lining 'easy' (Diagram 261). Match the hindarm seam, and connect the turnings lightly at intervals. Slip the hand through the lining armhole. Grasp one edge of the sleeve at the lower edge. Pull the sleeve through so it is inside the lining. Finish the lower edge of the lining by folding the raw edge to WS. Bring this over the raw edges of the sleeve hem. Keep the lining eased. Pin, baste and fell the folded edge so it rests about ¾ inch above the end of the sleeve (Diagram 262).

At the top end of the sleeve the lining must be kept free of the sleevehead fitting line until the sleeve is set into the jacket armhole, so flash baste the lining to the sleeve halfway between elbow and top fitting line to hold the two fabrics together at this level (Diagram 262).

After inserting the sleeves into the armholes and fixing any padding on shoulders and sleevehead, the top edge of the lining is gathered and drawn up on the fitting line to fit the armhole. Fold under the raw edge to WS. Pin, baste and fell this edge to the armhole stitching of the sleeve covering all raw edges of turnings and adjusting the fullness evenly over the sleeve head.

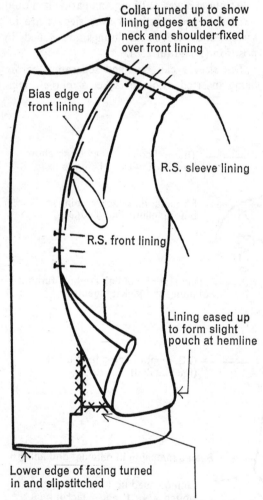

Front edge of lining being fixed to front facing on inside of jacket.

Collar turned up to show lining edges at back of neck and shoulder fixed over front lining

Bias edge of front lining

R.S. sleeve lining

R.S. front lining

Lining eased up to form slight pouch at hemline

Lower edge of facing turned in and slipstitched

Raw edges of facing and hem under lining fixed in place with herringboning

259

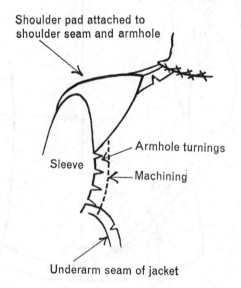

Shoulder pad attached to shoulder seam and armhole

Armhole turnings

Sleeve

Machining

Underarm seam of jacket

260

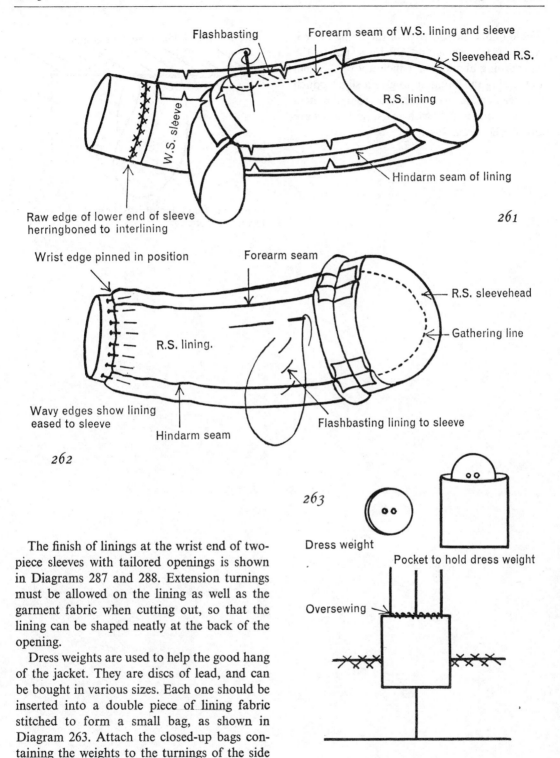

Flashbasting

Forearm seam of W.S. lining and sleeve

Sleevehead R.S.

R.S. lining

Hindarm seam of lining

W.S. sleeve

Raw edge of lower end of sleeve
herringboned to interlining

261

Wrist edge pinned in position

Forearm seam

R.S. sleevehead

Gathering line

R.S. lining.

Wavy edges show lining
eased to sleeve

Hindarm seam

Flashbasting lining to sleeve

262

263

Dress weight

Pocket to hold dress weight

Oversewing

Attach closed pocket containing weight to
seam and hem turnings

The finish of linings at the wrist end of two-piece sleeves with tailored openings is shown in Diagrams 287 and 288. Extension turnings must be allowed on the lining as well as the garment fabric when cutting out, so that the lining can be shaped neatly at the back of the opening.

Dress weights are used to help the good hang of the jacket. They are discs of lead, and can be bought in various sizes. Each one should be inserted into a double piece of lining fabric stitched to form a small bag, as shown in Diagram 263. Attach the closed-up bags containing the weights to the turnings of the side seams above the hem so they will be concealed when the lining is fixed in place.

Fold under the raw edge of the lining to WS. Matching the seams and CB lines, pin to the hem turning about ¾ or 1 inch above the hem fold, easing the lining up to give a slight pouch and keeping an even distance from the hem edge all round. Fell with invisible but secure stitches (Diagram 264).

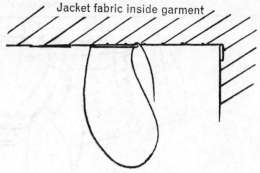

Jacket fabric inside garment

Felling the fold edge of R.S. lining to the garment

264

At one time tailoring was exclusively a man's craft. The skilful planning and drawing of patterns was, and is today, worked out with mathematical calculation and precision. Suitable cloth, woven to wear for a long time, was heavy to move and handle, whilst the art of hand pressing and tailor manipulation of the fabric with weighty goose irons and tailor's clappers (wooden blocks) needed brawn as well as brain. Modern living, with emphasis on speed in every direction, makes some of the laborious tasks of former times unprofitable so the craft of hand tailoring was forced to give way to the machine. The majority of tailored garments today are mass-produced. Almost all the hand processes can be imitated and worked by specially designed machines. Skilled hand-tailoring craftsmen and women are mainly found in the exclusive tailor's or couturier's workrooms where the individual client is prepared to pay for touches of originality and expert handwork.

A few of the techniques handed down by craftsmen tailors are recorded in this chapter for the benefit of those who wish to make their own tailored clothes. Most women and girls like to possess a well cut and tailored suit or coat; these, in good quality fabrics, are expensive items of wear round which personal wardrobes are built and colour schemes arranged. Tailoring processes are traditional and include tailored step collar and lapels, two-piece sleeves with button fastening back openings, and the working of tailoring stitches and buttonholes. Tailored pockets will be found in Chapter Nine and linings in Chapter Fourteen.

CHOICE AND PREPARATION OF FABRIC

Cloth for making the suit should be as good quality as possible, and responsive to tailor manipulation and moulding, such as woollen or worsted fabric, either 100 per cent or in blends with other fibres. (See also pages 14, 15 and 18.) Firmness of weave and handle together with sufficient softness in feel is advised. Test the weight too. Tailoring cloth is known to the trade by the number of ounces to one yard. An eight or twelve-ounce suiting is much lighter in weight when made up than a cloth of sixteen ounces. The latter may be very firm and durable, but can feel disappointingly heavy when worn. Modern clothing needs to be lightweight and must fold and pack into small space for travelling. On the other hand, too loose a weave can be tiresome in making up, through insufficient firmness to hold the intended shaping well.

Steampressing

Most good tailoring cloth is pre-shrunk nowadays, but in order to avoid press marks which may occur on smoothly finished suitings, it is advisable to steam-press the length of fabric before cutting out.

Open out the material. Lay the single thickness RS facing a clean blanket. Steampress the wrong side of the fabric methodically all over. If no steam iron is available wring out tightly a clean firm cloth of smooth white or unbleached cotton or linen. Lay the thoroughly dampened cloth over the fabric, starting at one end. Press all over with an iron hot enough to hiss when it touches the damp cloth, causing steam to penetrate the fabric. Lift the iron and set it down again, rather than pushing it to and fro. Move the position each time, so the steaming is evenly distributed over the whole surface. Allow the steam to escape and the fabric to dry thoroughly before using, so hang carefully to avoid creasing until the length of material is aired.

Interlining

For shaping by tailor manipulation using heat and moisture, woven lightweight tailor's canvas of natural fibres such as linen, or wool and hair, is desirable. Bonded interlinings will not mould to the same extent. Use them in suits of man-made fibre material, or where there is little or no shaping by moulding under heat and moisture to be done. As recorded elsewhere, darts and seams provide the means of fit and style instead (see Chapter Four, page 50).

Quantity required is the length of jacket from shoulder to hem.

Collar interlining

It is possible to buy special linen 'collar' canvas of heavier, firmer quality than the canvas used for the jacket front edges. This is usually sold by the straight thread, but it can be bought in special tailoring fabric departments already cut on the cross (since collar interlinings are always cross-cut), so $\frac{1}{4}$ yard collar canvas (enough for a step collar) would be shaped as shown in Diagram 265 when cut from the piece.

Tailor's linen tape

This is about $\frac{1}{4}$ inch wide and used for the bridle and for taping the front edges of the jacket. It can be bought in bundles or hanks at tailor's supply departments. Alternatively, strips of *tailor's linen* (distinct from canvas) can be cut to required widths on the straight grain, for the same purpose. For a jacket $\frac{1}{4}$ yard would be sufficient. Black, white or neutral shades may be bought from tailor's supply shops. Holland could serve the same purpose if linen is unobtainable.

To shrink canvas interlinings and tapes before using, soak in clean water. Press thoroughly dry. Canvas surface sometimes sticks when being pressed owing to a certain amount of dressing. Rub 'tailor's' soap (a particularly hard variety) all over the surface before ironing dry. This makes the canvas more pliable as well as smoothing the surface.

JACKETS

Cutting out

Use a well cut paper pattern as near to individual measurements as possible. Pin up and test on the figure before laying on the fabric. Any major adjustments should be carried out before cutting out, especially if the alterations entail extra material in length or width.

Find out right and wrong sides of the material, and if it has any nap or pile surface. In that case the paper pattern must be laid all one way, so the fabric shades evenly on the figure when the garment is worn. If the fabric has a twill weave (see Plates 2 and 3, between pages 24 and 25), this must run the same way on each piece of the garment, usually from the left shoulder across to the right hip on the wearer. Diagram 12, page 28, illustrates twill effect on skirts.

Sometimes when plain (not patterned) fabric has been woven with yarns of different colours, the hue changes when the material is reversed, or laid upside down. It is well to be aware of such points, in order to test material before dovetailing patterns so as to avoid disappointing results. Be critical about straight grain, which affects the balance and hang of the suit on the wearer. Fold the pre-shrunk material carefully with warp, or selvedge, and weft

grains at true right angles. The squared edges
of the cutting-out table will help in testing and
proving these (Diagram 13). Stripes, checks
or plaids need special care and attention in
matching and balancing correctly. See also
pages 31–2 (Diagrams 15, 16 and 17).

If using a commercial paper pattern, choose
the correct lay for the width of fabric and size
of pattern. Mark it conspicuously for easy
reference, and follow it carefully to ensure the
right parts of patterns are laid to folds. The
upper step collar is usually cut with CB to a
fold. NOTE: As this piece has to provide
sufficient fabric for rolling over on the crease
line allow (if possible) at least $\frac{1}{8}$ inch, preferably $\frac{1}{4}$ inch extra turnings to those provided
by the pattern. The under collar and interlining are both cut on the cross to the exact
pattern (Diagrams 265a and b).

Check that the straight grain indication on
each piece of pattern is correctly placed on the
fabric and that sufficient turnings have been
allowed, e.g. tucked or channel seams may
need wider turnings than those allowed by the
pattern (see pages 61, 62 and 70), according
to the desired finished effect.

NOTE: Cutting out sleeves is illustrated in
Diagrams 284a and b and given on page 186.
Cutting out skirts is described on page 195.

Pocket flaps or welts may match the weave
or pattern of the fabric when applied, or may
be cut to provide a decorative effect as well.
It is advisable to plan their position on the
fabric, but leave cutting the actual shapes until
after fitting, to ensure the right effect. (See
page 119, Chapter Nine.)

Balance marks are denoted by notches on the
edges of most commercial patterns. If the
fabric is notched inwards too, the seam turnings
are weakened. Either cut small triangles outwards, opposite the notches, or mark their
position with thread on each side of the double
fabric. After cutting out the garment, threadmark all centre and fitting lines, lapel crease
lines, pocket and buttonhole positions as well
as balance marks. Tailor tacking is the usual
method on double fabric, with centre lines in
straight basting. Curved edges such as arm-

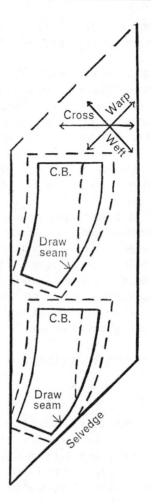

A Collar canvas cut on the cross and laid in single thickness

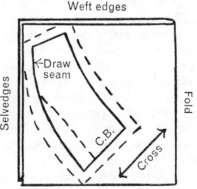

B Collar canvas cut on straight grain and folded double with selvedges together   265

holes and necklines can be preserved from stretching as described on page 45, Diagram 27.

Use the pattern of the front facings for the *front interlinings* following the same straight grain marks. The *side front* interlining pieces from the position of the front shoulder dart across to the armhole may be cut on the cross as shown in Diagram 266. Use the top of the jacket front shoulder and armhole for this, allowing it to reach about 2 to 3 inches down from the underarm.

Diagram 265a shows the placing of the *collar pattern* in two halves on the cross cut canvas so that both edges of the draw seam are on the selvedge grain. If using collar canvas cut on the straight thread, fold over the canvas so selvedges face each other as in Diagram 265b. When CB of collar pattern is laid on the cross the draw seam edge will be parallel to the selvedges.

For *interlining sleeves*, see Diagram 286a.

Assembling suit

Before any permanent stitching is done, assemble the jacket for first fitting. Pin and baste any darts first, tapering smoothly to the points. If the back is in several sections, pin and baste those seams next, placing correct sides together and matching balance marks at waistlines and top and bottom edges. Baste on the exact fitting lines of both sides of the fabric. Assemble each front separately in a similar manner. Fixing the back to the front sections, pin and baste the underarm seams, matching waistlines and balance marks, then armhole edges and hem. NOTE: The front shoulder is often slightly shorter than the back. Pin the neck ends together, then the armhole ends. Slightly stretch the front and ease the back pinning the fitting lines together. Baste in position.

For assembling sleeves, see page 186, and skirts, page 195.

NOTE: The skirt should be assembled and tried on for fitting with the jacket so the appearance of the whole suit can be judged.

Fitting

1. If shoulder pads are used, pin them in position before fitting the jacket. Have ready the right sleeve, assembled but not inserted. (See page 186.)

2. Try on the jacket right side out over the type of blouse or similar garment that would usually be worn underneath it. If the jacket is fitted wrong side out, the right half will be on the left side of the figure and vice versa. This may result in wrong balance and appearance, when worn right side out. Fold over and pin the centre front lines together. Make sure the jacket is on the figure correctly and the lower edges level.

3. Judge for appearance as well as fit. Line and proportion should be good. Appearance should be smooth, with no wrinkles in the wrong place, and sufficient room for ease of movement without strain.

4. Check the *grain of the fabric*. Weft grain should be horizontal, i.e. parallel to the floor, across the chest and back between the armholes. Warp or selvedge grain should run vertically down the centre front lines. If the centre back is cut to a fold, the straight grain position of CB must run vertically down on the figure. If there is a seam at CB this probably means some shaping has been incorporated. The line of the seam must run vertically down the centre of the back in this case.

5. Fit the right half of the figure, correcting left from right later, unless the left side of wearer differs from the right.

6. Judge for position and length of *darts* as well as fit. Positions may need altering, e.g. shoulder dart may appear too near the armhole side and would give a better appearance if moved nearer to the neck, whilst remaining the same in other respects, or waist darts may require lengthening or shortening, according to the figure of the wearer.

7. In the same way position and run of *seams* especially panel or decorative seams may require adjustment of position in order that the style lines may flatter the figure. *Side seams*

should run vertically. If they tend to swing either forward or backward, they must be un-picked and re-pinned. The fault may be one of balance. Either the front is too long for the back, or vice versa. These corrections may concern the shoulder seams as well as the underarm.

8. *Shoulders* should fit smoothly. Watch the current fashion line for width and judge if the armhole fitting line is correct in this respect.

9. *Armholes* should be comfortable with no bulging at sides or base.

10. *The back* should fit smoothly across the shoulders and between the armholes. Wrinkles across the top of the back may be caused by a square shouldered figure needing more room at the armhole ends of the shoulders. If sleeve pads were inserted for the fitting, remove them, and judge the fit again, as the shoulders of the wearer may not need them at all. If the wrinkles still persist across the top, the remedy may be to let out the shoulder seam at the armhole end. NOTE: If the jacket pattern was adjusted for this build of figure before cutting out, this trouble should not occur as allowance will have been made for the higher shoulder at armhole end.

Remember that movement of the arms in a forward position (e.g. driving a car, or riding a bicycle or similar position) causes extra strain across the back. Allow sufficient width for this.

11. At the *waistline* watch that the fastening position in front is at the correct level for good appearance, with no gaping. If the jacket is fitted, the waistline position should corres-pond with that of the figure, if anything slightly below, but not above. Allow sufficient ease for good hang. Too tight a waistline causes un-sightly creases across the figure. Sometimes folds across the figure just above the waist are caused by the back being too long for the front. The adjustment involves untacking both shoulders and underarm seams, lifting the back of the jacket up, and re-pinning on the shoulders, so it is shortened, and the creases disappear. This is a major alteration involving

the balance of the garment. Skilful refitting is necessary to give good lines again in the corrected positions of shoulder, underarm, and armhole.

12. Judge for smooth fit over the *hips* with sufficient ease to prevent riding up. This is particularly important on the 'not so slim' figures. Too close a fit may be most unbecom-ing, whereas a fraction more ease could ensure the elegance required when the jacket is worn.

Judge the length according to prevailing fashion and height of figure. Watch that it is level with the ground.

13. Slip the *sleeve* on to the correct arm. Pin the hindarm seam to the back balance mark and the forearm seam to the front balance mark on the armhole. Next pin the centre of the sleeve to the centre of the shoulder. (This may be slightly forward from the shoulder seam.) Pin round the rest of the armhole easing the sleeve-head over the top arm joint. The sleeve should hang smoothly down from the shoulder, follow-ing the natural position of the arm when held downwards. The weft grain across the top of the sleeve should be parallel to the floor. The selvedge grain should hang vertically from centre of sleeve downwards (Diagram 290). Judge the width and length of the sleeve, correcting where necessary before interlining and making the back opening at the lower edge.

Correct the left side of the garment from the right after the first fitting before permanent stitching is done. It is wise to try the jacket on again to be sure all is well before machining. If the figure is different on the left side from the right, both sides must be fitted, but usually only the right side is altered where necessary, and the left corrected from the right.

Further fitting may be necessary when the under collar is ready, and for the run of the armhole fitting lines before the sleeves are inserted. (Watch prevailing fashion for the latter.) The hem can be tested for level at this stage.

Fit when both sleeves have been basted into the armholes before machining. Remember to pin shoulder pads into position for this fitting, if they are to be worn in the finished jacket. The final hang is judged at this stage. Correct appearance is shown in Diagram 290.

Creases in diagonal directions mean the sleevehead is pitched either too far forward or backward. Untack the sleevehead. Move the top of the sleeve so the creases disappear—re-pin. Too short a sleevehead will cause a downward drag from the centre of the armhole on the shoulder. If the turning width is sufficient let out the top of the sleeve to counteract the creasing. Otherwise shorten the underarm of the sleeve by drawing the underarm seam through the armhole.

Too much length in the sleevehead causes folds across the top of the sleeve. This is remedied by shortening the sleevehead.

Insufficient width across either the back or the chest can cause strain across the sleeve. In either of these cases the armhole fitting line of the jacket needs letting out rather than the sleeve. NOTE: Whatever correction has been made, the final appearance of a smooth curve and becoming line to the armhole seam must be achieved.

Fit the jacket again when the linings have been inserted, before final felling, to judge the general hang, and to make sure they do not pull or drag anywhere incorrectly.

After fitting and correcting, machine the *darts*, tapering smoothly to the points. Secure the ends of thread and remove basting. Split open the folds of the darts, and cut as near to the point end as possible with safety to facilitate pressing. Lay the parts to be pressed WS uppermost over a tailor's ham. The curved surface will help in moulding such parts as the points of long shoulder darts whilst flattening

Canvassing front jacket

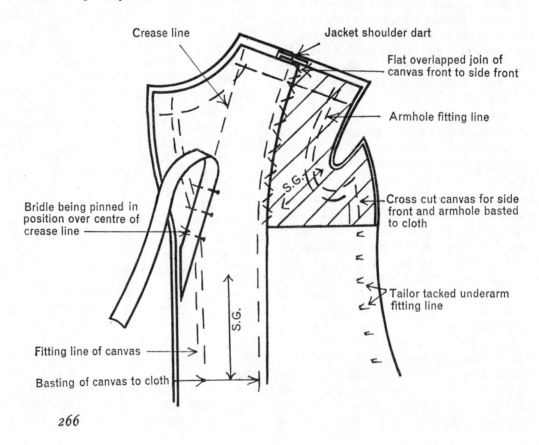

Crease line

Jacket shoulder dart

Flat overlapped join of canvas front to side front

Armhole fitting line

Bridle being pinned in position over centre of crease line

Cross cut canvas for side front and armhole basted to cloth

Tailor tacked underarm fitting line

Fitting line of canvas

Basting of canvas to cloth

S.G.

266

the seam line of the dart with the point of the iron over a damp pressing cloth. Having made sure the stitching line is flat on RS with no wrong fold being creased, press again more heavily on WS smoothly rounding the end of the dart over the bust line.

Fronts, or foreparts

1.   To make up the interlining, join the cross-cut side front to the forepart interlining by trimming the turnings to ¼ inch and overlapping the fitting lines corresponding to the shoulder dart (Diagram 266). Catchstitch the turnings on either side. For working catchstitch, see Diagram 36. Press the join over the tailor's ham. Lay the canvas forepart flat on the table. Over it lay the corresponding jacket forepart, WS facing RS canvas. Match and pin centre lines together and the shoulder dart to the canvas join. Match and pin the crease lines together. Working from the bust line upwards baste the front edges of the cloth to the canvas, smoothing it up whilst working, so as to keep it taut to the canvas with no wrinkles. Repeat from the bust line downwards. Baste the opposite edge of the canvas next, up through the dart position from bust line to the shoulder, and then down to the lower edge. Finally, baste round the armhole and small portion of the side line (Diagram 266).

2.   The *lapels* need special care.

As the crease line of the lapel is on the bias when worn in the crossover position it is apt to stretch, so a 'bridle' is made from pre-shrunk tailor's tape (or tailor's linen ½ to 1 inch wide), length equal to crease line plus at least 2 inches extra to continue on to the under collar later. Fold the tape or strip down the centre lengthways and press in a crease. Working from the lower end of the crease line on the canvas side of the garment pin the centre of the tape over the crease line, keeping the tape taut over the bias line (Diagram 266). Pin to within about ¼ inch distance from the neck fitting line. Using thread to match the garment fabric run a line of stitches through the centre of the tape on the crease line holding the tape to the gar-

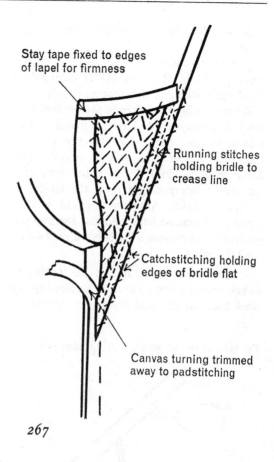

Stay tape fixed to edges of lapel for firmness

Running stitches holding bridle to crease line

Catchstitching holding edges of bridle flat

Canvas turning trimmed away to padstitching

267

ment. Keep the stitches taut, but not drawn up at all. Catchstitch the long edges of the bridle on each side to hold them flat (Diagram 267).

To make the lapel roll back softly into position and at the same time give support to the edges and corners, *padstitching*, a series of diagonal stitches, is worked from the canvas through to the cloth whilst the work is held in a curling position over the fingers of the left hand.

Each stitch picks up a thread or two of the garment fabric, whilst the thumb of the left hand presses the canvas slightly forward all the time. The effect of this padstitching is to make the underlayer of fabric contract so the lapel rolls back. Start padstitching from the edge of the bridle working the diagonal stitches in parallel rows upwards and downwards until the lapel is covered. Keep within the fitting lines. The rows become shorter as the space is filled.

NOTE: The needle is in a horizontal position for each stitch. Diagram 268 is enlarged to show the working of this process clearly.

When both lapels have been padstitched, they are well steampressed. Lay the jacket canvas side uppermost with the padstitched lapel on the pressing board. Lay over it a sufficiently damp pressing cloth. Using a hot iron of a reasonably heavy weight press the lapel flat, as far as the bridle. After pressing fold back the lapels on the crease lines, allowing them to roll softly. Do not press as a flat edged crease would spoil the effect.

3. To *stay* the front edges of the lapels and jacket, trim the canvas outside turnings of the lapel back to the padstitching as shown in

Diagram 267. Using tailor's stay tape, or ½-inch wide strips of tailor's linen (cut lengthwise), pin the strip to the outer edge of the lapel and continue down the front edge of the jacket. Catchstitch the inner edge to the canvas just inside the fitting line as shown in Diagram 267. Fix another strip across the top of the lapel, as far as the bridle.

4. When attaching the front facings measure and mark the 'step' on the top edges of the lapels so both are equidistant from the collar end to the point or end of the lapel.

When worn on the figure the seam edges of the lapels and jacket front should not show, so mark new fitting lines on the facings about ⅛ inch outside the original ones, on the turning allowance round the lapel and front edges.

Lay the front facings RS facing RS jacket.

Position of hands when working padstitch on jacket lapel

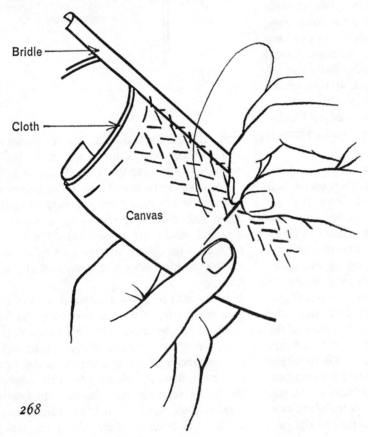

Bridle

Cloth

Canvas

268

Matching the new fitting lines of the lapel facings with the original ones on the jacket, pin and baste together using small stitches to hold and control the slight fullness round the lapels as shown in Diagram 269. The fullness is to allow the seams to roll slightly underneath when the facings are turned. Pin, baste and machine the front edge fitting lines from the end of the 'step' round the lapel and down the front edges, taking care to keep the exact shapes of both lapels. Remove basting threads. Snip the turnings to the stitching at the end of the step to release them for the neck edge (Diagram 269). Trim the turnings in layers to avoid thickness, cutting those of the canvas interlining as near to the stitching as possible down the jacket fronts.

Before turning the facings to RS open the seam turnings with the tip of a hot iron held over the edge of a damp pressing cloth. This will facilitate working the seam edges flat when the facings are turned through to RS. After pressing open the seams, cut off the corner turnings at the points of the lapels to within a few threads of the stitching. Turn the facings to RS. Working on the underside baste the seam edges of the facings round the lapels as far as the crease line (Diagram 270). Then reverse the seam edge and baste so it lies under the jacket front edge to the base of the jacket and cannot be seen on RS. Diagram 271 shows how the seams lie under the point of the lapel.

5. To press the lapel, lay it face downwards on the pressing board. Over it lay a partially damp pressing cloth. Press on the underside only as far as the crease line keeping the edge of the iron parallel to the crease line. Turn over to RS. Lay the lapel face upwards over

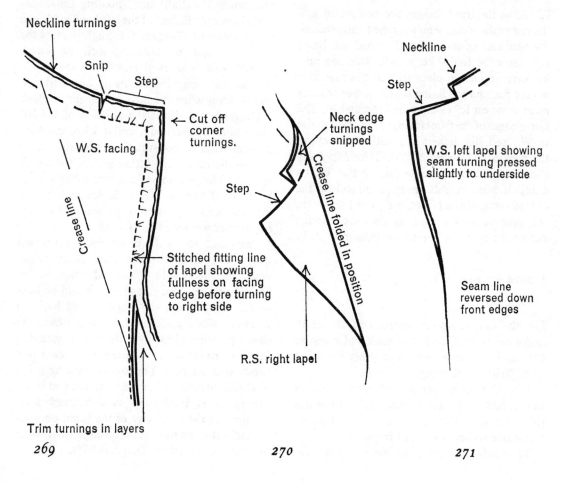

Neckline turnings

Snip

Step

← Cut off corner turnings.

W.S. facing

Crease line

— Stitched fitting line of lapel showing fullness on facing edge before turning to right side

Trim turnings in layers

269

Neck edge turnings snipped

Step

Crease line folded in position

R.S. right lapel

270

Neckline

Step

W.S. left lapel showing seam turning pressed slightly to underside

Seam line reversed down front edges

271

the tailor's ham to give it a curved shape. Again, steam press as far as the crease line using a piece of wool cloth next to the suit fabric, and the partly damp cloth on top, so as not to shine or press mark RS of the jacket. Alternatively, use a steam iron over the woollen cloth. After pressing the lapel, press the lower edge of the jacket face down on the pressing board in a flat position.

6. To finish the inner edges of the facings, fold back the lapels on their crease lines. Lightly pin or baste to keep them in their curled back positions. Lay the jacket front edge on the table with WS uppermost and lapel folded under. Smooth the facing in position. Pin and baste. The inner raw edge is herringboned to the canvas to hold it in place and later the lining will cover the raw edges. For working herringbone, see Diagrams 116a and b.

7. After the front facings are completed and the rest of the jacket seams stitched and pressed, the hem can be levelled and turned up. Baste and press the folded edge well. This can also be herringboned in place so that the raw edge is kept flat and the lining covers it. No stitches must show on RS (Diagrams 116a and b). The lower edges of the front facings are turned under to WS and slipstitched in position just above the hem edge (Diagram 259). Trim away any thickness of turning inside this portion before fixing. If dress weights are required to help the correct hang of the jacket, see page 169, where this process is explained, as they are inserted before the lining is completed (Diagram 263).

Tailored step collar

UNDER COLLAR

Lay the two cross-cut portions of the cloth under collar RS facing. Pin, tack and machine CB seam. Remove tacks and press the seam open. Trim the turnings to ¼ inch.

Trim CB seam turnings of each cross-cut canvas half to ¼ inch. Overlap CB fitting line for a flat join. Catchstitch the raw edges on either side to hold each half in place.

To attach the canvas to the cloth, lay the cloth under collar WS uppermost. Over it lay the canvas interlining RS uppermost and WS facing WS cloth, with CB fitting lines matching. Pin the crease lines together starting at the centre and pinning to each side. With matching thread run the two crease lines together keeping the threat taut but not gathered (Diagram 272). This stitching holds the under collar and interlining in position for working the padding of first the 'fall' and then the 'stand' of the collar. Fold the collar over on the crease line with canvas side uppermost and press the fold with finger and thumb, curving the collar in the way it will be worn.

Padstitch the fall in the same way as the lapels, using matching thread and working rows of diagonal stitches, inserting the needle horizontally each time. With canvas side uppermost and collar folded, start at the crease line, and work the 'fall' first, holding the collar curled over the fingers of the left hand as shown in the enlarged Diagram 273. Slightly press the canvas towards the stitching with the thumb as each row is worked parallel to the crease line so the underside contracts and curls inwards. Stop when the fitting lines are reached.

Diagram 274 shows the position of the left hand holding the under collar while working parallel rows of padstitching from the crease line to the neck edge fitting line of the stand. NOTE: The position of the crease line is kept to the right-hand side in padstitching both the fall and the stand. Both edges will curl underneath after working this process.

Press and shape the under collar (Diagram 275) by laying the padstitched under collar with the canvas side of the fall down on the pressing board. The crease line should be next to the worker and the stand folded back so its canvas side is uppermost. Using a sufficiently damp pressing cloth over the stand, turn the hot iron round so as to press the crease line firmly with its heel. This steam pressing helps to shrink the crease line. In so doing and while the collar is pliable in its dampened state manipulate the neck edge of the stand on each side of CB so as to stretch the edges slightly to fit over the shoulders (Diagram 275).

Undercollar - Canvas and cloth
Both are cut on the cross and joined at C.B.

C.B. seam of undercollar with turnings pressed open on W.S.

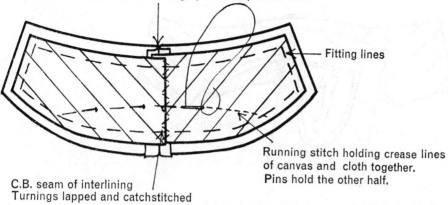

Fitting lines

Running stitch holding crease lines
of canvas and cloth together.
Pins hold the other half.

C.B. seam of interlining
Turnings lapped and catchstitched

272

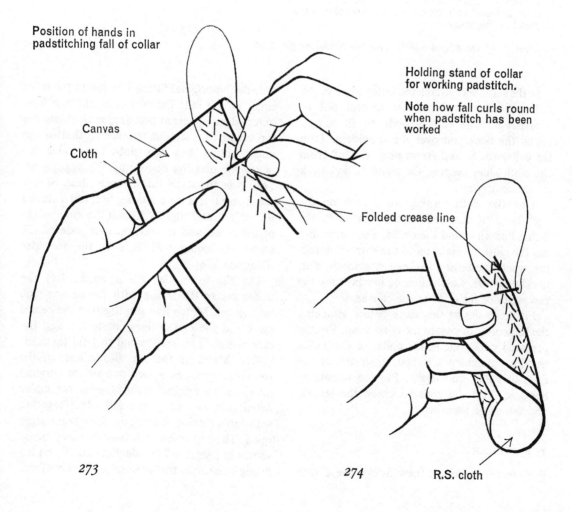

Position of hands in
padstitching fall of collar

Holding stand of collar
for working padstitch.

Note how fall curls round
when padstitch has been
worked

Canvas

Cloth

Folded crease line

273   274   R.S. cloth

R.S. undercollar showing crossway join at C.B.

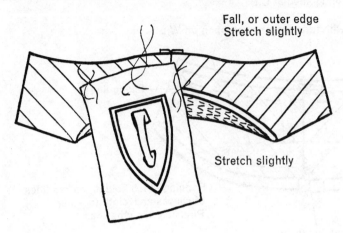

Fall, or outer edge
Stretch slightly

Stretch slightly

Damp pressing cloth causing steam under hot iron

Pressing stand from crease line fold with the heel
of a hot iron to shrink crease line and shape the
stand of the collar

275

Stretch the fall edges a little over the shoulder position

In the same way stretch the outer edges of the fall in similar positions. Be careful not to overstretch. The collar needs to fit snugly round the neck and over the shoulders. Turn the collar round and steam press the fall from the cloth side, keeping the stand folded back on the crease line.

Trim the cloth turnings to ⅜ inch on the neck edge of stand. Trim the canvas to the fitting line all round the collar. Fold over and pin the cloth turnings on to the canvas, notching where necessary to keep a smooth, flat, neckline curve. Catchstitch or herringbone the raw edges of the cloth to the canvas.

Fit the collar at this stage before attaching the top collar to ensure the correct set. Pin the prepared neck edge of the collar to the jacket neckline matching CB first, then the crease lines of collar and lapels. Pin the remaining neckline. Test the ends to check the length, and adjust if necessary.

TOP COLLAR

Prepare by marking a new fitting line ⅛ inch

outside the original fitting line round the three edges of the fall: the two ends and the long outer edge. By steam pressing, manipulate the top collar in a similar manner to that of the under collar. Lay the cloth top collar RS facing the pressing board and WS uppermost. Fold over the stand on the crease line. Shrink the crease line a little, having first run a thread through it, and slightly stretch the outer edges of the stand and the fall on each side of CB where the collar will fit over the shoulder (Diagram 276).

Lay the top collar RS upwards. Lay the under collar RS facing with the canvas side uppermost. Match and pin together the centre back and the crease lines. Baste through the crease lines from end to end to hold them together. Matching the new fitting lines of the top collar (marked ⅛ inch outside the original lines) to the original fitting line of the under collar, pin and baste the fall edges together with small stitches, leaving the draw seam edges open. The top collar will now be eased on as shown in Diagram 277. Machine exactly on the fitting line round the three sides, working from

Cut the top collar with $\frac{1}{8}''$ to $\frac{1}{4}''$ extra turnings all round as the fabric will need this allowance when the fall turns over the stand in the wearing position.

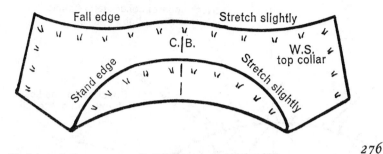

276

Shrink and shape crease line fold and slightly stretch the outer edges of both stand and fall to enable the collar to fit snugly over the shoulders.
(Do not stretch at centre back.)

the fall side. It is easier to control the fullness under the machine from this side. Be careful to machine accurately at the corners so both collar ends look alike. Remove basting from machined edges and from the crease line. Trim the turnings in two layers and cut away the corners to within a few threads. (The canvas has been trimmed to the fitting line already.)

As for the facing of the lapels, press open the collar turnings carefully, without creasing the collar, holding a pressing pad inside the collar to support it. Turn the collar through to RS. Work the ends and corners out to good shapes, matching each other. Working from the underside and keeping the seam edge rolling slightly underneath, baste round the three edges. Fold the turnings under on the fitting lines of both of the draw seam edges and baste these separately.

Baste the crease lines of the top and under collar together again. (It is important to repeat this in order to hold the three layers of fabric together on this line whilst pressing.) The top collar should now fit smoothly over the under collar on the fall side (Diagram 278). Laying it RS down on a pressing board with the fall edge nearest worker, press once more as far as the crease line to sharpen the three outer edges. Take care not to spoil the shape of the remaining parts of the collar.

Half view of top collar machined to undercollar round the fall edges, and showing fullness so when turned to R.S. the seam line can roll slightly underneath

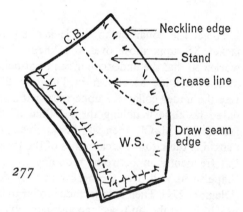

277

Draw seam edges of collar folded inwards on fitting lines and tacked ready for attaching to lapel

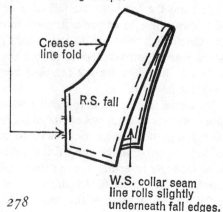

278

W.S. collar seam line rolls slightly underneath fall edges.

Position of jacket held over knee of worker for
attaching under collar stand to neckline of garment

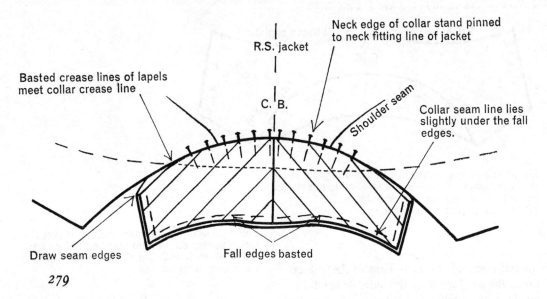

Neck edge of collar stand pinned
to neck fitting line of jacket

R.S. jacket

Basted crease lines of lapels
meet collar crease line

C. B.

Shoulder seam

Collar seam line lies
slightly under the fall
edges.

Draw seam edges   Fall edges basted

279

To set the collar on to the jacket, lay the jacket RS uppermost over the knee of the worker so that the under collar can be attached to the neckline as shown in Diagram 279. Lay the under collar RS uppermost with pre-pared neckline matching the neckline of the jacket. Pin at CB then at crease line ends matching these to the crease lines of the lapels. Pin frequently in between, retaining a good shape to fit well over the neck and shoulders (Diagram 279). Then fell the under collar to the neckline firmly and as inconspicuously as possible (Diagram 280).

Turn the jacket over. Bring the ends of the bridle from the lapels to the fall edge of the collar crease line to ensure a firm continuous line. Catchstitch the edges to the collar. They should reach approximately to a position op-posite the shoulders, leaving the back part of the crease line free.

The single fabric of the top collar stand is smoothed over to meet WS of the jacket neck. The turnings of the collar neckline (both under and top sections) must be snipped at the should-ers to facilitate reversing them at these points, in order to turn under for the draw seams, but lie flat across the back of the neck. Hold the

Felling under collar to jacket at back
of neck edge

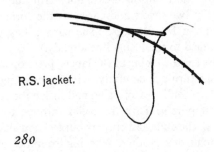

R.S. jacket.

280

raw edge in position between the shoulders by lightly herringboning it to the jacket, but do not allow any stitches to show on RS. The lining covers the raw edge eventually (Diagram 281).

The *draw seam* edges of the collar which have been folded under and pressed should now meet those of the lapel similarly prepared, edge meeting edge from the step to the shoulder where the turnings have been snipped. They are held together by the drawstitch illustrated in Diagrams 282a and b. This process should be worked so neatly on both under and upper edges that the finished appearance gives per-

R.S. collar and lapel edges prepared for drawstitching

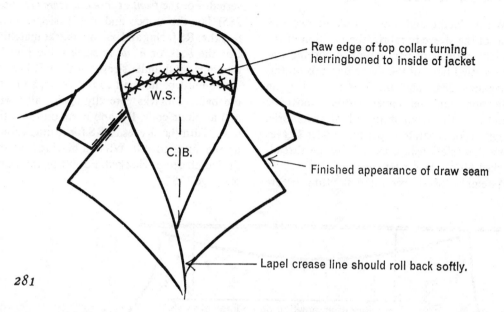

Raw edge of top collar turning herringboned to inside of jacket

W.S.

C.B.

Finished appearance of draw seam

Lapel crease line should roll back softly.

281

fectly even lines on both sides with no stitches showing. Diagram 283 illustrates the upper and under sides.

The collar and lapels are now pressed well over the tailor's ham.

Turned up undercollar showing draw seam of collar and lapel prepared for drawstitching

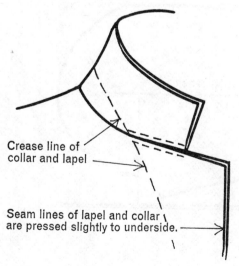

Crease line of collar and lapel

Seam lines of lapel and collar are pressed slightly to underside.

283

Drawstitch holding two folded edges together invisibly

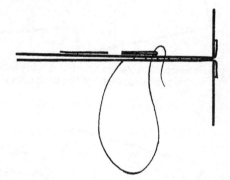

A Insert needle into upper fold opposite thread from lower edge.

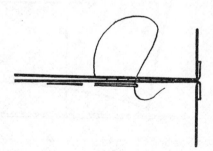

282 *B* Insert needle into lower fold opposite thread from top edge.

Two-piece sleeve with back opening

When placing and cutting out the two sections of the sleeve in fabric, the position of the straight grain is of paramount importance, as the eventual hang of the sleeve depends on this (Diagrams 284a and b). The straight grain indications on the paper pattern must lie parallel to the straight thread of the fabric. Diagrams of separate upper and under sleeves show this relationship, as well as the thread-marked fitting lines after cutting out.

Assemble the sleeves for first fitting before any interlining or permanent stitching is inserted. For the *front* or *forearm seam* (Diagram 285) lay the upper and under sleeve pieces together RS facing and balance marks matching. For the *back* or *hindarm seam* bring together the upper and under sleeve turnings RS facing. There must be no twist to the sleeve, so match the balance marks carefully again, also wrist and armhole ends. Pin and baste on the fitting lines. Turn the sleeves to RS for fitting, turning up the lower edge to WS and basting it so that the length can be checked. For fitting the sleeve, see page 175.

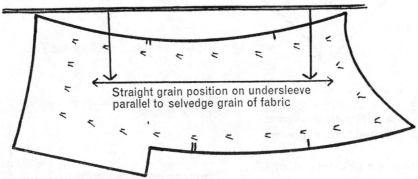

A   Position of selvedge grain of double fabric in relation to the correct placing of the undersleeve pattern

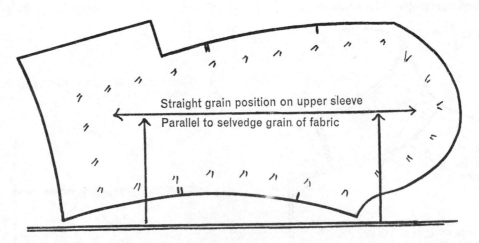

B   Position of selvedge grain of double fabric in relation to correct placing of upper sleeve pattern

284

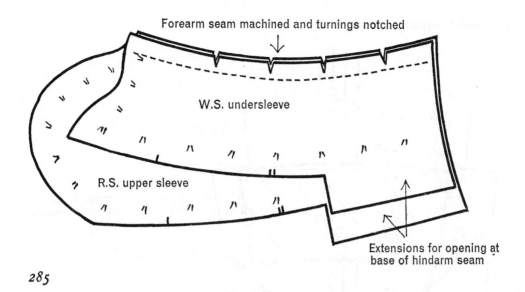

Forearm seam machined and turnings notched

W.S. undersleeve

R.S. upper sleeve

Extensions for opening at
base of hindarm seam

285

MAKING UP THE SLEEVES

After fitting, make any necessary adjust-ments, transferring corrected lines to the second sleeve. Then remove the basting from the hind-arm seams and open the sleeves out flat.

1.   Machine on the fitting lines of the forearm seam. Remove basting. The seam is slightly curved, so snip the turnings at elbow level and just above and below this to facilitate pressing the seam flat on WS. Trim the turnings to $\frac{1}{2}$ inch (Diagram 285).

2.   The *interlining* at the lower end of the sleeve is often a cross-cut piece of pre-shrunk canvas deep enough to reach the top of the opening, e.g. 3 or $3\frac{1}{2}$ inches by $10\frac{1}{2}$ or 11 inches across the sleeve so as to reach the fitting lines of the two edges of the opening. No turnings are allowed. Diagram 286a shows the canvas fixed to WS of the sleeve, one edge touching the hindarm seam fitting line on the overwrap side, whilst the other edge protrudes enough for the underwrap or button stand edge of the back opening. The lower edge of the canvas touches the fitting line of the wrist edge of the sleeve. Catchstitch the canvas in place (Dia-gram 286a).

Whilst the sleeve is laid out flat, finish the edges of the opening and wristlines by cutting across the turnings to within $\frac{1}{8}$ inch of the corners. Turn under the raw edges for $\frac{1}{8}$ inch to WS. Fold over the turning edges so the corners are neatly mitred. Catchstitch the raw edges to the canvas and slipstitch the mitred edges together (Diagram 286b). On the under-wrap side snip across the seam turning at the top of the opening to release it for the seam. Space and work the buttonholes as required for the style on the overwrap side. See page 192, Diagrams 294a–h for working tailored button-holes. Finished lower edge of sleeve on RS (Diagram 287) and WS (Diagram 288).

3.   Curl the sleeve round so the two edges of the *hindarm seam* are together RS facing. Matching the balance marks pin, baste and machine on the fitting lines. Remove basting. Snip the seam turnings as for the forearm seam. Press the seam open on WS over a sleeveboard or pressing roller. WS of finished sleeve before lining is shown in Diagram 289. Diagram 290 shows RS.

4.   The circumference of the *sleevehead* must be larger than that of the armhole, in order to fit comfortably over the joint of the top arm and shoulder. It should never be less than 1

Tailored two-piece sleeve opening at wrist

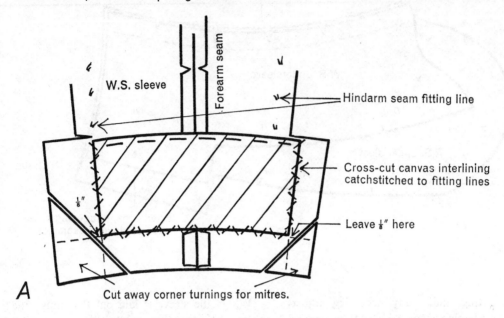

W.S. sleeve

Forearm seam

Hindarm seam fitting line

Cross-cut canvas interlining catchstitched to fitting lines

Leave ⅛″ here

⅛″

A Cut away corner turnings for mitres.

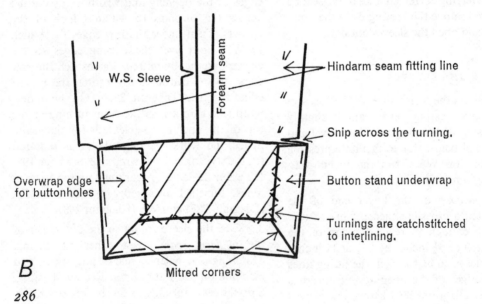

W.S. Sleeve

Forearm seam

Hindarm seam fitting line

Snip across the turning.

Overwrap edge for buttonholes

Button stand underwrap

Turnings are catchstitched to interlining.

B Mitred corners

286

inch larger and is often more. In wool fabric the surplus can be drawn up and the turning edges shrunk away as shown in Diagram 291. Use matching thread for inserting the gathering stitches on the sleevehead fitting line from hindarm seam to forearm seam. Draw up the

thread to fit the armhole into which it will be set, and wind the end round a pin. Place the sleevehead WS uppermost over the end of a curved pad or sleeve board edge, turnings next to worker. Wring out a pressing cloth with water. Place the damp cloth to cover the sleeve

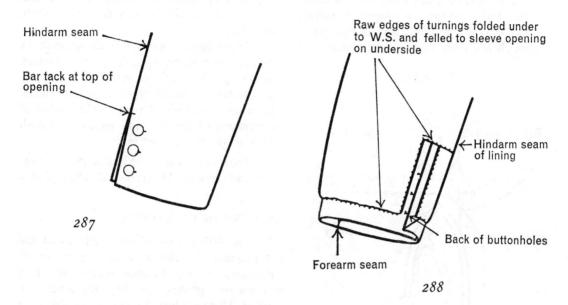

Hindarm seam

Bar tack at top of opening

287

WS opening with lining attached

Raw edges of turnings folded under to W.S. and felled to sleeve opening on underside

←Hindarm seam of lining

Back of buttonholes

Forearm seam

288

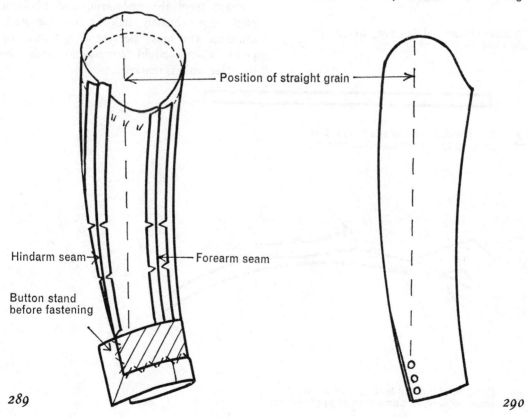

WS tailored two-piece sleeve before lining

RS tailored two-piece sleeve before lining

← Position of straight grain →

Hindarm seam→   ←— Forearm seam

Button stand before fastening

289

290

turnings. Steam shrink the surplus fabric by holding the toe of a fairly hot iron touching the wet cloth, and causing steam to penetrate the fabric. Diagram 291 illustrates this. Some fabrics shrink more readily than others, but with perseverance most wool materials respond to this treatment. When this is finished, the sleevehead will be seen to form a slight cup shape.

Where a large proportion of the fibres in the material are man-made, e.g. Terylene or Acrilan, shrinking will be difficult, and it may be necessary to take in the sleeve seams a little instead, in order to provide the right relationship of sleevehead to armhole and ensure a smooth fit when the sleeve is set in.

5. The *lining* of the sleeve is described on page 168 and shown in Diagrams 261, 262 and 288.

SETTING IN THE SLEEVES

1. The fitting lines of the armholes of the jacket must be clearly marked, also the indications of the balance marks or 'inset points' or 'pitches', as they are sometimes called. There are two of these for matching the sleeve seams: forearm pitch about 2 inches forward from the underarm, and hindarm pitch approximately halfway up the back armhole. On most sleevehead patterns the point which should correspond with the shoulder seam is marked.

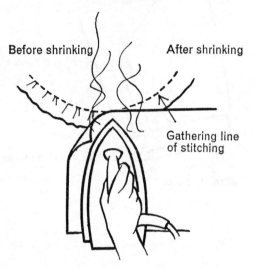

W.S. sleevehead

Before shrinking   After shrinking

Gathering line of stitching

Position of iron and damp rag when shrinking sleevehead turnings   *291*

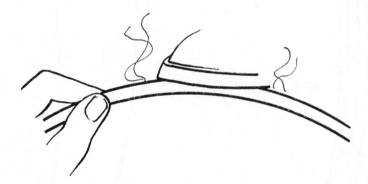

A   Straight edges of tailor's tape before shaping to fit armhole curve more smoothly

B   Position of holding tailor's tape to stretch outer edge when damp with edge of hot iron   *292*

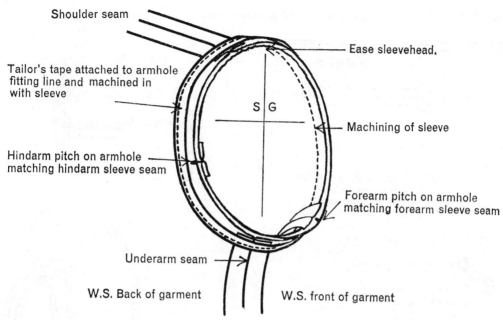

Shoulder seam

Ease sleevehead.

Tailor's tape attached to armhole
fitting line and machined in
with sleeve

S | G

Machining of sleeve

Hindarm pitch on armhole
matching hindarm sleeve seam

Forearm pitch on armhole
matching forearm sleeve seam

Underarm seam

W.S. Back of garment   W.S. front of garment

293

To hold the armhole firmly and give added support, particularly to the back where the strain occurs, a piece of tailor's linen tape can be attached as a stay to the fitting line on WS of the armhole. Diagrams 292a and b show how, before it is attached, the dampened tape can be shaped by stretching the outer edge under a hot iron. The tape will fit the armhole curve more readily after this treatment.

2. With RS facing and fitting lines meeting, pin the hindarm seam of the sleeve to the corresponding pitch on the back armhole, working from the sleeve side. Pin the forearm seam to the pitch on the front armhole likewise. Pin smoothly under the arm in between these points, matching fitting lines and continuing to work from the sleeve side. The two edges of armhole and sleeve should fit together without difficulty between these points.

3. Pin the centre of the sleevehead to the centre of the shoulder which may be about ½ inch in front of the shoulder seam. Pin the head of the sleeve from hindarm seam over the top to forearm seam adjusting the fullness evenly each side of the centre. This is where the

sleevehead must form a slight 'cup' over the top of the shoulder and arm joint although appearing to be completely smooth with no visible gathers. This is a process requiring good manipulative finger skill in controlling the fullness in the sleevehead whilst fixing it in the armhole. Matching the fitting lines of both sleevehead and armhole, tack in the sleeve with small stitches (Diagram 293).

4. When both sleeves have been inserted fit the jacket before machining to ensure they hang correctly without a wrinkle and are well balanced (Diagram 290). The shoulder pads should be temporarily pinned in position before the jacket is tried on, and removed again before machining (Diagram 260).

5. When satisfied with the hang of both sleeves, machine round the armhole from the sleeve side of the work, taking care to keep the armhole smooth. Remove basting. Press the seam open over a curved sleevehead pad (see page 40, Diagrams 23a and b) with the point of the iron, working over a damp pressing cloth.

6. When fashion dictates softly rounded sleeveheads, press the sleevehead and armhole

Tailor's buttonhole   Drawings c, d and e, show the workings of the stitch.

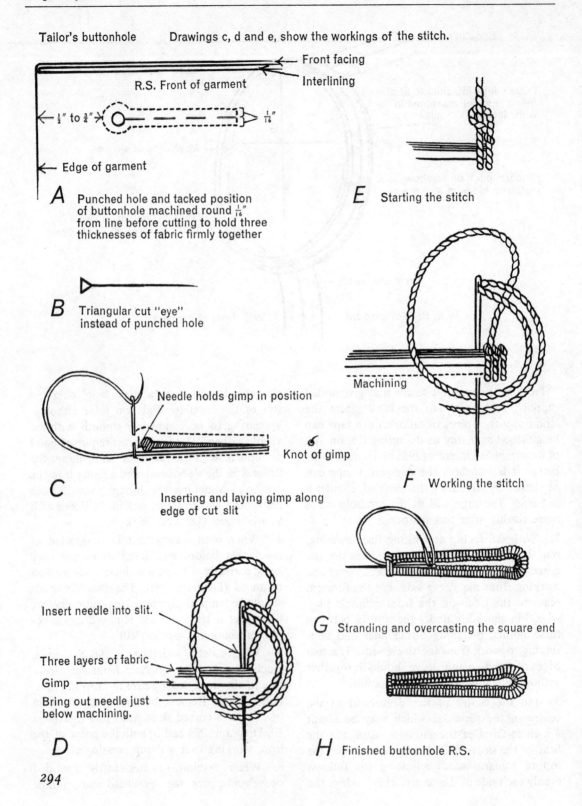

Front facing

Interlining

R.S. Front of garment

← ½" to ¾" → $\frac{1}{16}$"

← Edge of garment

A   Punched hole and tacked position
of buttonhole machined round $\frac{1}{16}$"
from line before cutting to hold three
thicknesses of fabric firmly together

E   Starting the stitch

B   Triangular cut "eye"
instead of punched hole

Needle holds gimp in position

Knot of gimp

C   Inserting and laying gimp along
edge of cut slit

Machining

F   Working the stitch

Insert needle into slit.

Three layers of fabric

Gimp

Bring out needle just
below machining.

D

G   Stranding and overcasting the square end

H   Finished buttonhole R.S.

294

turnings permanently inside the armhole. A softly folded pad of wadding is often inserted between the turnings and the top of the sleeve to help the rounded effect. Tear the wadding to thin the edges, rather than cut it. Using a strip about 8 by 2 inches, fold it almost in half lengthwise so the one edge slightly protrudes beyond the other. Press the fold up against the machine line on WS of the sleevehead, easing the wadding so it lies like a little cushion between the sleeve top and the turnings. Catch it at intervals to the turnings with light tacking stitches. The wadding is sandwiched between the sleeve and the lining, and eventually gives a softly moulded effect to the sleevehead.

7.   If square shoulders are in vogue, leave the turnings pressed open over the top of the sleevehead, for about 8 inches altogether. The rest of the turnings should be pressed into the armhole for the underarm portion. Shoulder and sleevehead padding will then be used to hold out the squared sleevehead edge as required.

For completing the lining of the sleeve at the armhole, see page 168.

Tailor's buttonhole

The name of this method of working firm strong buttonholes on fairly thick fabric (Diagrams 294a–h) is the result of generations of practising craftsmen in the art of tailoring. To master and perfect the process of hand working these buttonholes takes practice but adds pounds to the value of a smartly tailored garment when accurately executed.

Planning and spacing of buttonholes depends on the design and purpose of the opening and fastening. Both button and buttonhole sides must be planned so there is no gaping or puckering when the garment is fastened. These faults can also be caused through insufficient room at the round end of the buttonhole, or through the button being sewn too closely to the garment with insufficient shank or stem.

For this reason and because the fastening edges of tailored garments usually are interlined for firmness, causing three thicknesses

of fabric, an eyelet hole is made at the round or button shank end of the buttonhole (Diagram a). This is called the *eye* of the buttonhole. It enables the stitches with their firmly knotted edge to lie close to each other, making a strong round end to the buttonhole with sufficient room to fit the sturdy shank of the button. The easiest way is to punch these eyelet holes with a metal punch, such as that used for leatherwork. Otherwise make small triangular cuts with sharp-pointed scissors at the round end of buttonholes as shown in Diagram b.

The use of tailor's gimp is another difference between tailor's buttonholes and needlework or dressmaking worked buttonholes. The gimp is very fine round silk or rayon cord, obtainable by the yard in colours matching tailor's buttonhole twist from tailoring haberdashery departments. Its purpose is to hold the edges of buttonholes taut and prevent stretching. It also helps to give a firm rounded edge to the buttonholes. Buttonhole twist may be bought on reels or spools from draper's haberdashery counters, usually 12 yards on a reel. It may also be obtained from tailor's haberdashery departments where it is sold by the yard, each length having about six strands. So 'one yard of twist' when measured and cut gives a maximum length of six yards: six strands of one yard each. Because the thread is specially twisted for strength, it is apt to kink and cause knots in its length whilst the buttonhole is being worked. To remedy this, pull each single length of twist from under a warm iron whilst pressing down on a pad. Repeat two or three times before threading the twist into the eye of a needle. Length of thread is similar to that for needlework or dressmaking buttonholes, i.e., $\frac{1}{2}$ yard of thread for a $\frac{1}{2}$-inch buttonhole, $\frac{3}{4}$ yard for a $\frac{3}{4}$-inch buttonhole and 1 yard for a 1-inch buttonhole.

MARKING AND CUTTING

Mark out the buttonhole position by tacking through all thicknesses of garment (usually treble—garment fabric, interlining and facing). Horizontal buttonholes have one round (eyelet) end $\frac{1}{2}$ or $\frac{3}{4}$ inch from the edge of the garment (or half the width of the button) and one square end. Its length should be the diameter of the button plus $\frac{1}{8}$ inch.

If a punch is available, punch out the small eyelet hole at the correct end of the button-hole position, i.e. end nearest the permanent fastening edge.

STRENGTHENING THE HOLE

Before cutting the slit protect and hold the treble layers of fabric together by machine stitching or close back stitching with self-coloured thread $\frac{1}{16}$ inch from the marked tack line round the eyelet end and up the other side, as in Diagram 294a. Cut the slit with sharp-pointed scissors inserting the point in the eye-let hole and cutting exactly in the centre be-tween the two rows of machining. A straight clean cut is essential for good finish.

If an eyelet has not been punched before machining, cut the slit between the two rows of machining and then make a small triangular cut as shown in Diagram b. The buttonhole is worked from right to left with the cut edge uppermost.

INSERTING THE GIMP

Thread a large-eyed needle with a length of tailor's gimp, the colour as near to that of the garment as possible. Make a knot at one end. (This will be cut off later.) Diagram c shows the gimp inserted between the layers of fabric just beyond the buttonhole at the square end, i.e. end furthest away from the edge of the garment. Bring out the needle at the square end of the buttonhole so the gimp can lie along the cut edge. Allow the needle to hold the gimp in position at the round end whilst the first side is being worked. (NOTE: The edge of the garment will be towards the left-hand side of the worker.)

WORKING THE STITCH

Thread a second needle with buttonhole twist to match the fabric of the garment. (Length and preparation of twist is given.) Start at the square end, furthest away from the garment edge. Insert the needle between the layers of fabric bringing the thread out at the top of the slit and fastening on securely with a tiny stitch (Diagram d). Working from right to left insert the needle into the slit and bring out the point just below the line of machining. (Depth of stitch approximately $\frac{1}{8}$ inch.) Pass the double thread from the eye of the needle under the point of the needle from right to left (Diagram d). Draw out the needle and as the thread is pulled upwards work the knot tightly so it lies on top of the cut edge over the gimp and so protects the raw edge (Diagram e). Continue to work this stitch closely but spacing it so the knots touch each other and the gimp is covered (Diagram f). When one side has been worked withdraw the needle which holds the gimp. Gently pull up the gimp a little, so the worked edge of the buttonhole is tightened.

Continue to buttonhole round the eye keep-ing the gimp in position on the cut edge. Radi-ate the stitches, keeping them even in depth and sufficiently close. Work the second side as for the first. Gently pull up the gimp again to tighten the edge of the buttonhole. Then pass the needle holding the gimp through to the interlining and cut off the gimp so its end sinks back between the folds of the fabric. Also pull up the knot of the gimp (inserted at the start) and cut it off. Finish working the button-hole by inserting the needle into the knot of the first stitch and bringing it out at the end of the last stitch. Strand across the square end of the hole to keep the two edges together and in good shape. Overcast the strands for a neat unobtrusive finish (Diagram g). Buttonholing is sometimes used, but is rather more bulky.

The secret of a good worked buttonhole is the even depth of stitch and firmly drawn up knots of regular tightness. As with any skilled craft, proficiency is only reached through concentration and practice together with an understanding of the materials being used. The finished buttonhole is shown in Diagram h.

SKIRTS

The cutting out and fitting should be planned and executed in conjunction with the jacket.

Before cutting out, pin up and test the paper pattern against the figure of the wearer and adjust any portion that involves extra material either in length or width.

Cutting out

The correct grain of fabric on each piece of skirt is of utmost importance. It governs the true hang of the garment on the wearer. On straight-cut skirts the selvedge grain (or rib in jersey) should run vertically down centre lines. Weft grain must be horizontal at the hip level, i.e. parallel to the ground when worn. Checks or plaids must match at seams. See page 31 in Chapter One on cutting out (Diagrams 15 and 16). When using twill fabric the diagonal weave must run in the same direction on each piece of skirt, usually from left to right (Diagram 12). If the fabric has a nap or pile surface, e.g. mohair or corduroy, etc., each piece of pattern must be cut with the pile or nap lying one way (Diagram 19).

After cutting out, threadmark all centre and fitting lines as well as balance marks. Stay-stitch any curved edges in stretch fabrics, e.g. jersey, to prevent loss of shape.

Assembling and fitting

Take care to match all fitting lines and balance marks correctly. It is important to attach the waistline of the skirt to a temporary fitted waistband to hold the skirt in position on the figure. Otherwise, if the waist edge slips out of place, the fit of the skirt cannot be judged correctly.

See that the skirt is right side out and positioned correctly on the figure, i.e. centre lines falling in true centre. Pin up the placket taking care not to stretch the curved edge of the overlap. Observe the general hang of the skirt and whether the selvedge grain runs vertically down CF and CB and the weft grain at hip level is parallel to the ground, i.e. horizontal. Notice if the side seams run vertically. If they *swing forward* towards hem level, it means the back is too long for the front. Remedy this by lifting the *back waistline* at the centre, e.g. hollowing out from centre back round to centre front, until the seam hangs in its correct vertical line.

Backward swing means the opposite; the front is too long for the back. In this case lift the *front waist* at centre, and curve waistline gradually to centre back until the seam hangs in its correct vertical line.

Wrinkling at CB waistline caused by a hollow waist needs the skirt lifting at CB till the fit is smooth. Pin a new waistline, curving back to the original side seams.

A *prominent seat or abdomen* may cause tightness across the skirt at those levels, and strain the side seams out of their vertical line. Let out the seams and re-pin carefully. If there are panel or centre seams, it may be wise to let out a little at these also. Experience trains the eye in judging good true lines in correcting seams. Small adjustments in several seams are often better than too much at the sides only. Fit the right-hand half of the skirt, and correct the left side from the right, unless the figure is noticeably different on the left side. If so, fit both sides separately.

Making up

For *darts* or *dart tucks*, see notes on slacks, page 202, and pressing darts, page 42.

Seams will be according to the style and fabric. Panel seams may be 'plain open', 'tucked' (overlaid) as shown in Diagram 78, or 'slot' (channel) as in Diagram 57. Side seams are usually 'plain open' with turnings on WS finished according to fabric. (See Diagrams 64 to 69 and notes.) For pressing seams, see page 42.

Slits, vents and pleats are described in Chapter Eight. See Chapter Nine for *pockets*.

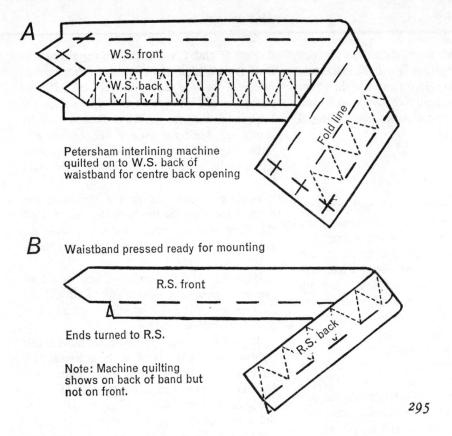

A

W.S. front

W.S. back

Fold line

Petersham interlining machine
quilted on to W.S. back of
waistband for centre back opening

B   Waistband pressed ready for mounting

R.S. front

R.S. back

Ends turned to R.S.

Note: Machine quilting
shows on back of band but
not on front.

295

Plackets or openings are usually closed with a zip-fastener. These are fully described in Chapter Six. If at the left side, the concealed zip opening is advised with strengthening stays and a guard of self fabric as shown in Diagrams 95 to 99. If at the centre back, the semi-concealed zip opening is often used. (See Diagrams 90 and 91 for preparation of skirt and Diagrams 82, 86 or 100 and 101 for preparation and fixing of zip-fastener.) For the neat invisible zip opening, see Diagrams 105a–e.

Setting on the waist

PREPARATION OF BAND

Interlining gives strength and support to the waistband. It can be skirt petersham bought by the yard in the desired width, or cut from previously shrunk tailor's canvas or bonded interlining fabric. NOTE: Elastic petersham can

be obtained in similar widths to cotton and Terylene petersham and may be preferred by those who do not like tight waistbands.

Two methods of attaching the interlining are shown; one in Diagrams 295a and b and the other in Diagrams 296a and b. Either would be suitable, but if machine lines or zigzag stitch are used, care must be taken to attach the interlining to WS of the back of the band, as otherwise the stitching would be visible on RS of the fabric; see Diagram 295b. If skirt petersham is used it should be plain, not boned, so as to make machining easier. Terylene petersham retains its firmness and does not shrink or stretch. Cotton petersham should be shrunk and pressed before inserting.

The approximate length of the waistband is the waist measurement plus 3 inches for under and overwrap ends. Press well on the underside (back) before attaching to the skirt. Clearly mark the fitting lines and balance points.

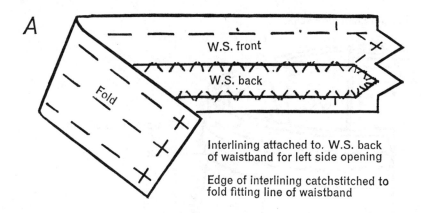

A

W.S. front

W.S. back

Fold

Interlining attached to. W.S. back
of waistband for left side opening

Edge of interlining catchstitched to
fold fitting line of waistband

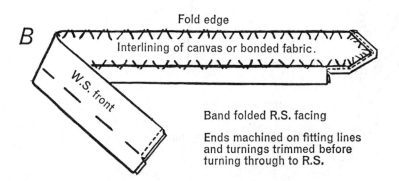

B

Fold edge

Interlining of canvas or bonded fabric.

W.S. front

Band folded R.S. facing

Ends machined on fitting lines
and turnings trimmed before
turning through to R.S.

296

Before the waistband is set on, the waistline of the skirt should equal the actual waist measurement plus 1 to 1½ inches for casc. When it is fastened, the waistband should be the exact waist measurement; the slight ease allows the skirt to hang smoothly with no drag.

MOUNTING THE BAND

Place RS band to RS skirt waist, raw edge of band uppermost and fitting lines together. The pointed end projects beyond the edge of the overlap. The square end is flush with the guard, on the underlap. Match balance marks. Evenly adjust the slight ease on the waistband. Pin and baste one thickness of the band to the skirt on the fitting lines (Diagram 297). Fit before machining to ensure the correct hang and smooth fit at the waist. Machine on the fitting lines. Remove basting. Trim turnings to ¼ or ⅜

inch, layering where necessary. Press open the waist seam to obtain a smooth, flat appearance on RS. Then press the turnings up into the band. Baste near the seam line to keep flat.

Fold under to WS the turnings of the free edge of the back of the band. Bring the folded edge to meet the machining on WS, enclosing the raw edges of the waist join. Pin and baste in position. Fell this edge by hand to the line of machining (Diagram 298). No stitches must show on RS. Press the band on WS.

FASTENINGS

Work a horizontal tailor's buttonhole at the pointed end of the band (Diagram 294; instructions on page 193). Sew a suitable button with a good shank or stem on the underlap, so the fastening will be smooth with no puckers or drag. Sew hooks and eyes in the positions

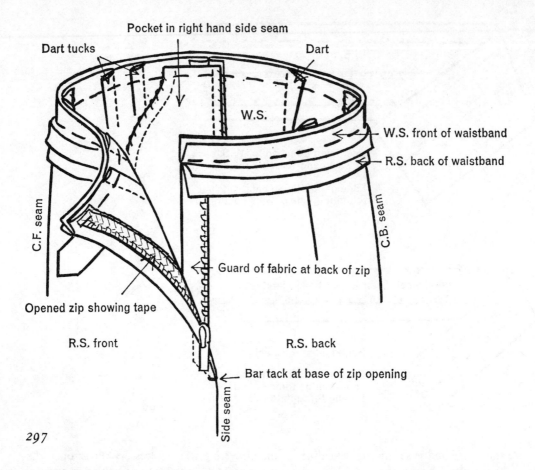

Pocket in right hand side seam

Dart tucks   Dart

W.S.

W.S. front of waistband

R.S. back of waistband

C.F. seam

C.B. seam

Guard of fabric at back of zip

Opened zip showing tape

R.S. front   R.S. back

Bar tack at base of zip opening

Side seam

297

shown in Diagram 298 so the square end of the band can be fastened first, holding the waistline firmly before zipping up the opening. This helps to prevent strain on the zip. When the button is fastened, the band neatly covers the top of the opening (Diagram 299).

Finishing

The finish of the hem depends on the style and fabric. See Chapter Seven. Treatment of seams inside hems is shown in Diagrams 62 and 63, hems for tailored skirts in Diagrams 112 to 117 and lined skirt hems in Diagram 123.

Linings are used extensively, especially in slimline skirts to preserve the shape and prevent seating in wear; see notes and advice given in Chapter Fourteen. Fully lined skirts are described on page 164. For treatment of a whole skirt lining at base of zip, see Diagrams 249 to 253.

For pressing during construction and finishing, according to fabric, see Chapter Two.

TAILORED SLACKS

Slacks have become an accepted part of a woman's or girl's wardrobe. For leisure wear or for warmth in winter as well as for sports, gardening and a host of other pursuits, slacks are chosen. They should be fitting yet comfortable, and smartly tailored.

NOTE: The following directions are for tailored slacks of cloth or jersey fabrics. They do not apply to 'stretch pants'. Stretch fabrics require special treatment in patterns, making up and pressing.

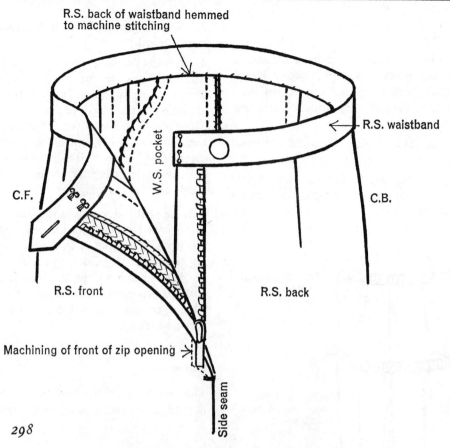

R.S. back of waistband hemmed
to machine stitching

R.S. waistband

W.S. pocket

C.F.

C.B.

R.S. front

R.S. back

Machining of front of zip opening

Side seam

298

Finished zip placket and waistband of slacks,
shorts or skirt

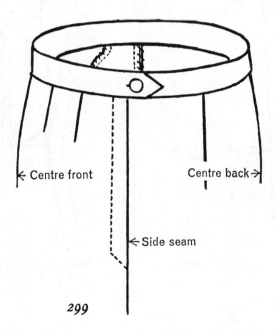

← Centre front

Centre back →

← Side seam

299

Measuring

In choosing or making a pattern for slacks, the measurements of the prospective wearer must be checked. Diagrams 300 and 301 show how to take the following principal measurements required:

1. Waist, taken closely round the normal waistline;

2. Hips, taken firmly but not too tightly round the fullest part of the hips, 8 or 9 inches below the waistline;

3. Side length, from waist to ankle, or required length;

4. Depth of crotch, taken in a sitting position from the waist to the chair (Diagram 301). This last measurement is important, as any alteration in the length of the pattern is made either above this level for a shorter or longer back, or below the crotch for shortening or lengthening the leg. This helps to ensure correct balance while giving the required length. See the dotted lines in Diagram 302.

Some of the processes in the construction of slacks have been described in other sections of this book. The order of work will vary according to style and personal preference. It is set out here so that any parts which can be constructed separately are completed before the whole garment is assembled, thus making for easier handling.

Cutting out

The general hang and balance of the slacks depend on correct placing of the fabric when

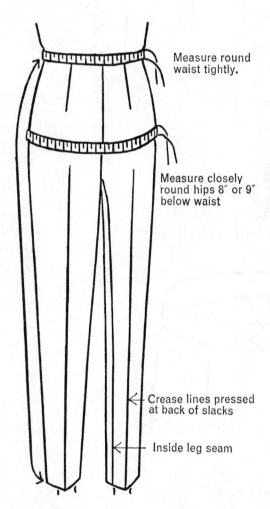

Measure round waist tightly.

Measure closely round hips 8″ or 9″ below waist

Crease lines pressed at back of slacks

Inside leg seam

Measure length from side of waist to ankle or required length.

300

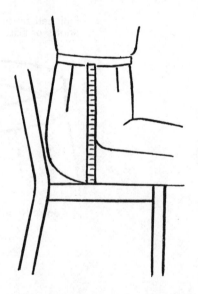

Measure depth of crotch from waist to chair seat.

301

cutting out. The straight grain, selvedge way (or rib in jersey) runs down through the centre of both pattern pieces of leg (Diagram 302) which are cut on double fabric to give right and left legs. The weft grain must be horizontal on the hip line. If corduroy is used, the pile must lie the same way on each piece of leg.

Assembling and fitting

After cutting out the slacks, mark all fitting lines and balance marks clearly. Assemble and fit the slacks before stitching any parts permanently. It is important to baste the waist to a temporary fitted waistband to hold the

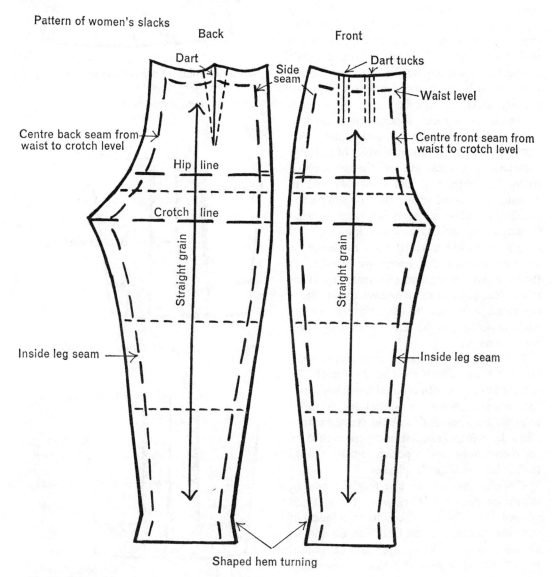

Pattern of women's slacks

Back   Front

Dart

Side seam

Dart tucks

Waist level

Centre back seam from waist to crotch level

Centre front seam from waist to crotch level

Hip line

Crotch line

Straight grain

Straight grain

Inside leg seam

Inside leg seam

Shaped hem turning

To shorten, fold tucks along the small dotted lines.

To lengthen, cut across the patterns on the small dotted lines and insert paper to give the required extra length.

302

slacks in the correct position at the wearer's waistline. The fit cannot be judged accurately unless this is done. Make any necessary corrections.

Making up

Darts or *dart tucks* must be evenly spaced each side of the centre seams. Match fitting lines accurately to ensure even lines of machining, even width and length for dart tucks and well tapered points for darts. Fasten off ends of machining securely on WS. Remove basting Press towards the centre seams on WS. For pressing darts, see page 42.

The choice of *seams* depends on the fabric. For wool (or similar) cloth or jersey, plain open seams are usual, with the raw edges of turnings neatened by overcasting or zigzag machine stitch. See notes and Diagrams 64a and b. Turnings on curved seams must be snipped or notched to allow a flat finish when pressed (Diagrams 53a and b). For washing fabrics of cotton or similar material such as denim or sailcloth, *machine fell* seams are advised, as they are flat, strong and self-neatening (Diagrams 76a, b, c and d). Whatever type of seam is chosen, it should be used throughout the garment. Construct the centre front and centre back seams first.

The *inside leg* and *crotch* seam crosses CF and CB seams which meet at the crotch. To achieve both a smooth tailored finish and comfort in wear, follow the suggestions given on page 58, Diagrams 51a and b for crossed seams. The side seams will be left partly unstitched on the right-hand side if a pocket is used and on the left-hand side for the placket.

The inset method of inserting the *pocket*, shown on page 115, Diagrams 145 to 151, is advised. If the fabric is thick, attach a facing of the same material to the front section and an extension to the back portion. Make the pocket bag of lining (Diagram 151). If a thinner material such as denim is used, the whole pocket can be made of self fabric.

The *placket* will be closed by a zip-fastener in the left side seam. The concealed method of

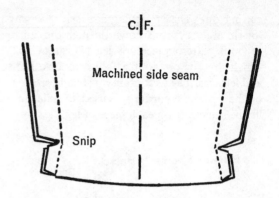

Shaped turning of hem allowance to fit leg of slacks when turned up

Layer turnings inside hem.

303

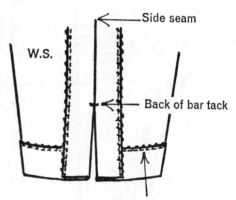

304   Fold edges sliphemmed

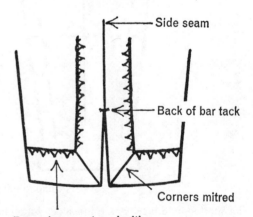

Raw edges neatened with zigzag machine stitches

305

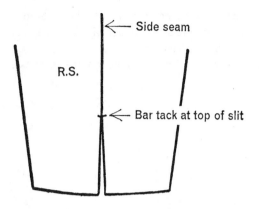

R.S. lower edge of slacks, with slit

306

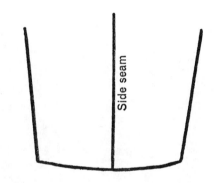

RS lower edge of slacks finished with hem turned up on WS

307

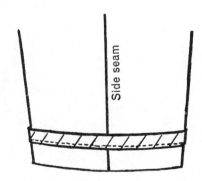

Raw edge of hem finished with ribbon seam binding

308

inserting the zip, strengthened with stays and backed with a guard of self fabric is shown in Diagrams 95 to 99 and described on page 78. NOTE: The zip-fastener must be long enough for its purpose; 9 inches is a good average length.

Setting on the waist

The waist is set on in the same way as for skirts; see page 196 and Diagrams 295 to 299.

Finishing

To finish the lower edges of the legs, the paper pattern should be so shaped that the hem allowance, when it is turned under, lies perfectly flat without puckers or fullness (Diagram 302). After machining the leg seams snip the turnings at the hem level nearly to the stitching to release them before pressing (Diagram 303). Several appropriate methods of finish for the hem are given. The choice depends partly upon the style and fabric. Diagram 304 shows a finish for slits similar to finishing slits in skirts described and illustrated on page 102. Corners could be mitred if desired (Diagram 305). A bar tack should be worked at the top of the slit for strength (Diagram 306). (For working bar tacks, see Diagrams 87a and b.) If no slits are required, as in Diagram 307, hems similar to those given for skirts on page 97, Diagrams 115a and b, using skirt seam binding, will give a finished effect as shown in Diagram 308. In each case press the fold edge of the hem on WS before finally attaching the free edge of the turning to the leg of the slacks. This will avoid any impression of stitches or turning edges showing through on RS. See pressing hems, page 42.

If desired, an instep strap of wide elastic can be attached to the inner and outer leg seams on the underside of the hems.

Finally, fold and press the crease lines down the folds of the centre front and back of the leg portions. (See Diagram 300.) As this pressing must be executed on RS of the fabric it is important to use wool next to wool (or similar self fabric) and lay the pressing cloth or cloths over this, according to the type of fibre and thickness of fabric. (See notes on pressing wool type cloths and jersey, page 43.) The folds may be basted in position and lightly pressed to secure correct placing. Then remove basting and press more heavily so no stitch marks show. Well pressed, accurately placed crease lines give a smart finish to tailored slacks.

vents, 102–4
viscose, 14, 15, 20, 25

waistband, 196–9
waist finishing, 77–8, 83, 164–5, 197–9, 203
   lining, 162–3
   seams, 77
warp, 14, 15, 29, 36, 172–3
warp knit, 36, Plate 5
water-repellent finish, 26
weft, 10, 14, 15, 29, 172–3, 175
   knit, 36, Plate 6
wool, chart, 18
   fibres, 14, 25, 37

mixture, 14
mothproofing, 26
pressing, 38, 41, 43, 171
woollen, 10, 14, 18, 171
worsted, 14, 18, 171

zips, buying, 72
   concealed, 78–85
   guard, 79
   invisible, 72, 85–7
   mitred tapes of, 73
   semi-concealed, 73–8
   stretching of, 72